PLAYING HURT

PLAYING HURT

My Journey
from Despair to Hope

JOHN SAUNDERS

with *New York Times* Bestselling Author
John U. Bacon

Da Capo Press

Da Capo Press
Hachette Book Group
1290 Avenue of the Americas, New York, NY 10104
www.dacapopress.com
@DaCapoPress

Printed in the United States of America
First Edition: August 2017
Published by Da Capo Press, an imprint of Perseus Books, LLC, a subsidiary of Hachette Book Group, Inc.

The publisher is not responsible for websites (or their content) that are not owned by the publisher.

PRINT BOOK INTERIOR DESIGN BY JANE RAESE
Set in 12.5-point Whitman
Editorial production by Christine Marra, Marrathon Editorial Production Services, www.marrathoneditorial.org

Library of Congress Cataloging-in-Publication Data has been applied for.
ISBN 978-0-306-82473-9 (hardcover)
ISBN 978-0-306-82474-6 (ebook)

LSC-C

10 9 8 7 6 5 4 3 2 1

To the memory of John Saunders,
a great brother, husband, father, friend

CONTENTS

Foreword, *Mitch Albom*   xi

Author's Note, *John U. Bacon*   xvii

Preface: Looking Over the Edge   xix

Introduction   xxiii

PART ONE
GROWING UP THE HARD WAY

1   An Oasis of Love   3

2   An Indecent Proposal   10

3   Playing with Fire   13

4   He Ain't Heavy   27

5   The Salvation of Sports   30

6   Looking for a Little Relief   36

7   My Two Selves   42

8   The Drug Business   47

9   Hurting Myself   51

CONTENTS

PART TWO
TRYING TO BUILD A BETTER LIFE

10	Moving Out, Moving On, Moving Back	57
11	Falling in Love	70
12	Go West	76
13	Getting Married	80
14	Country John Saunders	84
15	Chasing a New Dream	94
16	Making It in Moncton	99
17	Bright Lights, Big City	111
18	Big Man in Baltimore	118
19	A Family of My Own	132
20	The Worldwide Leader	139
21	Our Sister	144
22	Livin' in America	150

PART THREE
THE FAÇADE CRACKS

23	The Psych Ward	157
24	Dr. Dangerous	171
25	Falling Backward	175
26	Scaling Mt. Sinai	182
27	Learning to Walk	190

CONTENTS

28   A High-Stakes Stroll in the Park   200

29   Ready for Prime Time?   211

30   Testing, Testing   218

PART FOUR
COLLISION COURSE

31   The Damage of Doctor Dangerous Revealed   227

32   Let the Bad Times Roll   232

33   Stumbling Toward Unhappiness   238

34   A Day in the Doldrums   244

35   Peering Over the Tappan Zee Bridge   249

36   Back to the Bridge   254

37   Crunch Time   257

38   You've Got to Admit It's Getting Better   263

39   Jimmy V, Dickie V, and Cardio V   268

40   Learning the Best Lesson   277

Afterword, *John U. Bacon*   283

Acknowledgments, *John U. Bacon*   291

FOREWORD

A famous writer once said first impressions are always unreliable. That proved true for John Saunders and me. Our first encounter was in 2001 on the set of ESPN's *The Sports Reporters*, which back then was filmed early Sunday mornings on the second floor of a Times Square bar and restaurant. I greeted John, our new "temporary" host, who was filling in for the beloved Dick Schaap, laid up in the hospital.

Strong, I thought, *upon shaking John's hand.*

Must've been an athlete.

Nice guy.

Good voice.

Probably grateful for this chance.

Should be a decent sub until Dick comes back.

Those first impressions were as deep as a tissue—and about as significant. True, John had been an athlete (hockey player) and had a great, deep voice and a strong handshake, but (1) he wasn't crazy about doing the show, (2) he told his wife we were all egomaniacs, (3) he quickly went from sub to permanent because Schaap never returned, passing away tragically a few months later, and (4) he was far more than decent—he was exceptional.

Also, "nice guy" didn't begin to explain John Saunders.

It's like calling the *Mona Lisa* a "nice painting."

The book you hold in your hands is revelatory. That's not a word I'd normally use for sports-related autobiographies. Such books often recount famous games, locker room friendships, off-camera moments. They end with a "My Way" final chapter: *Regrets, I've had a few, but through it all, it's been a towering life that I wouldn't change.*

John was never going to write a book like that. John didn't live a life like that. Unbeknownst to many of us, including athletes, fans, and those who called him a good friend, John battled a raging demon most of his life.

This is a book about that.

Which makes it so much more than an autobiography.

◆ ◆ ◆

To sit by John away from the cameras or to chat in a restaurant or on an airplane going somewhere, you would never know the depth of his challenges. You would never know that his sleep was haunted, that he bunked in with pain, that his life was a series of emotional hurdles and physical abuses, or that his subconscious often took him to dark places.

Instead, you would think, *Here is the most affable guy, devoid of an ego, engaged with your conversation, a guy who loves his family, talks constantly about his wife and daughters, adores hockey and college football, and stands up for athletes other people criticize.*

He was all that. He was a joy. A loyal friend. A terrific storyteller. The kind of guy who was never too busy to do something charitable.

But he was more. And that "more" was like an anvil tied to his frame.

For one thing, John was in pain. Constantly. His banging career in hockey left him paying a lifelong price. A series of adult mishaps tortured his body even more. Diabetes tethered him to insulin shots. There were Sunday mornings when you'd have thought John played an overtime NHL game the night before. His voice was groggy, his beefy frame sagged, his shoulders were killing him, and his hands shook. His energy level was barely enough to get an insulin needle into his skin.

Yet by the time the cameras rolled, he'd somehow inflated, his full-strength baritone filled the room, and he arrested the lens with a welcoming smile and complete command of the set.

The turnaround was astonishing.

But, as John tells us in these pages, it was a double life. He'd grown used to sucking it up and toughing it out, to hoisting a smile and keeping the chatter going. Professionally it wasn't an act. John truly loved broadcasting and his front-row seat to major sporting milestones. He truly enjoyed the coaches and fellow broadcasters he called his friends.

But you cannot lose your shadow, no matter how they adjust the lights. And John's shadow of early abuse and teenaged depression dogged him as an adult. His attempts at treatment remained largely a secret, as did certain hospital stays and dark battles with suicidal thoughts. But this was who John Saunders was—along with his much-admired professional reputation.

And not long ago he decided to come clean. To tell his story, demons and all.

So he worked with John Bacon and wrote this book.

And then he died.

◆   ◆   ◆

When we got the news that John was gone at the too-early age of sixty-one, we were stunned. *We just saw him. He seemed fine. He seemed happy.* After finding our footing, the panelists on *The Sports Reporters*—and its longtime producer, Joe Valerio—all agreed. The entire Sunday show would be about John. That's pretty rare, to dedicate a full show to a host. But *The Sports Reporters* was a kind of family. And we all felt that strongly about the man.

Still, I can tell you that, even as we prepared our topics, we didn't know exactly how John died. It was shrouded in a certain mystery, the way, it turns out, much of his life had been. Our tributes to him were laudatory, highlighting his gifts, his talent, his patience, his wisdom, his loyalty, his friendship, his big voice and even bigger heart.

But we barely mentioned his depression. We didn't talk about the battle of his life. That is a story only John could tell. And as it turned out, he had just finished telling it—to the written page.

And so you have it here. I could spend endless words talking about John the conversationalist, John the funny storyteller, John the loyal Canadian arguing for more hockey topics, John the father who got teary eyed when he spoke about his daughters' accomplishments.

But only John can tell his real story because so much of it was inside his mind, a wrestling match between the majesty of living life and the tempting peace of ending its pain. It took him to the brink, to hospitals, to a bridge over troubled waters. He almost jumped.

But he brought himself back home.

Remember this: John planned on living. Which means he fully intended to discuss this book, to speak openly about his revelations, to take them with him for the rest of his years every time he sat behind a microphone and in front of a camera. To live openly with what he termed the mental illness that had plagued him.

That, friends, is an incredible act of courage.

As it turns out, it was his last—and his most important. This book is not just the journey of a man, his loves, his talents, his road to success; it is also a cautionary tale to others with John's problems and an open embrace to those battling their own demons, a way of saying, "You are not alone."

You never felt alone with John. He lifted you up. Made you feel good. Made you happy about this thing we call the human race because he was the most human of us, the most decent, and, as it turns out, most brave.

I said this book was revelatory. The biggest revelation is that, come the final page, you have even more admiration for John

Saunders than you had coming in. That, for those of us who knew and loved him, is a pretty amazing feat.

Mitch Albom
Author, journalist, longtime panelist
ESPN's *The Sports Reporters*

AUTHOR'S NOTE

After John Saunders passed away in August of 2016, I continued to work on the manuscript with the help of his family, friends, and physicians. But in the end this is John's story, told from his point of view, based primarily on his recollections. Of course, memories can differ. Also, while the events depicted here are true, some names and identifying details have been changed, and some dialogue has been reconstructed.

John U. Bacon

PREFACE

Looking Over the Edge

It was mid-February 2012, the time of year when we northerners become convinced that winter will never end. For me the winter of 2012 was already the longest of my entire life.

I was driving to the Tappan Zee Bridge, twenty-five miles north of Manhattan. The bridge is just a few miles from our home in Westchester County, where we've lived since 1999.

My wife, Wanda, and I raised our two girls here. Our oldest, Aleah, had just graduated from Fordham University. Her little sister, Jenna, was finishing her freshman year at my alma mater, Ryerson University in Toronto.

Maybe a dozen times a year we take I-87 to cross the Tappan Zee Bridge to visit the Palisades Mall in West Nyack, New York. We also use the bridge on our way to Canada, my "home and native land," as the anthem says. When they built the Tappan Zee in 1955 it was supposed to last about half a century, and it's already surpassed that. Engineers have deemed it one of the most decrepit bridges in the country, and it looks like they constructed it from an erector set. There's nothing pretty about that bridge.

But when you're on it, you have to admire the view. The Hudson River is one of our nation's great jewels, and if you take your eyes off the road long enough to follow the river south, you can see the faint skyline of New York City on the horizon.

But on this day I wasn't driving toward the bridge to go to the mall or visit Jenna in Canada or admire the Hudson. I wasn't even planning to drive to the other side.

On this particular day I was a beaten man. On top of a life-long battle with depression, I had still not fully recovered from a brain injury I'd suffered on September 10, 2011, on the set of *ABC College Football*. After a break in the Alabama–Penn State game, I stood up too fast, blacked out, and fell backward onto the tile floor, with my head taking the impact. I endured six months of grueling therapy just to relearn how to walk and talk and read and write.

Six months later the lingering effects of the injury were evident whenever I made a mistake during our broadcasts by mixing up names or getting the score wrong—the kind of simple errors that guys who've been on TV for a few decades aren't supposed to make. Each time I screwed something up, a few anonymous critics on Twitter would hammer me. That's part of the business, of course, but after a few months of this I concluded that the one skill I could always count on, the thing that had saved me so many times, my ability to talk on TV, was slipping away from me.

To mitigate my depression I had undergone years of therapy and medication from a battery of doctors—some great, some not. But on this morning I woke up as deeply depressed as I'd ever been. That was when I decided to drive to the Tappan Zee Bridge.

I told myself I wasn't going there to jump off the bridge. I was only going to take a look over the side. When I got to the bridge I drove to the highest point and stopped, just as I'd planned. Suddenly I felt a great urgency. With cars whizzing past and the police sure to show up at any minute, I realized if I was going to peer over the edge to see what it looked like, I'd have to do it *now*.

But after I got out of my car and walked to the side I encountered girders and fences designed to keep people from jumping. I realized that killing myself this way would take more effort than I had anticipated.

I made my way through the first layer of obstructions and got close enough to see the river below. Once I finally looked over the edge, I saw a drop of about 140 feet, equivalent to a fourteen-story skyscraper. The river's rough gray surface looked more like concrete than water.

I stood there motionless, taking it all in.

When I realized I could do it, that I could jump from the bridge, I got scared. I turned around, got back in my car, and drove off, heading for home.

On my way back I decided that whatever I was going to do, it wasn't going to be *that*.

But what *was* I going to do?

INTRODUCTION

This decade two active professional athletes have announced that they were gay. This was a first for the NBA, the NFL, or any major American professional league. Commentators frequently declared that those announcements broke the last taboo in the macho culture of American sports.

But there remains another: the taboo that tells men they must never confess that they suffer from mental illness, which is why men are far less likely to seek help than women.

In this book I openly discuss my lifelong battle with depression and how it nearly cost me my life. *Playing Hurt* is not an autobiography of a sports celebrity but a memoir of a man facing his own mental illness, and emerging better off for the effort. I will take you into the heart of my struggle with depression, including insights into some of its causes, its consequences, and its treatments.

My story unfolds like most of our lives do, among family, friends, and colleagues. But I will also take you places we don't usually visit: the therapists' offices, the hospitals, and the psychiatric wards where the real work of recovery is performed.

I invite you behind the façade of my apparently "perfect" life as a sportscaster, with a wonderful wife and two healthy, happy adult daughters. I have a lot to be thankful for. Trust me, I know it, and I am truly grateful. But as my trip to the Tappan Zee Bridge shows, none of those things can protect me or anyone else from the disease of depression and its potentially lethal effects.

People only see what's on the outside. When you're depressed, as Robin Williams was, the pain and darkness you feel on the inside can eclipse everything you have going for you on the outside. When Williams ended his own life, everyone asked, "How could he do that? He had so much to live for!" But given the pain he must have been experiencing, instead they should have asked, "How did he manage to live that long?"

◆　◆　◆

Mine is a rare story: that of a black man in the sports industry openly grappling with depression. I will share the good, the bad, and the ugly, including the lengths I've gone to to conceal my private life from the public.

So why write a book now, one that will compromise the very privacy I've worked so hard to protect?

Because, once and for all, I want to end the pain and heartache that comes from leading a double life. I also want to reach out to the millions of people, especially men, who think they're alone and can't ask for help.

Any doubts I had were erased in the spring of 2013, a little more than a year after I considered jumping off the Tappan Zee Bridge. That spring I boarded a train to attend the first National Conference on Mental Health, hosted by President Barack Obama. At the conference I was joined by celebrities, politicians, and others who have dedicated themselves to the cause of mental health. I met a lot of remarkable people who had suffered from mental illness and had the courage to talk about it.

When I got home that night I eagerly told my wife and daughters about my big day. After our girls went up to bed I sat alone at the kitchen table. As the warm glow from the day's events began to cool, I thought about what I was hiding, and I felt like such a hypocrite.

Why didn't I have the guts to tell the truth about my own life?

With each minute that ticked by, my shame grew. I realized I needed to come clean.

So I'm going to tell you now.

PART ONE

◆ ◆ ◆

Growing Up
the Hard Way

CHAPTER 1

An Oasis of Love

MY FATHER, BERNIE SAUNDERS, WAS A GIFTED ATHLETE, a serious baseball player, and a semi-pro football player before becoming a handyman and an aspiring entrepreneur. He was also good enough at the bass fiddle to play in a jazz orchestra and a jazz trio.

My parents met through family members and hit it off right away. My mother was a beautiful jazz singer. Occasionally they played gigs together, and before long they decided to get married.

They knew they wanted to have a family and started right away. My father wanted to name their first baby for his best friend, Oscar Peterson, one of the greatest jazz pianists of all time. But my mother didn't like the name Oscar, so when I was born on February 2, 1955, they compromised and named me John Peterson Saunders. They also asked Oscar Peterson to be my godfather, which is pretty neat. I called him "Uncle Oscar," and he was very good to me.

My parents' love for music filled our home. My father was always playing his 78 rpm records and reel-to-reel tapes in the house. My mother serenaded us with Billie Holliday or Ella Fitzgerald classics. Almost every chore or lesson was done to music, and many of my earliest memories involve their favorite songs.

For the first ten years of my life my family moved back and forth between Toronto and Montreal. My brother, Bernie, was born a year and a half after I was, and our sister, Gail, came along three years after Bernie, in 1959. My mom smoked and drank during her pregnancies, which was not unusual back then, but perhaps as a result I developed asthma at a young age, and Gail was born two months early.

When we brought Gail home from the hospital my mom held her over her shoulder in the passenger seat. (There were no infant car seats in 1959.) I was four, Bernie was three, and we were sitting behind Gail, kissing her tiny hands and smelling her. We were both completely smitten from the start.

Our mom warned us, "Oh you, you love her now, but wait until she starts getting into your stuff!"

"She can do whatever she wants!" I said, and I meant it.

Sure, there were times when Gail could be a pain in the neck, like any little sister, but the three of us were incredibly close.

The following year, when I started kindergarten, I walked the four or five blocks to school by myself, which was also pretty common. I remember being *so* happy to be starting school! I liked the teachers, I liked my classmates, I liked the structure, and I liked learning. As soon as I learned to read, I always had my nose in a book.

But most of my early memories aren't happy ones.

A few weeks into first grade I went to the kitchen for breakfast, still fired up about going to school, and sat down across from my father. At the time my dad was still my hero and the toughest guy I knew.

But now I saw him sitting at the kitchen table, his head in his hands, quietly weeping. I had never seen him cry before. This was stunning to me. I thought my dad was Superman, and Superman never cried.

I asked him, "What's wrong?"

"Nothing. Get out of here."

"Why are you crying, Daddy? Are you okay?"

He raised his voice. "I told you! *Nothing!*"

My mom overheard him and came rushing into the kitchen, crying and screaming that Dad didn't care about his family, he only cared about himself, and that he was going to leave us to live with his mistress.

She said, "He's been screwing a woman at work."

I had no idea what that meant. I wasn't even sure what my father did for a living, though we later learned he'd been the manager of a car wash.

Dad just took it, hanging his head, while mom kept yelling. I burst from the kitchen and hid in my room, hoping the shouting would stop.

The Cleavers we weren't.

◆ ◆ ◆

Both our parents believed in corporal punishment, which was pretty common then too, but they also practiced "corporal problem solving." A slap to the side of the head was an easier way to stress the urgency of a simple task—such as fetching their cigarettes or grabbing their drinks—than asking nicely.

One day, when I was five or six, I was snooping around in my parents' bedroom, the way kids do. When my mom caught me I gave her some backtalk, which was never smart. When she reached for a belt, I ran out of the house.

I was running so hard that I had an asthma attack. When she caught up to me I was bent over but managed to gasp, "Look at what you made me do!"

"Oh yeah?" she said. "I'm going to *whoop* that asthma out of you!"

She started whipping me with the belt, wherever she could land it. Now, when parents spanked their kids in the sixties, no one gave it a second thought. But this beating was bad enough that even the neighbors came out of their houses to watch.

This incident aside, it was more common for Mom to discipline Bernie and Dad to discipline me. With Bernie, Mom would occasionally take off her belt and use it on his backside—sometimes with the buckle—which occasionally caused him some embarrassment the next day in gym class when his friends could see the marks she left. Mom believed that if you spared the rod, you spoiled the child.

Our dad picked on me the most, perhaps because I was the oldest and had the biggest mouth. Oh, and I got in trouble the most, too. My brother almost never talked back or got in trouble, so he was rarely the target of my father's rage.

Sometimes Dad would order me to strip to my underwear and then whip my backside with a leather belt. But that was better than being forced into a tiny broom closet and then left there sitting in the dark to think about what I'd done. Huddled in that closet, my chin resting on my knees, I would repeat to myself: *You deserved it.* By the time my father finally let me out I had convinced myself that I *did* deserve it. I figured my dad had to come down so hard on me because I was manufactured wrong. It wasn't his fault, I decided—it was mine.

If I was stupid enough to mouth off—and I was, many times— his fists proved the most convenient weapon. But even when I knew I had it coming, I refused to give him the satisfaction of crying, stubbornly keeping a stiff upper lip. This allowed me to emerge from his beatings with a shred of dignity, which was essential for surviving those years. But over time that ingrained the habit of self-denial, of never admitting when I was hurting, and that would have serious side effects years later.

Despite scenes like that, what's amazing is that I still thought we had a great family. Kids have a remarkable ability to block out the bad stuff and focus on the good stuff. They can also learn to blame themselves instead of their parents for whatever's wrong.

Taking the blame for our problems allowed me to believe my family was stable, even normal. Better to think I was the problem than my family was. I often bragged to my friends how great my family was, probably trying to convince myself as much as them.

But scenes like the ones above made me wonder sometimes if our parents were not quite as perfect as I'd thought.

◆　◆　◆

I always had allies, lots of them, starting with my brother and sister. And I'd accumulate more over the years: teachers, coaches, and, always, plenty of friends—*good* friends. But my first and most important supporter was my mother's mother, whom we called Nanny. Her father was half-Cree, half-black. The rest of her family made it to Canada via the Underground Railroad. Nanny and Grandpa lived in a neat, big home in Scarborough, a nice suburb just outside Toronto.

Nanny's presence in my life was a true blessing. In a childhood filled with uncertainty and fear, she provided security and lots of love. When I was with her I had no doubt that I was loved, I had nothing to be afraid of, and the only thing I had to do was be myself. Nanny and our Grandpa, a warm and funny guy, made our trips to their home special.

I always thought Nanny's soft, comforting voice was like an angel's and that she was the best cook to walk the face of the earth. Her Thanksgiving and Christmas feasts were legendary: turkey, ham, macaroni and cheese—I can taste them even now.

I don't know what Nanny thought of her oldest daughter, my mother. To this day I really have no idea why my Nanny and my mom were so different. But I do recall thinking that Nanny must have been aware of the differences between her immediate family and ours.

When I was around five I was riding in Nanny's car when she accidentally turned the wrong way down a one-way street.

"Darn!" she said as she pulled over.

I corrected her. "You 'appose to say *shit*. Daddy always says *shit*."

"Oh, dear! You shouldn't say that!" But she couldn't stifle her laughter.

Nanny's shining spirit cut through a dark world. Even her smallest gestures—putting a hand on my shoulder, inviting me to sit on her lap—showed her love for me and made me feel so good.

Nanny was dignified, graceful, and elegant. She kept her long hair pinned in a bun. I often begged her to let it down so I could stand behind her on the couch for what seemed like hours, brushing her shiny hair, which was jet black with silver threads. While I ran the brush slowly through her hair she'd ask me how I was doing in school, who my friends were, and what I liked to do. I soaked up the attention, which was incredible therapy for me. I felt so calm, so safe, so loved. It's a real blessing to think someone cares about you more than anyone else in the world. Nanny made me feel like I was somebody, so when I was with her, I dared to think maybe I wasn't such a bad kid, after all.

I loved to read, and Nanny often asked me to read to her. She liked to teach me her favorite passages in the Bible. Other times I'd just pick up a magazine and start reading out loud, just to show her how much I was learning. She'd brag about me to my father.

"Bernie, you should be so proud of this boy! He's so smart!"

If my father was in a good mood, he might mention how many hits I'd had in my last baseball game. Sports were his main vehicle for praising Bernie and me.

Once, when I was seven, I was playing with Nanny when my father told me to go to the store to fetch him a pack of cigarettes. (Again, not uncommon in 1962.) When I reluctantly peeled away from Nanny my father became irritated with my dawdling and raised his voice.

"I told you to go to the store, and I told you to go *now*! Get going, before I—"

"Before you do *what?*" Nanny snapped. In an instant her soft, beautiful brown eyes turned hard as diamonds. "If you lay *one hand* on that boy, you'll have to take *me* on next."

I'd never seen anyone challenge my father like that. I had no idea Nanny could be so strong. I was impressed, but also afraid. I knew what my father was capable of, so I was worried he might haul off and hit Nanny. But even if he didn't, I knew I'd pay the price later.

He stared at her for a moment, then dropped it. I knew worse could be coming for me after Nanny was gone, but for a brief moment I savored my first victory over my father, even by proxy.

◆　◆　◆

My grandpa was a small, wiry man, maybe five-foot-six, with an infectious laugh. Even in Canada, where racism was much less rampant than in the States, he had endured a lot of humiliation in his job as a railroad porter, yet he always seemed to shrug off the slights and kept a positive attitude.

After thirty years he retired from the railroad and took a job as a skycap at Toronto's airport. I'd like to imagine this little guy manhandling those huge bags. They said he also had a way of making his customers smile, and he cherished every dime tip he received.

From my grandparents I learned how to treat people with consideration and respect. They constantly reiterated their fundamental values: "Don't ever lose sight of your principles," and "Don't let anyone step on you." Coming from two people who'd experienced untold offenses while keeping their self-respect firmly intact, this carried a lot of weight.

I loved going to their home so much that I often fantasized about living with them.

CHAPTER 2

An Indecent Proposal

COMPARED TO NANNY AND GRANDPA'S HOME, OURS often seemed strange and scary. On the rare occasions when all of us were there at one time, we had no center, no gravitational force pulling us all together. The Hallmark card photo of five family members sitting around the table for dinner or watching a game or a movie together simply didn't exist for us.

To be fair, part of this was the era. Kids were on their own a lot more in the sixties than they are now, so we made our own fun.

Bernie and I protected Gail, but if she wanted to play with us, she had to learn to play our way. When Bernie and I were playing hockey in the basement Gail and our cousin Loretta would beg to join in. We compromised by having Loretta stand in one spot and Gail six feet to her left. We'd say, "Don't move," and they became the goalposts.

Occasionally we'd fire a puck off one of the girls' shins, which would start the play-by-play: "Saunders with the shot . . . ohhhh, and it hits the goalpost!" Bernie believes that was my first play-by-play, so I owe Gail for that too! Gail and Loretta never flinched because they didn't want to be sent away. Playing together was enough to keep all of us happy.

＊　＊　＊

One of my father's friends, whom I'll call Pete Doby, had a half-dozen children. When we started visiting their spacious home in Toronto, Bernie and I were babies, and two of Doby's daughters, whom I'll call Laura and Carol, might have been ten and nine. During a visit about seven years later Laura and Carol asked me, Bernie, and two other boys if we wanted to see something. I was hoping she had some toys or candy, so I said, "Sure." While the other boys followed Carol, I tagged along with Laura downstairs to the guest bedroom in the basement.

She closed the door behind me and unfastened her blouse and bra. "Get on top of me," she said.

Laura asked me to stroke her breasts and kiss them. I did it, partly out of curiosity, partly out of pleasure, and partly out of fear. Each time I visited she would take me down to the guest bedroom for more, while the other boys would go with Carol or come with me. These encounters were mysterious, exciting, and troubling all at once. They left me feeling very confused and unsettled, but I certainly didn't think of it as abuse.

After each encounter Laura admonished me, "You can't tell anyone. If you do, I'll be sent away." I didn't dare say a peep.

One night she whispered, "Come into the bathroom with me."

When I walked in I saw that she had left the lights off. I stumbled into the room, blindly feeling along the walls. When I reached her she took my hand and guided it beneath her skirt, then inside her panties. To my childish mind, it felt like a netting of some kind, hot and moist.

"Take your pants off," she said. Her hands were all over me, touching my genitals. I achieved an erection, but that just confused me more. Laura made me put my fingers into her vagina until she had what I now know was an orgasm.

These occasional encounters continued for almost three years, only stopping when my father moved us to Montreal for a new job. I had never heard of women molesting boys, so I dismissed these memories as just another part of my strange childhood. But the effects of those too-early sexual encounters would stay with me the rest of my life, affecting my feelings about sex and my relationships with women long into adulthood.

Moving to Montreal, however, also cost me many visits to my grandparents. When my family left Ontario for Quebec, I lost Nanny—my protector, my shoulder to cry on, and the first person I felt gave me unconditional love. If my grandparents had been with me throughout my childhood, I might have made better choices and far fewer mistakes.

CHAPTER 3

Playing with Fire

WHEN WE MOVED TO MONTREAL WE SETTLED IN A working-class, bilingual suburb called Chateauguay (pronounced *SHAT-a-gay*) about fifteen miles from the city. Dad told us his new job was going to pay a lot more and would change our lives forever.

We moved into a split-level, four-bedroom bungalow across the street from a dairy farm. Coming from our cramped quarters in Toronto, it was a welcome change. We lived in a great neighborhood, surrounded by a lot of kids our age. We played sports every hour we could, but our two favorites were hockey and baseball.

Our father's father, a Jamaican immigrant, was a tall, athletic man. My father and his four brothers all played football and boxed. Uncle Danny had been Canada's amateur middleweight champion, and my father had been a star running-back for a minor league affiliate of the Hamilton Tiger Cats of the Canadian Football League. It seemed like Dad could jump over any hurdle and could run backward faster than anyone in our neighborhood could run forward. When you're a kid, that's the stuff of legends.

My dad really liked coaching our baseball and football teams, and it showed. He knew his stuff, he took it seriously, and he was the kind of guy all the neighborhood kids loved. But he had a knack for knocking me down at my best moments.

When I was ten or eleven our town built a couple of Little League ballparks. We had a game there when everything was finished except the outfield fence. They had laid down the gravel warning track and built the fence frame, but they hadn't put up the plywood boards yet.

When I hit a towering fly ball that just kept going back, the left fielder gave chase until he ran into the fence frame, and the ball sailed over his head. Home run! As I rounded the bases I looked into the dugout, hoping to witness my dad's approval. I was pleased to see him laughing.

But when I got to the dugout I found out why he was chuckling. "You dummy, the fence isn't finished! You just hit a ground-rule double!"

The umpire had signaled a home run, as he should have—the ball didn't go *through* the fence, after all, but *over* it—but my Dad made the official scorer mark it down as a double. Instead of celebrating his son hitting the first home run at the new park, he seemed to get more pleasure sending me back to second base.

He wasn't afraid to dress me down in public, but more frequently his punishments were meted out in private. If he told me to do something and I hesitated or questioned his order, he would furrow his eyebrow, which created a crease across the bridge of his nose. Then he'd slowly narrow his eyes, as if sizing up his prey. I knew what was coming next, so I'd start to run, usually for the perceived safety of my room. But that wasn't very smart because then I was trapped, so I'd grab pillows to protect myself against the blows I knew were coming.

When I was younger he'd hit me with an open hand, usually on any part of my body that I'd failed to protect. I'd duck and dodge and try not to cry, but pulling that off was almost impossible when the guy you thought was Superman had reduced you to a squirming lump of fear. The older I got, the harder he hit me.

It could be hard having my dad around, but it could be even harder when he wasn't. A few years after we moved to Montreal our dad started shuttling back and forth to Ohio. He did this, he told us, to make his fortune in prefab homes. His frequent absences made it harder for us to pay the rent, keep food on the table, and explain to our friends why our dad wasn't around. Whenever they asked, I told them, "He's working long hours in Ohio so he can create a better life for us," because that's what he had told us—and I desperately wanted to believe him.

He started out by alternating two weeks in Ohio with two weeks at home. Then it was three weeks in Ohio and just one week in Chateauguay. Before long our father had become a casual, infrequent guest in his own home. The famous threat, "Just wait 'til your father gets home," took on an entirely different meaning when that could take weeks—and when Dad did get home, absence seemed to make his heart grow harder.

When I was around twelve my father had returned after a few weeks away and started giving us all chores to do. I unwisely suggested that, because he wasn't around much anymore, he no longer had any right to tell me what to do. That's when I saw the all-too-familiar furrowed brow and squinting eyes. This time the open hand became a fist. When he started punching me, naturally I clenched my hands, as if preparing to punch him back. This only enraged him more, and he punched me ever harder. As an added humiliation, he punctuated every blow with a cutting remark.

"Why can't you learn to keep your mouth shut?

"This is your own fault!

"Why are you so dumb?"

Long after the bumps and bruises faded, what stayed with me was a deep, unshakeable feeling of worthlessness. Despite all the beatings, I never thought my father was the problem. Instead, I concluded that I deserved them because I must have been a horrible kid.

Bernie and I almost never talked after my father beat me, but on a few occasions, when we knew I was in for hell, we managed to team up, steal the belt hanging in the closet, and hide it from our dad. My relief was short-lived, however, because my dad would just resort to his fists.

Our sister was probably most affected by my father beating me. Gail's room was above mine, so when she heard the commotion begin, she'd run down the stairs, hoping her presence would be enough to get my father to stop. If it wasn't, she'd start screaming over my father's shoulder, urging me to shut up so maybe he'd stop. And if that failed, she'd sit at the top of the stairs with her head in her hands, sobbing.

When Dad had finished he'd walk past her as if she wasn't there. Then I'd follow to reassure her that I was okay.

"But why can't you just do what he says," she'd ask, "and then he'll leave you alone?"

I'd tell her I'd try to next time or I'd say I just didn't know how. Maybe there was just something wrong with me, I said. Even worse, I believed it.

◆　◆　◆

My mother wouldn't intervene in my father's punishments. When my father wasn't around, I didn't fear our mother the same way, so I had more freedom to do what I wanted. As a result, two distinct John Saunders began to emerge. There was the good, public John Saunders, a careful young man who did well in school and went to church. Nanny and Grandpa were very religious, and our parents raised us to love God and believe in the Bible. I grew up very devout. On our grade school debate team I argued strenuously for God's creation of man and earth in six days, and I won.

Then there was the private, devilish John Saunders who was willing to try just about anything for a kick. That included science experiments, but not the kind you'd expect from a ten-year-old. I wasn't growing roots out of potatoes or looking under a microscope to watch sugar crystallize in water—I was combining everyday chemicals to concoct explosives.

I had learned that mixing sulfur, saltpeter, and charcoal powder—all available at our local drug store, where my mom took me to buy the components—produced gunpowder. With my good buddies Ralph and Robin I'd played around with the mixture for about a year, using it to fuel rockets constructed out of paper and aluminum foil. Sometimes, when I was bored, I'd amuse myself by setting off small explosions, just to see things blow up. And I discovered that if you put copper powder in gunpowder, it burned like a rainbow. Pretty neat.

But I didn't stop there. One day in the spring of 1966, right before Easter, I packed a plastic lemon-shaped bottle with gunpowder and took it to an open field across the street, where I showed it to Bernie.

"It's a grenade," I bragged.

Bernie was naturally curious. I started a match and lit the homemade fuse—obviously not the smartest move. In an instant, flames soared up my face. I panicked and dropped the plastic lemon. A second later it exploded upward between my legs, scorching my jeans and my thighs.

"I'm on fire!"

Bernie looked almost as shocked as I was. He stared at me, petrified. I ran across the street to our house and banged on the glass door. Inside I could see my mother talking on the phone with one of her friends.

Our mom didn't have many rules, but she was strict about one thing: my brother, sister, and I were only to enter the house through the basement so we wouldn't track in mud. At that moment, however, with my legs on fire, obeying that rule was not my top priority.

I kept screaming and banging on the door. She looked up from her phone conversation, mildly perturbed, and pointed downstairs. She couldn't see what the problem was. Finally I ran down the cellar stairs to the basement, then up two flights of stairs, howling. Seeing that my hair was singed, my mother told her friend on the phone to wait a second and brushed the ashes off my head.

"Now get back outside," she told me, and returned to her call.

"No—my legs!" I screamed.

She looked down and saw the real damage and hung up the phone. She threw dishwater on me to douse the embers, which sent me into immediate shock. My eyes grew fixed, and I shook like a cold puppy. When the police arrived they tried to put me into their cruiser, but then they realized I was going to need medical help during the trip to the hospital. We had to wait an agonizing twenty minutes for an ambulance. I shook and sobbed while my mother looked on, finally grasping the seriousness of the situation.

During the ride to LaSalle General Hospital I passed in and out of consciousness. When I was awake I felt an incredible searing pain, which I later learned was the result of third-degree burns. The wound went deep into my flesh. The skin of my inner thighs looked like raw hamburger meat, and I had suffered extensive nerve damage.

I stayed in the hospital for three weeks. The doctors gave me painkillers, but the worst part of my recovery was the daily process of taking the dressings off and putting new ones on to prevent infection. It was forty-five minutes of torture. But what I remember most from my hospital stay was that my father never visited me.

I still idolized him, which forced me to invent increasingly elaborate stories for my buddies to explain why he wasn't around. I could fool my friends, but lying in that hospital bed, as the days became weeks, it was getting harder to fool myself. I saw other fathers visiting their children down the hall, sometimes staying overnight in uncomfortable chairs. I could no longer ignore the contrast: my father had better things to do than drive back to Montreal to visit his oldest son in the hospital.

We spoke on the phone exactly once, very briefly. I was afraid he'd be furious with me because I was sure to miss out on a lot of sports that spring and summer. He didn't shout, as I expected him to. He chastised me in a finger-wagging sort of tone. "Whatya doin', dummy?" But he never let me have it, perhaps because he felt some guilt about not coming to see me.

When Easter Sunday arrived I was still in the hospital. My mother brought me a Cadbury Creme Egg—a real treat—and said, "It's from your father." I knew it was a lie, and she probably knew I knew, but we both played along.

Lying there alone each night in my hospital bed forced me to confront proof of my biggest fear: there was something wrong with me—something that made me inherently unlovable. I spent every night crying. Not from the burns but from my dad's indifference. I had never experienced physical pain as severe as those burns, but the emotional pain was worse.

I did learn one important lesson from my time in the hospital: I'd better learn to look out for myself.

◆   ◆   ◆

Despite all this, because Dad was so passionate about coaching our teams, I still thought that down deep he loved me and that we were buddies. Bernie has told me that Dad bragged about me often. I'm sure Bernie's not lying, but it's very hard for me to imagine that. It just isn't consistent with the man I knew.

Three months after I got out of the hospital, well into the summer of 1966, my skin was slowly recovering, but my scars were still so bad that they bled and required fresh bandages each morning and night. Raw flesh remained exposed, some of which I couldn't feel due to nerve damage. One day out of curiosity I picked up a comb and sank it into my wound. I felt nothing.

I couldn't run, and I certainly couldn't play football. But when my father came back from Ohio for a few days he told me I had to play. My mother didn't protest.

"Dad, please," I pleaded. "Let me take just this summer off."

But football was my father's first love, and he insisted. I wasn't ready, but I wanted to live up to his expectations. I agreed to return.

I was our team's lead running back, so on our first day of practice I took most of the snaps. Near the end of the scrimmage I saw my father arguing on the sidelines with his assistant coach, Mr. Delaporta. After a few minutes Dad waved me over to join them.

When I started walking toward them my father yelled, "We don't walk in practice, boy. RUN!" So I ran the final few yards, despite the excruciating pain in my legs.

"What did I do wrong?" I asked.

"Mr. Delaporta doesn't think you've healed from that stupid accident. He thinks I should feel bad because you were dumb enough to play with fire and tried to blow your balls off!" He laughed. "Mr. Delaporta doesn't think you should play this year."

A wave of fear swept over me. If I hinted that Mr. Delaporta might have a point, my father would feel I had shown him up in front of his friend—and I knew what that would mean after we got home. I was trapped. So I looked Mr. Delaporta in the eye and said, "I feel fine. I *begged* my dad to let me play."

"John," Mr. Delaporta said sternly. "Look at your uniform." I didn't have to look down. I knew what he wanted me to see.

"John, your *legs*."

Slowly I lowered my head to look at my white football pants. Blood had soaked through my bandages and was leaking out the bottom of my pants down my shins.

"Bernie, he can't play," Mr. Delaporta insisted.

But Dad wasn't budging. "This is a tough kid," my father told him. Then he turned to me. "You want to *quit*?"

My legs were in agony, but I knew better. "Dad, I'll never quit."

I played that entire eight-game season, including two practices a week. No matter how much I bandaged the burns under my uniform, I bled through my white pants every time. I often heard opposing coaches and parents openly question whether the kid with the blood-soaked pants should be playing.

My father gave them all the same answer: "It's none of your business. I make the decisions regarding my son." Back then that was enough to end the conversation.

But playing with open wounds prevented my skin from healing very fast or very well. By the time football season ended, I had developed huge keloids, rubbery scars that often come with badly healed burns. Mine were about three inches thick on both inner thighs, so they rubbed against each other when I walked, which made the pain worse.

When hockey season approached, my mother took me to some specialists in Montreal. They tried a series of experimental procedures, injections, and medications to see if they could reduce the keloids. One of the treatments involved a device that resembled a power drill with a tiny needle on the end. The doctor stuck the needle into my huge scars and flipped the "ON" switch, spinning the needle to spread the medication throughout the scars. The twice-weekly procedure was excruciating. Worse, it didn't help.

I played hockey that winter, and my dad coached me in baseball the next spring before he returned to Ohio. But before he left he made sure I knew who was boss, one more time.

My burns still hadn't fully healed, but I was playing well, and our team led the league. I pitched and played third base. Bernie was a great shortstop. One of our best friends, Rick, played first and was a star left-handed pitcher who could throw a wicked curve ball, very rare at that age.

In the championship game, with two innings to go, our team was cruising along with a 4–0 lead. I was pitching, and feeling a little cocky, I started to joke around on the mound. I struck out two but then grooved one that a big kid knocked over the fence: 4–1.

In the seventh and final inning the first batter knocked a ground ball to my brother, who tossed him out. Two outs away from the championship. I struck out the next batter, but the catcher missed the ball and the batter stole first. We still had a 4–1 lead, though, so the next batter caught us by surprise when he bunted. We couldn't get anyone out on the play, so now we had runners on first and second, with only one out, and the tying run at the plate.

Against the next batter I threw a breaking ball off the fists, just where I wanted it. He backed up and smashed it deep into center—an impressive piece of hitting for a sixth-grader.

If it was gone, they'd have tied the game, but it stayed in the park and our center fielder made a great catch. Both runners tagged up and advanced a base. Now they had runners on second and third, with two out. A single, and our lead would be cut to one.

But none of this stopped me from clowning around on the mound. My friends played along, but not Bernie. If he'd learned nothing else from me, it was when to keep his mouth shut and avoid our dad's wrath.

I wasn't worried when I walked the bases loaded, even though that brought the winning run up to the plate. Then my father walked to the mound.

"Stop acting like a stupid idiot," he told me.

I just stared at him and said, "I can handle this."

From that exchange alone I knew I'd be in trouble when we got home, but I remained defiant.

The next batter crushed a fastball into the left-center field gap, far out of reach. That brought in the runner from third base, who jogged home to make it 4–2, and the runner from second base, which cut our lead to 4–3. While those two crossed the plate the runner on first base ran to third base and the batter made it to second. He was now the winning run, and a single would probably bring him home. Our opponents were going crazy, jumping around in the dugout, thinking they were about to take the title.

Again, my father came to the mound. "See what acting like a jackass has accomplished?"

I didn't buckle because there was nothing he could do to me on the mound. I also knew my buddy Rick, our best pitcher, had already pitched the day before, and the rest of our pitching staff was not very good, so Dad had little choice but to keep me in.

"Wait and see," I told him, with more brass than brains. "I'll strike this guy out."

He walked back to the dugout, fuming.

First pitch, on the inside corner: called strike.

Second pitch: a swing and a miss. Strike two.

We were one strike away from winning the championship—or one single away from losing it.

Before the next pitch Rick and my brother visited me on the mound. Rick and I started joking around, acting like the game was already over—but not Bernie. My father glowered at me from the dugout, just like I knew he would, then started walking toward the mound to chew me out again. I thought he might even pull me from the game, out of spite.

But before he could cross the baseline onto the field, the runner on third base took off for home plate. I was so shocked that I shot-putted the ball to the catcher. The runner beat my throw easily to tie the game.

Or he would have, if my father hadn't called a time-out when he'd left the dugout. The umpire had the guts to make the right call, which sent the runner back to third base.

After all the commotion, when my father finally got to the mound, he fired his words through gritted teeth: "If we lose this game . . ." he began. He didn't finish his sentence because he didn't have to. We both knew what he meant.

With two strikes, two outs, and two men in scoring position, my next pitch broke so much it hit the dirt as the batter swung and missed. Strike three! But when the ball hits the ground, it only counts as an out if the catcher gets the ball and tags the batter, or throws him out at first base.

Our catcher caught the ball and tagged the batter. The umpire made the call: "Out!" Game over!

We were the Little League champs of our small town, but we felt like we'd won the World Series! We poured 7-Up over each other, including Dad, who seemed as happy as I'd ever seen him. He looked over at me and smiled at his oldest son, who'd just won the deciding game. Perhaps I'd been forgiven.

After the game I sat in the car with him.

"How do you feel about your performance?" he asked. I knew he was referring to my behavior as much as my pitching.

"Dad, I'm sorry I almost lost us the game," I said. That was what he wanted to hear. And at the time it seemed like it might be enough to satisfy him. We drove off to meet the players and parents celebrating at the best pizza joint in town. I was having such a great time with the team that, as my father got up to leave, I asked if I could stay with my friends and walk home later.

My dad actually agreed, so my buddies and I ate more pizza and then went to Rick's house, where we tossed a football around for an hour or so. It was probably the best day of my life—up to that point.

At about ten I left Rick's house and got a ride home. When we pulled up in front of our house I could see my father waiting in the kitchen. When I walked in he didn't seem angry but just gazed at me calmly.

"John, you helped win a championship," he said, "so I've got an idea for next season. Instead of playing third base when you're not pitching, I'd like you to play catcher. You've got a strong arm, and you could throw out runners trying to steal second," something few Little Leaguers could do.

When I wasn't pitching I liked playing third, not catcher, but I was too tired to argue. It had been a great day, he hadn't brought up my hot-dogging, and I felt no need to push it. I mumbled my agreement, then headed for bed.

"Hold on," he said. "Let's toss the ball some before you go to bed."

At that hour, already tuckered out, that was the last thing I wanted to do, but I couldn't refuse him. We headed out into the backyard, lit by a single bulb attached to the house. I reached for my glove.

"You won't need that," my dad said.

He started out by lobbing the ball to me, soft enough for me to catch it barehanded. After a few throws, he paused, the ball gripped between his fingers. His expression turned cold, and he started throwing harder and harder. I caught every toss barehanded.

I knew he wanted me to quit, but my pride wouldn't let me. Seeing that I was not backing down, he hauled back and threw it with everything he had. My dad was in his midthirties, still in good shape, and he could whip it. I was sure my bare hands would shatter. But I caught each burning pitch, tossing the ball back to him and opening my hands for another.

Unsatisfied with my stoic response, he started pitching the ball so it dropped a foot or so in front of me. I couldn't catch these pitches even if I had a glove. The first few I fought off with my hands, which started to sting. My knuckles began to swell and bleed, but I was determined not to give in. My father then went to a full wind-up but kept bouncing his pitches off the ground, which hit me in my cheek, my nose, my throat. I took them all.

Finally I stood up from my crouching catcher's position to leave. I'd made my point. I was tough, but I'd had enough.

He just stared at me. I knew from his glare that if I left, he'd follow me into my bedroom, close the door, and I'd be in for another beating. So I crouched back down to field more pitches, pitches that felt like punches. I could no longer catch any of them, but I was able to take most of them off my chest and keep them in front of me, like you're supposed to, until one pitch bounced up off my hand and then hit me square in the mouth. I started bleeding.

We kept going. Finally, after a half-hour of "practice," he was satisfied that he had broken my spirit and called it quits.

When we walked back into the house I didn't dare say a word, but he did. "You'll think twice," he said, "about ever showing me up again."

When I woke up the next morning my pillow was covered in dried blood. I went to the bathroom to look in the mirror. My eye was swollen shut, and my mouth looked like I'd gone fifteen rounds with Muhammad Ali.

When my brother walked past the open bathroom door he saw me, stopped, and asked, "What *happened?*"

At this age I still didn't want to paint our father as a bad guy, so I lied. "Rick and I were tossing the football around. One of his passes went through my hands and hit me."

I washed up as well as I could and went to the kitchen to have some cereal. My mom was sipping coffee at the table, but she stopped cold when she saw me. I could see the shock on her face, but she didn't say a word. She knew better, too.

When my father appeared, he laughed. "What's the matter with you?"

I didn't answer him. I didn't even look at him. I returned to my room, closed the door, and started to cry. My dad had turned the best day of my life into one of the worst. After a few minutes my mother knocked on the door, came in, and sat on the bed.

"John, do you know why your father hits you?" she asked.

"Yeah," I said. "'Cause I'm a big mouth who doesn't know how to be a good son."

She shook her head. "It's because *his* father used to do it to him." She told me his father used to knock him down, then kick him in the ribs with his steel-toed work boots.

This didn't help me understand my dad any better or forgive myself, either, as perhaps she'd intended. No, my first thought was this: *I will never have any children.* Because if there was even the slightest possibility that I was going to do to my children what my father did to me, and his father had done to him, I could never live with myself.

If someone was going to break the cycle, it was going to be me.

CHAPTER 4

He Ain't Heavy

BERNIE HAS ALWAYS BEEN MY BEST FRIEND AND MOST trusted ally, but he still did whatever he could to antagonize me, like little brothers do. Then I naturally responded like big brothers do. I've always been thicker than Bernie, who's always been lean like our dad, so he'd call me fat or simply go into my room and toss my stuff all over the place. I would respond by beating him up, while he'd try to run away.

One day we were sitting at the kitchen table slurping Kool-Aid when I accidentally spilled some on Bernie. He acted like he was going to toss his Kool-Aid on me. I dared him to do it—and that's all he needed to hear. A split-second later he splashed his Kool-Aid all over my shirt. Before it made its way to the floor, I jumped up, and he took off, bursting out of the house.

He was a much faster runner than I was, but I had greater stamina. I chased him half a mile before I caught the back of his T-shirt and beat him up pretty good. I felt I needed to remind him who was boss, falling into the same violent patterns as my father.

Before we became teammates on the local travel hockey team, the Chateauguay Bantams, we played on rival teams when we were twelve and eleven. Every time our teams faced each other we ended up having a fight. After that season the league drafted a policy—still in effect all these years later—specifying that brothers had to play on the same team. Now there's a legacy we can be proud of.

My rule for Bernie was simple: if he was asking for it, I could pound him, but I wouldn't let anyone else touch him. This principle was put to the test the day Bernie, about fourteen at the time, came home bleeding badly from his nose and mouth. When I asked him what had happened, he said one of our French neighbors had beaten him up. When I asked why, Bernie replied, "For nothing. I didn't do anything."

Now, I knew better. Bernie was in the habit of starting things and then taking off. But even if he'd started it, my rule still held: no one else laid a hand on my brother.

My mother called the police, who drove us around the neighborhood in a cruiser, looking for the guy who had bloodied Bernie. I secretly hoped the officer wouldn't find him because I wanted to hand out my own brand of justice. When the police took us home, empty-handed, they told me if I found the guy I should call them instead of starting another fight. I agreed, but I had no intention of following their orders.

As soon as the police drove off I set up shop on our side porch because I knew this guy would have to pass me on his way home. At fifteen I was probably six feet tall and 180 pounds—not someone to mess with. I had another advantage: I was willing to wait all night. Sooner or later the guy had to come home.

Sure enough, about an hour later this guy cruised by on his bicycle. He was a tall, thin kid with black hair almost down to his shoulders, just like his mother's. I immediately ran to the street to cut off his path, and I didn't waste any time with words. I dragged him off his bike and started beating the hell out of him. I ground his face into the pavement and scraped it back and forth while punching him with all I had. It was less a fight than a thrashing.

Suddenly his parents arrived on the scene and began cursing me in French. My hockey teammates had already taught me all the bad French words, so I got the gist of it: his father was threatening to do the same to me if I didn't let his son go.

With that I realized I'd done enough damage to make my point. I let go of the kid's shirt and stood up—but I wasn't finished. I stepped toward his father and told him if he didn't want some of what I had justly given to his son, he had better take his family home, and they had better not speak one word to any member of my family again.

"If you see any of us," I said, "you better cross the street, or there'll be more of the same."

The kid looked at me, and then his parents—but he kept his mouth shut, his dad didn't say anything, either, and they all walked home. They only lived a few houses down the street, but they never talked to us again.

In the process I learned how much I loved my brother, but I also learned I had more of my dad in me than I realized—or wanted. The violence shot up inside me with such speed and power, like a volcano erupting, that it alarmed me. With that much anger inside me I knew my fears of repeating my father's mistakes were justified.

But for the time being, the attack served its purpose. Word got around pretty quickly: even with Mr. Saunders gone, you'd better not mess with the Saunders boys.

CHAPTER 5

The Salvation of Sports

BY THE TIME I REACHED MY TEENS I HAD BECOME PRETTY skilled at living this double life. At school, in church, and in front of adults I almost always did the right thing and seemed confident, stable, and reliable. In private I was pretty much the opposite. This dual personality helped me survive some rough years, but it came with a price.

With each passing year my counterculture habits took deeper root. With our visits to our grandparents increasingly rare and our father spending more time in Ohio, I was free to indulge my growing interest in music. I graduated from the Monkees to psychedelic bands like Led Zeppelin, Iron Butterfly, and my favorite, Jimi Hendrix. I even wore a big afro with a headband like Jimi's.

In that era a passion for "Purple Haze" often meant embracing the drug culture too. My friends had older siblings who talked constantly about the joys of marijuana and often offered me drugs, but I didn't indulge for one reason: I shared my father's belief that I had a future as an athlete.

After we moved away from my grandparents my favorite sanctuaries were hockey rinks, baseball parks, and football fields. At their best, sports can provide a rational and sane universe: Do right, get rewarded. Do wrong, get punished. The scoreboard is blind to race, religion, and everything else but your performance. Sports also offered my best chance to get my dad's approval, but even when I didn't, I seemed to get everyone else's.

Hockey has always been my favorite sport, as it is for most Canadians, but especially for me because my father knew nothing about it. He couldn't coach me, so he couldn't correct my every mistake, the way he would when we drove home from baseball or football games. All he knew was that I was usually the best player on the ice, and there was currency in that.

I remember one game, when I was thirteen, I started with the puck behind our net, then faked my way through the entire opposing team, finished with a move that left their goaltender floundering, and tossed the puck into the open net. On the bench one of my teammates asked, "How did you *do* that?"

I thought for a few seconds, then said, "I don't know." It just came naturally.

Even when Dad acted unimpressed with my performance, if I scored a hat trick, those small triumphs temporarily blocked his ability to put me down. And if he didn't always reward me for doing well, others would.

When Bernie and I were on the same Pee Wee all-star team, we played in a big tournament in Hull, Quebec, just across the provincial border from Ottawa, Ontario. There must have been five thousand or so people packing the stands. When I skated around the ice for warmups it felt like I'd just entered another world. I played great that weekend. By the end of the tournament it seemed like everyone was cheering for me. When people think you're special, especially when you don't often think you are, it's a very powerful drug. Sports can do that for you.

When parents tell their children they're special and they're loved, those children tend to grow up feeling good about them- selves and usually don't have a burning need to gain the approval of the rest of the world. But if you don't grow up with that sense of security, then the next-best thing is to get it from thousands of strangers cheering for you.

I don't think I would have pursued sports as a career if I wasn't searching for something I couldn't get at home. Unlike some of my colleagues at ESPN, I didn't get into this field because sports consumed me. Most of the guys I work with worship the legends we grew up watching, and they dreamed of doing what we do now. When my good friend Chris Berman was a kid he was so taken by the idea of becoming a sportscaster that he used to play "Sports Announcer" in his backyard, using a pencil for a microphone.

That wasn't me. Obviously I love sports, but probably not as much as many of our viewers. I don't watch every game, I can't recall every pitch, and I can't recite statistics from the fifties. Growing up, sports provided a way for me to get noticed and, I hoped, a chance to make big money in the pros.

The appeal of this dream went beyond a need for acceptance. Whatever money Dad was making in Ohio, he wasn't sharing much of it with us. Whenever our phone rang I assumed it was a bill collector. To this day I have a Pavlovian reaction that a ringing phone means bad news. A bailiff occasionally visited us at our door with legal judgments against our father for failing to pay outstanding bills. By the time I was eleven I had already learned that if I didn't touch the summons, it could not be served.

And yet in the midst of this struggle our parents always produced great Christmas mornings. Dozens of great gifts—hockey skates, baseball gloves, Gibson guitars—propped up our tree as if we were rich. But a few months later we would inevitably have to pawn our new presents to pay the rent.

As my father's visits dwindled, he'd call my mother and say that he had wired money for us and that we could pick it up at the Western Union office in Montreal in a few hours, or sometimes in a few days. We'd receive this as great news. *We're saved!* We'd pile into the car and drive to the Western Union office downtown. For our first few trips our mother, Bernie, and Gail waited in the car while I headed inside. I took a deep breath and straightened my shoulders. I quickly got this routine down. When I got to the front of the line I'd ask, "Is there a money transfer for Saunders from Bernie Saunders?

The clerk had his routine down too. "No. Nothing yet."

The cashiers felt sorry for me, the boy whose deadbeat dad told us he'd sent the money and who couldn't figure out why it hadn't arrived. Thinking that Dad's wire would come any minute, sometimes we waited until Western Union closed. Then we drove home, dejected, just to return the following morning, full of foolish hope. Once in a great while there would actually be a wire waiting for us, which was just enough to keep us coming back for more. Usually I walked out empty-handed. That brought us to the last act of this tired play: the silent, sullen car ride home.

I grew weary of this pretty quickly and started ducking out of these all-too-predictable trips by staying at a friend's house. That forced Bernie to take over my role, with the same demoralizing results.

Over time I learned to field just about everything my father could throw at me, including his fists. But I never could understand why he left us hungry. I resented every night we sat at the kitchen table peeling potatoes, one of the few foods we could afford, even though our mom turned these into delicious potato pancakes.

But while peeling those potatoes I told myself that, whatever I did for a living, I'd be able to buy all the things I dreamed of having as a kid. And not just food but a nice, big home, a reliable car, and new clothes. You can get those things by being a doctor or lawyer, of course, but money alone wasn't enough for me. Being a nobody at home fueled my ambition to be *somebody*, to be recognized and respected. So I dreamed of being an actor or a rock-and-roll legend or a hockey star. It might have been a misguided ambition—what were the odds?—but it drove me. I was determined never to be a nobody again.

But even hearing five thousand fans cheering for you at a Pee Wee hockey tournament in Hull, Quebec, was no substitute for my father's approval. In the middle of this tournament, during one of the best weekends of my life, I remember looking up in the stands and wishing my dad had been there to see me score and hear all the people cheering for me. I fantasized that he would be there and finally tell me I had impressed him.

◆ ◆ ◆

Of course, the scoreboard might be coolly objective, but the coaches don't have to be. Most coaches play favorites, which is why I loved playing for a coach named Roger St. Onge on a Bantam travel hockey team, for players in grades eight and nine. He was a young man, probably in his late twenties, but he had the look of a hockey lifer. He wore his black hair combed straight back, with a two-day beard and a windbreaker from one of his old teams. Coach St. Onge didn't speak very much English, so he kept it simple, "John, Bernie—go!"

But his philosophy was just as simple, and I loved it. Coach St. Onge was completely consistent and fair. With him my performance directly determined his actions: play better, and I got more ice time. Play worse, and I got less. This sounds straightforward, but how many coaches actually do that, every game, with everyone on their team? With Coach St. Onge, hockey gave me things I couldn't seem to get anywhere else, including structure, a sense of fairness, and male role models.

I was a very good running back, pitcher, sprinter, and high jumper, but for me hockey eclipsed them all. Montreal is home to the Canadiens, the Yankees of hockey, and our area produced serious players. Peter Quinn, two years older than me, played at Dartmouth. Steve Heggison, one year older, got a full ride to Providence College, where he played for Lou Lamoriello, the future president of the New Jersey Devils and now the Toronto Maple Leafs. If you played well in Chateauguay, you could make a better life for yourself.

By high school I was one of the best players in the area. Ivy League teams out east and Midwestern programs like Michigan and Michigan State were courting me. Not only did I believe hockey would give me my best chance to get to college, but I also had no doubt that I'd make it to the National Hockey League.

But my hockey dreams were about to run into two major obstacles. One I couldn't control. The other I could, but I chose not to.

CHAPTER 6

Looking for a Little Relief

LIKE MOST TEENAGERS, I STARTED TO RELY LESS ON MY parents and more on my friends. Fortunately I've always had good friends. By eighth grade my loose circle was evolving into a smaller, tighter group of trusted allies—Gerry, Vincent, and Barry—and we've remained close to this day.

For the first time in my life I felt like I belonged to a group of people who *chose* to accept me. These guys became my family. They liked my ideas and thought I was intelligent enough to engage in a real conversation.

Our relationships with our fathers varied, but none of us was very close to his dad. In those days that was more the norm than it is today. Vincent had about ten younger brothers and sisters, so he was as much a father to them as a brother and had to be responsible. But Barry and Gerry went out of their way to do the opposite of whatever their parents wanted. Gerry's mom remarried; his stepdad was a stand-up guy who became a true father to her kids, but he and Gerry still argued a lot.

Despite all this, I envied them for having fathers at home, a reliable supply of food on the table, and strict rules they had to follow. Even if they hated obeying those rules, they gave my friends some structure—something all kids want, even as they rebel against it. Our family had rules, but I didn't follow them, and if my dad wasn't home, there weren't many consequences. So the rules quickly lost their power.

But none of that stopped me from pretending that I had it much better than my friends did. I'd ask, "What time do you guys have to be home tonight?"

"Midnight. What about you?"

"Well," I'd boast, "my dad's in Ohio, and my mother doesn't care what time I get in." This was an exaggeration: we did have a curfew, but if I came in late, Mom didn't say much, if anything.

This was every teenager's stated fantasy. But as my friends grudgingly left the street and headed back to home, I was the jealous one.

Like a lot of teenagers, we liked flirting with danger. When I entered ninth grade my dream of being an NHL player cheered by thousands became less important than fitting in with my small circle of friends. Barry, Vincent, Gerry, and I made our first forays into drugs at our town's grocery store. Someone told us we could get high by chewing nutmeg, so we stuffed our pockets with as many bottles of the spice as we could carry and gathered beneath a highway overpass.

"All right, who's going to go first?"

I was fourteen and still hadn't had my first beer or cigarette. Neither had the others. Gerry dared to go first, and soon enough we were all chewing the nutmeg, eagerly anticipating the psychedelic paradise we'd heard about. But the truth is that chewing nutmeg is like eating sand and tastes like the bottom of a bird cage—with about the same effect.

"Anybody feel anything yet?" Gerry asked.

We waited. Nothing. But nobody wanted to be the first to admit he wasn't catching that "spice high." We all wanted to be the first spice boy, so we all acted like it was working.

"Hey, this is pretty good!" I lied.

"Definitely feelin' it!" another said.

But when Gerry asked if anyone wanted any more, we all said, "No!"

When we got to Billings Regional High School in the late sixties the conventional wisdom held that when it came to drugs, there was little middle ground. Marijuana would rot your brain and lead you to even heavier drugs, which in turn would lead to addiction. Start smoking pot, and soon you'd be shooting heroin. I have no idea if the domino effect is true, but I can tell you this much: nutmeg *definitely* leads to harder drugs.

The four of us were amateurs, but our friends' older siblings were experienced. One night, soon after we started hanging out with them, I helped polish off a gallon of homemade red wine, about the worst stuff you could imagine. I woke up hours later inside a tent in Vincent's backyard. I was severely hungover, and my face had somehow been smashed up, with a long scrape and a fat lip. I had no idea how it happened until my friends informed me that, after chugging the bottle, I tried to ride a bicycle from the handlebars. No one was surprised when I fell face first into a rock in Vincent's front yard. Well, that explained that.

I could have learned a lot from that one night: drinking alcohol can be dangerous, chugging a gallon of red wine more so, and homemade wine is to be avoided at all costs. And if you break all these rules, you probably shouldn't hop on the handlebars of a bike and try to ride it. But the only lasting lesson I took away was a lifelong aversion to red wine.

Even in the late sixties most of my classmates would not smoke pot. What motivated me to cross that line was a need that went much deeper than achieving fame on a hockey rink. Getting high provided a temporary escape from feeling sad and worthless, my dominant emotions at that age.

Many people have fleeting thoughts of suicide, especially teenagers. For me the desire to die started to take hold at this age and followed me for decades. In hindsight it's obvious that I was depressed—and yes, adolescents can suffer from depression, which is a more serious condition than typical teenage moodiness. It can be more dangerous, too, because often the decision to end one's life is impulsive, and teenagers are more impulsive than adults. But in my teens I was no more aware of being depressed than a fish is aware of being in water.

I knew I felt bad, though. I even thought I knew why: I was a bad kid, an inadequate son, a defective person. If *you* are the problem, your problem is pretty hard to escape.

It was in one of my various basement bedrooms that the sick feeling in the pit of my stomach became much more intense. As I lay on my bed I felt even more alone in the world. I'd drop the record player needle onto a Jimi Hendrix album, like *Are You Experienced?* or *Axis: Bold as Love*. The music helped me sink into my favorite daydream: that I could close my eyes and never wake up.

I could still retreat into the disguise of the good kid. I could ace a test, run for a touchdown, hit a home run, or score a goal, but the pleasure these things provided didn't last. I knew my dark side was always waiting to make a roaring comeback. I decided that if I was going to get some relief from feeling horrible all the time, I needed more than a good grade or a good game. I needed something else. So I started smoking pot with my friends.

What I initially got out of drugs wasn't the buzz but the feeling of acceptance. If I had the approval of this group of friends, I thought, did the disapproval of my parents really matter? I might have been high as a kite, but I felt like my thinking had never been clearer.

However, the more pot I smoked, the harder it was to keep up my double life. I had been raised to fear God, do my best in school, and lead Chateauguay's Little League teams, but all those things mattered less and less. After all, what did I get for all my hard work and self-denial? A dark, lonely basement room where I could wallow in my solitude.

But when I smoked pot and stayed out all night I had a ball. I was hanging out with the only people who seemed to think *I* mattered. They didn't like me for my grades or athletic ability but for who I was—something I hadn't felt since we moved away from my grandparents.

Our Gang of Four became part of a larger group that included Ralph, Robin, Richard, and a few others: the resident potheads at Howard S. Billings Regional High School. None of our families had much money, but if you had to be lower middle class, this was the time to do it. In the late sixties wearing the same worn jeans to school every day was considered cool. The rich kids were trying to look poor, not the other way around.

While the kids who had a bit of money waited in the cafeteria line for their food, our gang walked past them with the same boring sack lunches we took to school every day. If my friends and I came into a few bucks, we'd visit a food truck around the corner that sold French fries and a Quebec delicacy called *poutine*, which is fries smothered in gravy and cheese. But we soon faced a lunchtime dilemma: How could we afford fries and still have enough money for pot?

Gerry came up with the bright idea of panhandling. It wasn't that unusual to see long-haired kids on the street asking for spare change, and plenty of folks passing by would throw a few coins their way. The four of us proved to be pretty good at this. We were smart and entertaining—or so we thought—plying reluctant givers with a little song or a joke, which often nudged them to reach into their pockets for some change.

We weren't above begging for cash from classmates' parents, either, or even friends. We certainly didn't feel that our pride or reputations were at stake, and sometimes we walked off with enough money to get fries *and* pot. Now that was a good day! But when we didn't have enough for both, we chose the grass.

◆　◆　◆

I found that I could drink or smoke my pain away, at least for a little while, but my sadness never disappeared. It just retreated for a bit, then came back even stronger. That was when a voice began telling me, *Stop at the next depot and get off.* Killing myself seemed the only option that could end my pain, but the idea of actually doing it scared the hell out of me.

I preferred fantasizing about dying in spectacular fashion than planning how I might actually do it. One of my favorite scenarios was imagining myself behind the wheel of a red Triumph sports-car doing 100 miles per hour, flying past the Indian reservation between Chateauguay and Montreal, a stretch of highway that was once called the deadliest passage in Canada. Just a small slip of my wrist, I figured, and I would be airborne, hurtling over and over, until I died in the glorious wreckage.

You might think my death fantasies would end with the self-absorbed satisfaction that comes with vengeance: "Look what you made me do!" But mine always ended with the feeling of relief because I thought my death would make life easier for my family, like removing the family stain. So in my fantasy the spot gets removed, and our family picture becomes perfect again.

At least when I was high I wasn't thinking of ending my life. For many people drugs can lead to death by reducing their inhibitions to act on their suicidal impulses or through an accidental overdose. But for me getting high was fun and actually moved my thoughts away from death.

Finding a way to get high soon became an obsession for all of us. Because we lived near Montreal, it was never difficult to find pot. We just had to find a way to pay for it. When we realized the money we were bringing in from panhandling wasn't keeping up with our spending on drugs, we had to come up with something else.

CHAPTER 7

My Two Selves

IN QUEBEC STUDENTS GRADUATE FROM HIGH SCHOOL after grade eleven, so our tenth grade is similar to junior year in American high schools. When I was in tenth grade I was elected class vice president. I was really into student council and worked hard at it. I was playing good hockey, which I still figured was my best chance to get to college and make a name for myself.

After Coach St. Onge my most important hockey mentor was none other than Jacques Demers. Yes, the same coach who led the Montreal Canadiens to the Stanley Cup in 1993. I first met Jacques at the Phil Myre Hockey School in Montreal when I played at the Bantam level, after eighth grade. Jacques basically ran the summer camp. In the winter he coached our town's top Junior team, the Chateauguay Wings—the pride of our city, composed largely of eighteen- and nineteen-year-olds.

Once, between skating sessions, all the campers my age were sitting in a classroom with Jacques drawing plays on the chalkboard, explaining some basic strategies. When he asked a question about a particular formation, I was the only one who had the answer. He smiled at me, then looked around the classroom. "See dat?" he said, in his thick French Canadian accent. "Dat's why he's going to be playing for my Junior team one day!"

For a sixteen-year old, that was an amazing thing to hear. My buttons were popping. But did he really mean it? I learned that, like Coach St. Onge, when Jacques told you something, his word was good.

The next year I played for Les Aisles' Midget team, just a level below the Junior team, with a promise to come up as soon as I was ready. Jacques was a very smart coach, but his calling card was his amazing enthusiasm, which was contagious. When we learned he lived around the corner from us, we couldn't resist visiting him occasionally.

What we didn't know then—what no one knew until Jacques confessed in 2005—was that he was illiterate. He couldn't read. Imagine how smart you have to be to work around a handicap like that and manage to become head coach of five NHL teams. When I read the news of his illiteracy, I gained even more respect for him—for his cleverness, for his determination, and for having the courage to confess publicly.

In his autobiography Jacques explains why such a smart guy could be illiterate: his father beat his mom and him, which made him so anxious he couldn't learn. "All I wanted from my father was to treat me with love," he writes. "Not to beat me up when I did something wrong. Not to beat up my mom. It really hurt me because he took away my childhood."

That sounded familiar. No wonder we connected so well. Jacques believed in me, and he often told me I was a legitimate pro prospect.

The support I received from Jacques's boss, Mr. Bougee, the manager of the Chateauguay Wings, was far more conditional. Whereas Jacques was an athletic, dashing, well-dressed guy with a stylish moustache, Mr. Bougee was a big, frumpy man. He also knew more about me than Jacques did—which was not to my advantage.

After practice Mr. Bougee told me he'd heard rumors that I was hanging out with drug users, which was really only the half of it. I wasn't just hanging out with them; I was one of them. He added, in a stern voice, "If you want to play for us, you better keep yourself clean."

My only real dream at that age was to become a professional hockey player, and the Chateauguay Wings represented the best route to get there. So I lied and told Mr. Bougee there was no truth to the rumors. I'm sure he didn't believe me.

"You got de talent and aptitude for dis game," he told me. "And dat's a rare combination, especially at your age. I've seen only a few with your understanding of de game. You can go as far as you want in hockey, even play in de NHL. Don't blow dis by doing something stupid."

If I had listened, it might have changed the course of my life. But his wise words just wafted away like the smoke from the joint I'd smoke ten minutes after I left his office.

◆　◆　◆

My NHL dreams would soon face another obstacle, this one not of my own making. In our football team's season-opening game, our kicker boomed it, and I ran downfield to make the tackle. I thought I had the runner lined up, but when he cut sharply I missed him and hit the ground hard. My left shoulder popped out of its socket. The pain was worse than anything I'd ever experienced playing sports before.

Riding in the ambulance I began to hallucinate. At the hospital the doctors twisted and pulled my arm for two hours, trying to jam the ball joint back into its socket. It was an excruciating process—and for nothing. After all that, when they wheeled me into the X-ray room, I simply stood up, and my shoulder magically popped back into place. It still hurt, but nowhere near as badly as it had.

To make sure the joint healed properly, they put me in a cast from my waist up to my neck, like a turtle shell. I missed the entire football season. After I recovered I returned to our midget hockey team, where I was one of the league's best players. It helped that

I played with Bernie, one of the scoring leaders. I was one month away from being called up to the Juniors, Jacques's team, for the 1970–1971 season.

In February of 1971 we were playing on the road against one of our big rivals. When my brother scored the go-ahead goal, I skated over to congratulate him—while an opposing player snuck up from behind and flattened me. I went down hard, ripping my left shoulder from its socket for the second time. In an instant my chance to join Demers's Junior team vanished.

After they put me back in the cast for another six weeks I had no reason to go to practice. I suddenly had all this unexpected free time, and I used it to smoke pot. While my friends worried their parents might find out, I worried my coaches would. But none of those fears stopped us.

After our meager stash ran out, we stumbled on a way to get more, for nothing. When classmates asked us for pot, it didn't take a rocket scientist to realize we could sell it to them and smoke the profits—never mind that risked being arrested by the police or roughed up by competitive dealers.

We started small. We calculated that if we could get just twelve people to give us ten bucks each, we could get high for free. To get things started, we even threw in a little extra for our first custom-ers. Our plan worked—maybe too well. Our classmates soon beat a path to our lockers, which angered the professional dealers in our town. We went ahead anyway, and it wasn't long before we were taking in more money than we could ever spend smoking pot.

We each had a hundred dollars burning holes in our wallets, making us feel like high rollers. I bought new clothes, posters, and records. Even better, at sixteen I started putting some food on my family's table. Mom never asked where the money came from. If anything, she seemed pleased, maybe even impressed. Occa-sionally she asked me for a few dollars "to pay a bill." On more than one occasion I opened the drawer where I stashed my pot and proceeds and found I was short a few bucks. It would have been hard for someone to find the cash and not see the stash.

I never said anything to her, and she never asked. I was making good money, smoking a lot of pot, and my mom was leaving me alone. Why rock the boat? I had a good thing going, and it didn't make sense to spoil it over a few missing bucks.

The drug business was good, but having gotten a taste of easy money, we wanted more. My friends and I started scheming ways to bring in more cash, although we also did a few dumb things, I'm afraid, just for the thrill of it. We hit a new low when we robbed a classmate's house and sold his father's musical instruments to a guy in Montreal who gave us fifty cents on the dollar.

We also organized a system to steal record albums from the local department store—possibly the stupidest item you could pick, given its unwieldy shape—and eventually we were caught. Although the store's security cop didn't call the police, he told our parents. My mother slapped me and told me to stop hanging out with these kids, blaming them more than me.

But if I was proud of the idea that I was raising myself, I was doing a very poor job of it.

CHAPTER 8

The Drug Business

WE WISELY GOT OUT OF THE B&E BUSINESS, AND WE stopped stealing after security broke our "album ring," but we continued selling pot, which was more dangerous. We'd started out just wanting to get high for free, but we quickly became minor league drug dealers. We were making so much money that we couldn't help but wonder how much more we could make if we "turned pro."

What we should have been wondering was who knew what we were up to and how long it would take before someone caught us—or attacked us. Classmates who liked getting high knew they could get it from us. Classmates who didn't get high told their parents and teachers about us. Before long it seemed like everyone knew what we were up to. Ignoring these signs, we charged full speed ahead.

In January of 1970, about a month before my sixteenth birthday, Gerry, Vincent, and I hitchhiked to Montreal, where we met with a dealer named Claude. He sold us joints made of hash and tobacco, which proved to be a big hit with our friends. After a few more successful deals he introduced us to LSD, but it wasn't very lucrative because our classmates were scared of it. We found bigger profits selling mescaline, a natural herb that functions much like LSD. As an organic drug, mescaline had greater appeal to our more cautious classmates, and it sold like hotcakes. The problem was that Claude couldn't get his hands on as much mescaline as we needed. But once our classmates tried mescaline, it wasn't hard to convince them that its artificial cousin, LSD, was safe. We sold plenty after that.

I was not above dropping acid at the start of the school day and soaring through my classes high as a kite. Why not? Thanks to my shoulder injury, my hockey career was on hold anyway. In tenth and eleventh grade I probably took more than two hundred acid trips.

LSD fulfilled my daredevil instincts, gave me a cheap thrill, and dulled the pain of depression. Now, to be clear: I was responsible for my decisions, and suffering from depression doesn't make taking drugs right, or even smart. The last thing a depressed person needs is a drug problem on top of his other problems. But tell that to a sixteen-year-old.

And sure enough, I almost got into real trouble with the police when they decided to inspect my school locker. Luckily I'd been tipped off, and I moved my stash just in time. When they asked to inspect my locker, I couldn't have been more cooperative—"Why, sure, officer! Why do you ask?"—which probably irritated them even more. But they found nothing.

We also had a close call with some friends of Claude's who happened to possess a very long knife they were not afraid to wave under our noses. If any of these situations had gone wrong, I might be in jail, or dead. I certainly wouldn't be on ESPN. The fact is that I was pretty damn lucky. And I was even luckier when you consider that I never got into any car accidents on drugs or tried to jump out of a window, which many have.

But no depressed person can wipe out their problems with alcohol or drugs. These substances just kick your problems down the road, but they resurface, again and again, and they come back stronger each time.

◆ ◆ ◆

Throughout my shoulder recovery Jacques Demers stuck with me, although I'm sure he didn't know my whole story, or even half of it. Perhaps he saw himself in me, a kid who needed someone to believe in him.

As soon as I returned to the ice I blew out my left shoulder again during a hitting drill designed to toughen us up. Mr. Bougee wanted to cut me from the squad because he didn't want to save a spot for a defenseman in rehab. Fortunately Jacques stood up for me and wouldn't let him cut me. But even after my shoulder had healed well enough that I could play, Mr. Bougee kept delaying my return. When it became clear that Mr. Bougee was holding me up, I went to Jacques and explained that hockey was probably my only way to get to college.

Jacques was sympathetic, but his hands were tied, so he told me to go to another team, La Prairie, ten miles away but in the same league. I met with their GM, who said, "You look great. Can you play Monday night?"

"Sure!"

But when Monday night came, the paperwork still hadn't been finished. I missed that game, then another game, then another. A couple of weeks later, when the season ended, I'd never gotten in a game for La Prairie or Jacques's team, Les Aisles. I ended up playing for a local travel team, a crucial notch below Juniors, so no scouts watched us. At the end of the season I ran into La Prairie's coach, who explained why they couldn't play me: Mr. Bougee wouldn't release me from Les Aisles—and he wouldn't let me play for Jacques either.

In 1973 the Chicago Cougars, one of the brand-new World Hockey Association teams, asked Jacques to become their director of player personnel. Before he accepted, he had a lot of questions about working and living in the United States. He knew our dad spent most of his time working in Ohio, so he asked Bernie and me about the opportunity, which we encouraged him to take.

When he accepted, Bernie and I walked around the corner to his house to give him a pair of cufflinks. We loved him and missed him immediately. But we would both see him again.

CHAPTER 9

Hurting Myself

SELF-MUTILATION IS USUALLY ASSOCIATED WITH TEEN-age girls. The most common method is to use an old-fashioned razor blade to make small cuts on the arms or thighs, just deep enough for blood to surface.

One night, feeling despondent, I grabbed a wire hanger from my closet and beat it against my legs as hard as I could, first with my pants on, then eventually on my bare legs. During gym class the next day I couldn't hide the damage I'd done. When the boys gawked at the deep welts on my thighs, I told them, "We had a rough game of street hockey last night."

After I returned home that day I went into my room and did it again, whipping my legs with the hanger until the skin welled up with blood. I flinched as each blow sent a stinging shot straight through my thighs. When I felt I'd finally given myself my appropriate punishment—for what, who knows?—I stopped and sighed, as if I'd finally scratched a hard-to-reach itch.

I don't know why I started hurting myself. Some experts say people who hurt themselves are deprived of feeling, so feeling pain is better than feeling nothing. Others say it's an act of anger turned inward. Or maybe I was picking up where my father had left off, punishing myself when he was not there to do the job himself.

When Dad was around, life was never dull. One night, when he was at home, I rode my bike about five miles to visit a friend, Susan, the daughter of my dad's best friend. I planned to hang out with her until about ten and then be home for my eleven o'clock curfew. Now, curfew was rarely enforced when our father wasn't home, but when he was, things were different.

Susan and I weren't interested in each other romantically. We just liked talking with each other. Before we knew it, time had flown by, and it was 11:30, but I thought it would be okay with Dad because her parents could confirm that I'd been at their house the whole time. Nonetheless, I pedaled home as fast as I could. Halfway there I spotted my mother's station wagon crawling around a turn. Then it hit me: she wouldn't be going out when my father was home. As the car pulled up alongside me, the driver's door flew open and my father jumped out.

"Where the hell have you been?"

He yanked me by my collar, pulled me off the bike, and threw me to the pavement. I instinctively covered my face. He was madder than I'd ever seen him, kicking me hard in the side.

"You stupid no-good waste! You've got all this talent, and all you do is screw around. If that's what you want, then you'll get it, all right! I'll be happy to help you."

Our car shielded him from onlookers. He must have kicked me six or seven times before I jumped up and cocked my fist as if I was going to fight back, but that didn't stop him. He threw me up against the car and punched me twice on the side of my head, then ordered me to get in the car while he loaded my bike in the back.

I was obviously defeated, but he wasn't finished. Like a lot of black guys in the early seventies, I had a huge Afro. Everyone who wanted to be a rebel wore their hair big.

"Tomorrow morning you're going to get a goddamn haircut," he told me.

That bothered me more than the beating. My Afro was part of my identity, and I dreaded the comments I'd get at school when my friends saw I'd shaved it. When we got home he went upstairs to bed. I sat at the kitchen table, tears rolling down my face.

As usual, I blamed myself: *Why do you make him do this to you? All you had to do was make a phone call, and none of this would've happened.* Then I heard someone coming down the stairs. As I brushed away my tears, my father sat down at the table across from me.

I spoke first, blurting out, "I'm sorry."

"John, you think I *like* to beat you? I just want you to be all you can be, and you can't do that without discipline. You need to learn you can't do whatever the hell you want."

I wanted to say, "I do whatever I want when you're not here," but I'd had enough for the night, so I just listened.

"I don't want to be away from you guys," he said. "I'm just making the best life I can for you."

This statement ignored the fact that we seemed to have much less money, not more, since he'd basically moved to Ohio. I had learned to fear my father, but I still held tightly to the memories of the long afternoons this man spent teaching me the art of pitching a perfect curve ball or how to make the proper cut down the field with a football tucked against my chest. That father had to be in there somewhere.

"You can keep your hair," he said, then he rose from the table and went to bed. That was it.

I still wasn't tired, so I went to my room and played a Led Zeppelin album at a very low volume. I grabbed a hanger from the closet, but then a new idea came to me. I grabbed a pack of matches, lit the entire pack, and held the flames to the hanger until the matches burned down to my fingers. Then I pressed the hot wire into the bare skin of my shin.

The pain was excruciating, but I held it there until the wire cooled. As I removed it, flesh fell from my shin. I could see into the wound. It reminded me of burning my legs with the explosives.

I lay down on my bed.

I feel so alive now. The more I'm able to take, the stronger I become.

I felt some peace. At least I was in control of the pain instead of it controlling me.

◆ ◆ ◆

A few weeks later, on a spring afternoon, I was walking home from school again when it looked like we were having a yard sale. Our family's possessions had been piled by the curb: our living room sofa, our lamps, our dishes, our coffee pot, all my clothes and hockey jerseys, even my little sister's stuffed animals.

My mom and I had barely spoken in months, but when I saw her sitting on the curb with her head in her hands, I couldn't help but feel sorry for her again. When she looked up, her eyes said it all.

The landlord had changed all the locks. On the front door he'd hung a sign that read, "EVICTION NOTICE." We'd spent six years in that house, the most time we'd ever lived in one place.

"Your father hasn't paid the rent for six months," she told me. "Take a good look around," she said, waving her hand in the air. "Because you'll do this to your family someday. You're just like your father."

That was her way to cut me the deepest, because she knew it was my worst fear—and there was some truth to it. I was already developing my dad's two worst traits—violence and absence. If I was going to avoid repeating his mistakes, I felt I needed to get out of Chateauguay, ironically enough, and get a fresh start.

PART TWO

◆　◆　◆

Trying to Build
a Better Life

CHAPTER 10

Moving Out, Moving On, Moving Back

WITH HIGH SCHOOL WINDING DOWN I HAD TO MAKE A big decision. Thanks to my banged-up shoulders, my drug use, and a couple of lost seasons, my hockey prospects had dropped considerably. I'd visited the University of Michigan, but the feelers I'd previously received from Dartmouth, Princeton, and Providence College had all dried up.

My dad told me he knew someone at Indiana University, where they were planning to upgrade their hockey program from club to varsity status. Without any better offers, I decided to go to Indiana. To our dad's credit, he knew the value of a college degree and pushed Bernie and me to use hockey to get an education. He even promised to pay a good chunk of my expenses.

The summer between high school and college I got a job collecting night crawlers just outside Chateauguay. They called us "worm farmers," which was a nice way to say, "worm pickers." At dusk I strapped on a miner's hardhat and aimed my headlight into the dark leaves. One by one I plucked the worms from their holes with my hands and collected them in cartons the size of take-out boxes. For each box of writhing worms the boss gave me 75 cents, Canadian. That was enough to convince me it was time to get a college education.

At night I played in a competitive summer hockey league to get ready—the first real hockey I'd played in a couple of years. When Jacques Demers, who had returned to do some scouting for his new team, the Chicago Cougars, saw me at the rink, he called me over. "You're playing de best I've seen you play!"

Near the end of the season the family of one of my high school friends, Jerry Findlay, moved to Toronto. Because I was still eager to get out of our apartment whenever I could, I jumped at Jerry's invitation to bike the entire 350 miles from Montreal to Toronto. We did it in three and a half days, sleeping in a tiny tent each night on the side of the road. I was in better shape than I'd been in years.

When I returned to Montreal I discovered we had been evicted once again. My mother had found another studio apartment for her, Bernie, Gail, and now me for a few weeks. When I entered the place I saw a tiny room filled with boxes and a couple of mattresses piled on the floor. I was not eager to stay long.

Although Bernie and I could fight like dogs, we always had a tight bond, and Gail was our baby. Because our dad left for Ohio when she was only five or six, she barely knew him, which was both good and bad. I tried to be the understanding older brother who offered sage advice—"Do as I say, not as I do!"—and a shoulder to cry on.

Because Bernie was around a lot more than I was, he took it upon himself to keep bad guys away from her—and he was good at it. Gail prayed that her dates would pick her up when Bernie wasn't home because he could scare her dates so much that the date sometimes ended before it started. I knew as long as Bernie was living under the same roof as Gail, she was safe.

❖ ❖ ❖

Right before I left for Indiana, the first week of August 1973, the University of Michigan's new head hockey coach, Dan Farrell, called me at home. How he found me after all our moves, I have no idea. When I picked up the phone I was surprised to be talking to Michigan's head coach—and even more surprised by what he said.

"Hi John. This is Dan Farrell at Michigan. I just wanted to wish you good luck this year. And if you ever change your mind and want to attend Michigan, we'd love to have you."

My heart went cold. "What are you talking about?"

"Well, frankly, I just don't understand why you'd turn us down for a school that doesn't even have a true varsity program."

"I don't know what you mean," I said.

"Your father called me last week and told us you're going to Indiana."

I couldn't believe what I was hearing. I tried to compose myself and not screw up whatever might have remained to screw up.

"Coach, I don't know anything about this. Can I call you back?"

"Sure," he said, "but I need an answer today because we're about to give your spot to another recruit."

I called my father and calmly asked about Coach Farrell's call.

"Oh, I'd been meaning to talk to you about that," he said casually. "You've got to go to Indiana. Michigan can't give you a scholarship."

"But I don't want to go to Indiana."

"You'll do what I say or else you can forget all about college. You're going to Indiana!"

I put down the phone and started to cry. But then I pulled myself together and called Coach Farrell. I had three choices: I could follow my dad's orders; I could say yes to Michigan's offer of walking on, without a scholarship; or I could forget about college and try out for one of the Junior teams in Quebec or Ontario and try to get to the NHL that way.

My confidence was so low that I decided to take the path of least resistance. I didn't have the energy to fight with Dad again, and being a big fish in a little pond might have some advantages. So I told Coach Farrell I appreciated his offer, but I'd be going to Indiana after all. He sounded surprised, but he told me to keep in touch, and if I ever changed my mind to let him know and he'd see what he could do.

Indiana University is famed as a basketball school, but in 1973 Bobby Knight had only been there for a couple of years and had yet to win any of his eleven Big Ten titles or his three National Championships. Indiana also had a new football coach named Lee Corso, who would become a fixture on ESPN's *College Football Game Day*. They would both become great friends, but you wouldn't have guessed that when I showed up on their campus in 1973.

Indiana's registration period began in mid-August, so I packed up my few belongings and my hockey equipment, hopped in my dad's car, and headed for Bloomington. It felt good to be starting a life of my own. As soon as I arrived I realized this could work out very well. Indiana University has a gorgeous campus filled with friendly midwestern folks and stately limestone buildings, all showcased in the cult classic *Breaking Away*.

After my dad left I got a ride out to the rink, which was far off campus: a rickety, three-sided building with something that looked like a hockey rink inside. I saw a sign that said, "HOME OF THE INDIANA HOOSIERS." It was their rink, all right. My jaw dropped. This was basically an outdoor arena with three walls and about a thousand seats. Meanwhile, five hours northeast in Ann Arbor, the University of Michigan was converting its famed Yost Field House into an eight-thousand-seat arena, which quickly became one of college hockey's best barns.

Baffled, I called Indiana's coach for an explanation. He told me not to worry because they would soon be playing in Assembly Hall, the basketball team's new home. I wasn't sure if I should believe that or not.

I returned to campus, found my dorm room, threw my bag down, and flopped on the bed, defeated. But as I lay there, I started to focus on the positive. *It won't be so bad*, I thought. *It's*

*a nice place and a great school, and my dad offered to chip in. This
could still work out.*

I was wondering when my roommate was going to check in
when I heard a key turn in the door. The door swung open, and in
walked a huge kid, who had to be a lineman on the football team,
followed by his parents. I stood up and held out my hand to greet
him. "Hey, I'm John, from Montreal. I'm a hockey player."

All three of them stopped in their tracks. No one shook my
outstretched hand.

"I'm not staying with no fuckin' nigger!" the kid said to his parents. "Can't believe Coach roomed me with a goddamn darkie!"

His father tried to calm him down. "Don't worry, son, we'll get
this straightened out."

They talked about me as if I was in another room.

"I mean, I know I have to *play* with them," the son said, "but I
don't have to *live* with them."

I turned to the mother for a sympathetic look, figuring she was
my best chance. She made for the door. "Let's get out of here," she
said.

As soon as they left I wanted to get out of there too, so I went
to see a movie, *Last Tango in Paris*, starring Marlon Brando. I'd
heard it had a few nude scenes with an actress named Maria
Schneider—scandalous at the time. But as soon as the movie
ended I couldn't remember one thing about it because I was still
consumed by the scene in my dorm room.

Back home racists like that were like dinosaurs—you heard
about them, but you didn't think they still existed. I'd been called
"nigger" on occasion, usually by a hockey opponent looking for
anything he could think of to rattle me. But I had never tasted real
racism until I set foot in that Indiana dorm room.

When I returned to my room I saw that all signs of my new
roommate had vanished. Apparently the idea of living with me
was more than he could bear.

How the hell do I get out of this? I needed to escape from the
place I'd just escaped to. I decided I wasn't going to wait around

to see who would be my next roommate or when the rink might get finished. I picked up the phone and called Coach Farrell at Michigan.

"Hi Coach, this is John Saunders. Do you still want me to come to Michigan?"

"Absolutely," he said. He explained that I'd have to come as a walk-on, with no scholarship money, but if I made the team, he'd see what he could do. I had no idea how I would pay for school, but I was desperate, so I told him I was coming regardless.

"Great!" he said. He promised to meet me at the bus station.

When I phoned my father he exploded. "Why can't you do anything right? Don't expect a damn dime from me. You're on your own!"

I hung up.

◆　◆　◆

I loaded up my bags and got on a Greyhound. Just as Farrell had promised, he was there to greet me in Ann Arbor—a welcome sight. He dropped me off at the Bell Tower Hotel, which is where the big-name musicians stay before they perform right across the street at Hill Auditorium. Farrell said he'd try to find me a dorm room as soon as possible. No guarantees, but his good intentions were clear. Like Coach St. Onge and Jacques Demers, Farrell was a man I felt I could trust.

After a few days in the hotel I moved into a dorm on the other side of campus, far from the rest of the freshman hockey players. I met them the next day for dry-land training. I was now part of something big. No one has won more NCAA hockey titles than Michigan, and the university speaks for itself. Even though I was a latecomer, the guys on the team were great. Most of them were fellow Canadians, and the American guys wanted to act like Canadians. After all, hockey is *our* sport!

A week into the fall semester we had to take physical exams the same day the basketball players did, and they seemed curious about this black guy lined up with all these white hockey players. Campy Russell, the basketball team's star player and the nephew of Michigan's all-time great Cazzie Russell, approached me and said, "You're a hockey player?" I nodded shyly, not sure what was coming next. The room turned silent. Then he asked, "Man, how can you stand up with those knives on your feet?"

Both teams busted out laughing. Coming off my brief experience at Indiana, this felt great.

We started dry-land training about six weeks before we hit the ice. We ran sprints, we ran distances, and we lifted weights, things the NHL hadn't even thought of, yet. Dan Farrell, Wisconsin's Bob Johnson, and Minnesota's Herb Brooks were all way ahead of their NHL counterparts on and off the ice. College hockey was entering a golden era, and these guys were leading the way.

When we got to dress for our first practice in the former Yost Field House, built in 1923, I was so excited that I dressed quicker than everyone else so I could be the first Michigan player to step on the ice at the newly converted Yost Arena. I knew Farrell planned to red-shirt me that season—which meant I'd be practicing with the team but not playing in any games—but I hoped to impress him so much he'd change his mind.

I was in for a shock. If I was a bit behind my new teammates at off-ice conditioning, it was nothing compared to the gap I noticed as soon as we hit the ice. I had always been the biggest guy on my teams, but most of these guys were at least as big as I was, and they moved at speeds I'd never seen before. Meanwhile I was paying the price for all the time I'd spent away from the rink the past few years, due to injuries and other priorities.

We had a large freshman class of ten guys, five of whom would go on to play a combined thirty-two years in the National Hockey League, part of the first wave of college players to break into the NHL. I had joined some pretty fast company, and I was struggling just to keep up.

To start the season we played a few exhibition games, when even red-shirts can play. Farrell gave me plenty of chances to show my stuff, and I held my own—but not well enough to take anyone's spot. The best game I played was against Western Michigan University, which was starting first year as a varsity program. I threw my weight around and handled the puck with some agility. But when Farrell posted the final varsity roster, I wasn't on it. I would practice with the team that season but not play in any games.

That was tough, but what made it even tougher was that I'd become good friends with two other freshmen, Dave Shand and Rob Palmer. Both were from the Toronto area and came ready to play. After the first game the *Michigan Daily* announced, "PALMER SPARKLES IN DEBUT," so I immediately christened him "Sparky." The nickname followed him into the NHL and to the present day. As Palmer says, however, "It could have been worse. Saunders could have called me 'Sparkles.'" Be thankful for small blessings, Spark.

Because my dorm room was so far away, Rob and Dave let me crash on their dorm room floor. They had no problem getting girlfriends, while I extended my unfortunate knack for becoming "just friends" with just about any girl I met, but never more than that.

Compared to living with a racist roommate at Indiana, even sleeping on a dorm room floor at Michigan was quite an improvement. I could eat in the cafeteria too, thanks to Shand. We were about the same size, but he was white with shoulder-length hair, and I was black with a big Afro. He'd get in line before me, flash his meal card to the guy checking at the door, then pass it back to me, and I'd use it. The guy checking was either happy to play along or he had really, really bad vision. I've always liked to assume it was the former.

Sparky and Dave treated me as an equal, which gave me some confidence when I sorely needed some, even though they were already stars while I was sitting in the stands. Still, it wasn't easy watching my friends play, while I sat out. I missed my brother and sister. I missed my friends. And I missed taking drugs to forget about everything for a while.

Self-medication wasn't a term we used back then, but that was exactly what I had been doing. That's one reason why, when I had to go clean during my semester at Michigan, my depression deepened. Self-medicating isn't a good idea, of course, as it just delays your troubles and makes them worse, but stopping cold turkey was hard.

I also felt like a stranger in the States. By the time I arrived on Michigan's campus in 1973 we were just a few years removed from inner-city riots igniting across the country, including Detroit, and the University of Michigan was one of the hottest campuses for racial turmoil. In 1969, a few months after football coach Bo Schembechler arrived in Ann Arbor, Jesse Jackson met with the Michigan football players and tried to persuade them to boycott the team. They declined, telling him the program treated them fairly, but protest was in the air. The next year the Black Action Movement (BAM) shut down the campus for eighteen days.

Just three years after that I'm walking across campus with Dave and Sparky when we passed three black women walking together. Being Canadian, we all stepped to the side so they could pass. They looked at me and nodded, which was the code at the time among black students to show solidarity. Fresh from Canada, I had no idea about this custom. I didn't know I was supposed to nod back. When I didn't, all three women turned to yell at me.

"Who do you think you are?" one of them said. "Just 'cause you got some white friends doesn't make you better than us!"

Her friend started in. "You keep trusting those honkeys, and you'll get stabbed in the back. Stay with your own, *brother!*"

I was speechless. Just a couple of months earlier I had faced old-school racism from my white roommate at Indiana, and now I wasn't black enough? I didn't have anything like the consciousness of other black students at the University of Michigan because I hadn't experienced what they had, which added to my sense of isolation.

I wasn't playing hockey. I lived on the other side of campus. I didn't have a girlfriend, and I was being called out for not being black enough. As fall wore on, things seemed to get harder on all fronts.

Returning from hockey practice one chilly November after-noon, I passed a group of black students hanging outside my orig-inal dorm room, where I only checked in occasionally to get a few things. They began taunting me, calling me "Oreo," "sell-out," and "wannabe." They accused me of thinking I was better than they were because I hung out with white guys. They probably didn't know those guys were not just my teammates but my closest friends on campus.

My temper, never dormant long, flared up. I turned to one of the larger, more vocal members of the group. "You don't know shit about me," I told him. "You couldn't survive the life I've lived." This got his attention, so I kept going. "You're at one of the most prestigious universities in the country and you're not an athlete. I'm guessing your parents had enough money to send you here, and now you want to bring *me* down? No, I don't think I'm better than any of you. But I want an education too, and the only way I can get it is by playing hockey. If that means my friends are white, well, it's what I've lived with my whole life."

Everyone went silent. I walked away, savoring my minor tri-umph. But when I returned to my dorm room that night, I found a bag of Oreo cookies tacked to the door. I stormed down the hallway, screaming for whoever did it to show their faces. Once again, no one made a peep.

I tore open the bag and placed a single cookie beneath the door of every room in my hall. On a large sheet of paper I scrawled a challenge and posted it on the hall bulletin board: "LET'S MEET & SEE WHO IS MORE OF A BLACK MAN."

A few days later I was heading out of the dorm to go to class when four black students stopped me. They grabbed my arms and escorted me back into someone's room, where they had me sit in a chair in the middle. I knew I was in trouble, so I tried to talk my way out of the situation. I explained that in Canada I was only one of a handful of blacks at my high school but had very

few problems. Growing up with generally harmonious race relations, I told them how shocked I'd been to face blatant racism
from white students. I told them my story about Indiana, and said
I understood why they felt the way they did.

They weren't impressed. Two of them jerked me up out of the
chair, and the biggest guy slugged me in the ribs as hard as he
could. Then they took turns punching me. No one touched my
face. I guess that would have been evidence. After a few minutes
they left me in a heap on the floor.

One of them turned back to me and said, "Now maybe you
understand how strongly we feel about race relations. If you don't
have us on your side, you have nothing. The same white people
you call your friends are calling you a nigger behind your back.
WAKE UP!"

The next day, in the locker room, I told my teammates some
of what had happened, but not all of it. I was careful to leave out
the actual beatdown because I knew if these guys heard about one
of their teammates getting messed with, they'd defend me. That's
what hockey guys do. It wouldn't be about race for them but about
team solidarity. The rest of campus wouldn't know that, though,
and would probably assume it was racially motivated. The last
thing I wanted to do was start a race riot.

I did tell my Canadian teammates a few of the attackers' lines,
which they thought were bizarre. They had seen my black classmates try to entice me to sit with them, and some had harassed
me when I didn't accept their invitation, but the idea that sitting with my white teammates would invoke anger in people who
didn't even know me was truly foreign to my teammates. "Why
do they care who you hang out with? Tell them they're welcome
to join us." It was a different world for them too.

I felt a lot more comfortable in the locker room surrounded
by white Canadians than I did in my dorm surrounded by black
Americans who thought I wasn't black enough. Obviously most
of our history was the same, starting with slavery. In Canada we
had similar black churches, food, and music. But our history after

reaching Canada is largely one of inclusion, not segregation. And that was where my experience differed from that of my black American classmates.

Perhaps understandably, they weren't interested in learning about my life north of the border. That was fine. But I couldn't put aside the unfair assumptions they'd made about me, and that was a problem.

With my first semester at Michigan coming to a close, I assessed my situation. Coach Farrell told me I had little chance of getting any scholarship money second semester. I wouldn't get into any games until my sophomore year. I had good friends on the team, but no girlfriend. And I had no friends among my black classmates—and no prospects for making any. When I added it all up, I started to think I wasn't going to make it at Michigan.

Sitting in the stands made me more depressed than anything else. I'd been playing hockey since I was four, and on every team I'd been on, if you weren't playing much now, you probably never would be. It never occurred to me that in college hockey, you had to wait your turn. Freshmen usually didn't play much, if at all. The seniors generally carried the team. But when your two best friends are freshmen who are playing all the time, you think that's how it works. Throw in the fact that I'd missed most of my last three hockey seasons, and I had a lot of catching up to do, and this would be a hard place to do it.

As finals approached, I made up my mind. I walked from my dorm down State Street to Yost Arena to give Coach Farrell my decision. When I told him I was quitting, he was surprised and disappointed, but he wished me good luck. No hard feelings.

I wish I'd had the strength to fight my way through the issues at Michigan and to stand up for who I was. But I let myself get discouraged by racial problems, loneliness, and the gap between the starters and me—things I could have mitigated if I'd just kept working.

When I returned to my dorm room I called the head coach of Western Michigan, Bill Neal. I asked him if he remembered the black player on Michigan's team who played in the exhibition game against them earlier that season.

"Sure I do."

I told him I wanted to transfer to Western. He immediately said yes and invited me to a game they were playing in Kalamazoo the next night.

The following day I drove my "new" used car, a beat-up Oldsmobile Delta 88, through a serious snowstorm one hundred miles to Kalamazoo. I liked Western Michigan immediately, and this time I knew what to do when I got a small nod from another black student. All it took was a nod back, and I was one of them.

I had managed to get another fresh start the following fall.

CHAPTER 11

Falling in Love

AFTER I COMMITTED TO ATTEND WESTERN MICHIGAN IN August of 1974 I had to kill eight months in Montreal surrounded by my family and friends. I knew it was a potentially dangerous gap of time, given all my old habits that could easily resurface. On the drive back to Montreal I also worried my friends and former teammates would think I was a failure, washing out after only one semester, and I wondered where I could play that season, and where I would live.

Before I returned, my mother had decided to move Bernie, Gail, and herself from Montreal into a two-bedroom apartment in the tiny town of Ajax, outside Toronto. This time they moved because of the rising French separatist movement, which threatened to split the province of Quebec from the rest of the country. Among other goals, the movement wanted to make French mandatory in Quebec high schools. Bernie was a decent student but had difficulty passing French, which could jeopardize his chance at a college hockey scholarship—and his chances were much better than mine.

Ajax, Ontario, was on my way back to Montreal, but I didn't stop to see them. I missed Bernie and Gail, but not enough to risk speaking with my mother for the first time in the four months I'd been away. I preferred it that way. Whether this was another sign that I was "just like my father" remained to be seen.

Instead I returned to Chateauguay, where the mother of my Little League baseball buddy Rick insisted I stay with them. She made me feel welcome, and she wouldn't take a dime. I will forever be grateful to her.

As soon as I got back, just before Christmas, I went down to talk to Mr. Bougee, the general manager of the Chateauguay Wings. This time he was more than happy to take me back. No, he hadn't changed his mind about me, but the Wings were terrible that year, and he could use all the help he could get. So within days of returning I was back on the ice playing competitive hockey, which always lifted my spirits.

But soon I was running with my old friends again, and that meant smoking a lot of grass and dropping acid just about every other day—not the kind of habits typical of top college players. I started to toy with the idea of not enrolling at Western Michigan after all.

Far more seriously, I revisited the idea of killing myself, which still came up occasionally. I didn't scheme ways to do it, but I daydreamed about dying in a car crash or falling off a bridge. The idea of dying rarely left me for long, but the drugs I was taking numbed me enough to keep me going.

Fortunately I had some new distractions. I had been the first in our gang to escape Chateauguay and I used that to my advantage when trying to romance the ladies with talks of exploits that I no longer had to make up. But no matter how hard I tried, I still became every girl's best friend instead of her boyfriend.

With only two games left in the Wings' season, I decided I'd had enough—another sign of immaturity, depression, and my remarkable lack of focus. For our next game I didn't even call and tell them I'd be missing. I just didn't show up. When Mr. Bougee called me afterward I told him I needed to get away. I knew that didn't sound good, so I added that I had to get a job to help pay for the coming year's tuition at Western Michigan. Needing to get away and needing to get a job aren't exactly the same things, but I didn't care, and by then he probably didn't care very much about me either. I can't say I blame him.

So in March of 1974 I told my friends and Rick's family goodbye, swallowed my pride, and headed to Ajax to move in with my mother, my brother, and my sister to save some money before enrolling at Western. Jamming four family members into a two-bedroom apartment made it easy to get on each other's nerves, especially as they'd been living with each other for years, while I'd been making only cameo appearances. It wasn't long before I had an outburst that I'm ashamed of to this day.

My sister was still the sweetest girl on the planet, but while I'd been away she'd started to grow up. She was almost fifteen, but she looked older and was trying to act it too. During my frequent absences Bernie watched her like a hawk, but one evening she stayed out past her curfew, which bothered me more than it should have. After all, she was a good kid, and Bernie had been the one holding down the fort, not me. But I still saw her as an eight-year-old girl and couldn't fathom why she'd be out that late on her own.

When Gail finally walked through our door I stood up immediately and confronted her in a way I never had before. Instead of being the gentle listener, I acted like my father: obnoxiously self-righteous, even mean. It was a side of me Gail had never seen, so it shouldn't have surprised me when she returned the insult.

"John, you've been gone such a long time, I can't believe you've turned into *Dad!*"

No sooner had the words escaped her mouth than I slapped her across her face.

We stared at each other in disbelief. My mother started in, but I yelled at her to shut up. Tears welled in Gail's eyes. I stammered an apology, but I quickly realized that even if she might forgive me, I could never forgive myself. I had just provided compelling evidence that Mom was right: I was just like my father. If true, I was also right: I should never have kids.

I ran from the living room, stuffed some pot and a bottle of whiskey in my bag, and left the apartment. I walked to a nearby shopping mall, found an outdoor bench toward the back, and lit up a joint. *Who the hell had I become? Was I destined to become my father?* I felt the burn of whiskey at the back of my throat. The only things I cared about—hockey, my friends, and now my sister—were slipping away. I finished the bottle and passed out on the bench.

Hours later a police car pulled up. The officer rolled down his window and hollered at me, "Get on home, kid!"

I got up and started walking. It was approaching dawn when I crept into the apartment as quietly as I could. Everyone was still asleep. I slipped into Gail's room because I wanted to be the first person Gail saw when she woke up. I sat at the foot of her bed and watched her sleep, feeling dead inside.

At dawn Gail woke and her eyes met mine. I opened my mouth to tell her I was sorry, but she beat me to it.

"I'm sorry," she said. "I watched Dad beat you. Call you disgusting names. Say how you were no good. I know that what I said hurt more than any slap to the face."

That was wonderful to hear, but it only made me feel even guiltier.

"I'll never forgive myself for hitting you," I said, and started to cry.

She hugged me. I asked her if she'd braid my hair later that day, something she did to make my Afro fluffier.

"Sure," she said.

She smiled and fell back asleep. We were okay.

◆　◆　◆

That morning I headed out to look for work. My dad had offered to pitch in for tuition again, but I wasn't sure how much he could afford, so I figured I had six months to scrounge together enough money to cover my first year at Western Michigan. Ajax had some factories, so I shaved, ironed my slacks, and set off to find a job.

I started my search at Bailey Engineering, which produced silicon boards and connectors for electronic equipment. When they offered me a job moving parts from one assembly line to another, I was thrilled. One of my stops was the silk-screening room, where workers painted numbers onto parts. That's where I met Fran Smith, an attractive woman in her mid-forties who wore her bleached-blond hair in a tight bun. She ran the department, and we hit it off immediately. During breaks we'd laugh and cut loose.

I'd been on the job for a month when I found Fran working alongside a younger woman who seemed to share the same bottle of bleach. But unlike Fran, this woman wore her locks loose. She was a little taller than Fran and very shapely. When I approached, she turned from her work, locked eyes with me, and smiled. I thought, *Visits to this room are going to be more frequent.*

"This is my daughter, Delia," Fran said. "She used to work here and is coming back, starting today."

We exchanged polite smiles and went about our business. But I was soon spending all my breaks and lunches with Fran and Delia.

At the end of work one day Delia told me that she and a bunch of her friends were going out that night and invited me to join them. At twenty-two, Delia was three years older than I was. She'd recently ended a bad marriage to a man she said she never loved. I told her the ex-husband thing didn't faze me, and from that first night out we began spending every free moment together. Delia was adamant about one thing: "No sex." I held out hope that this rule wouldn't last forever.

When Delia and I began dating I was surprised when Fran turned cold. Delia told me that her parents didn't approve of her dating a black man.

When I confronted Fran she said, "You're a great person, but my husband and I just don't think it's right."

But they couldn't stop us. Delia moved out of her parents' home and into a cheap apartment. I was nineteen years old and I finally had my first true girlfriend. For me, 1974 seemed like an endless summer of love. While Delia was an instant hit with my mother and Gail was indifferent, Bernie didn't like her, and our father wanted me to stay away from girlfriends altogether, lest they distract me from becoming somebody. But I didn't care. I was in love.

The night before I headed to Western Michigan Delia asked me to stay at her place. For the first time, we made love. We woke in each other's arms the next morning, and I kissed her goodbye.

"I love you," I whispered. It was the first time I had said that to any woman—although I had no idea what love really meant. She told me she loved me too, and planned to visit me as soon as she could. When I returned to my Mom's home that morning I found my father loading up his car for our trip to Kalamazoo.

"Guess you slept with your little whore," he said. I squinted—a habit I'd learned from him. Not getting the hint, he continued. "Last thing you need is to get mixed up with some man's ex-wife. She's used up. Damaged goods. She just wants to screw her way into your life."

"You don't know anything about her," I said, seething. "You can go screw yourself."

We endured the eight-hour drive to Kalamazoo in icy silence. My father never raised his gaze from the road, and I never looked at him. After crossing the American border at Detroit he finally spoke. "You know, your focus should be on hockey and school."

"You missed your chance to give me advice," I told him, glaring out the passenger window. "Just drive."

When we reached Western Michigan I couldn't even mumble a goodbye.

CHAPTER 12

Go West

BY SEPTEMBER OF 1974 I WAS IN LOVE FOR THE FIRST TIME. I was attending a university with a brand-new Division I hockey program, and I was living in a dorm room with some of my hockey teammates. Compared to where I'd been just a couple of years earlier, this representeded progress on all fronts.

But no matter how well things were going, I could still see my low moods were lower than my friends'. So I loaded my class schedule with psychology courses, hoping to sort myself out.

I was grateful for a fresh start, but most of the players at Western were faster, stronger, and just plain better than I was. Something had to change—and it had to start with me. Western's off-ice training was just as tough as Michigan's, which came as a shock, but I was determined to work my ass off to stand out.

On our first day of dry-land training I met two of the team's best freshmen, Neil Smith, a tall, blond-haired guy with a Fu Manchu moustache, and Bob Gardner, a high-flying left wing with a big shot and an even bigger grin. Neil came up to me and said, "I heard you're from Toronto."

"Ajax," I said.

"Ah, that's not Toronto!" He ran off to start our run, while I was thinking, *What an ass!*

Despite all the tangible signs of progress I'd made, I still felt inadequate. To avoid that horrible feeling, I stayed in bed—which only made everything worse. Sometimes I'd stay in bed until it was time for practice, and then I would get up and pretend to be everything I wasn't: confident, friendly, and socially skilled. But most of the time I felt so unsettled, I actually wanted to throw up, and sometimes I did.

My teammates had no idea how I felt, even though we lived together, ate together, attended classes together, and played together. Soon Neil, Bob, and I became best friends, known around campus as "The Three Musketeers." Outside of class and practice we engaged in the typical college fun. The drinking age was eighteen, and local bars charged ten cents a glass for draft beer, so how could we resist?

Delia and I wrote each other letters every week, and she visited a few times. She had my heart, but at nineteen I wasn't oblivious to the looks the hockey players got from the flocks of pretty girls eager to meet us. Unlike at Michigan, where football was king and basketball a close second, at Western, hockey was the most popular sport.

I fought temptation, trying to be true to Delia. I thought my familiar role of being every girl's "best friend" might finally pay off and I could keep things platonic. But after I lapsed one night, I hadn't anticipated the guilt that overcame me, which felt like I'd swallowed poison. When I confessed to Delia, she was hurt, but she said her love was strong enough to forgive me—a great gift. After that I was tempted a few times but never succumbed again.

I was only beginning to sense how my far-too-early introduction to sex at age seven was affecting my relationships with women. I was fine with dating until things turned physical. Sex for me was unconnected to my feelings, something mechanical, something shameful. In all my relationships this would surface as an obstacle I would have to work past.

◆　◆　◆

After I procured a beat-up Oldsmobile 88 on campus, I managed to collect enough parking tickets that the university police actually arrested me—not exactly the kind of thing a man hoping to become a responsible adult does. Sitting in my jail cell, I recalled that my father had promised if I ever got tight on funds, he would send me some cash to help out. He had told me to open a checking account so he could wire me money directly, and this time he came through. I don't think I could have stayed in school without his help.

But as soon as I got out of jail I was broke again. I called him for more money. "The money's on its way," he assured me.

Thinking my problems had been solved, I cashed checks at a few stores to get some essential things I'd been putting off. A few days later I received an angry phone call from a grocery store telling me the check had bounced, and I was banned. The calls soon came in from stores all over town, with my name posted in each place as a deadbeat. When I called Dad he stammered that there must be some mistake, because *of course* he had sent the cash.

I felt like a fool. And here I was, collecting parking tickets, doing a bit of jail time, and bouncing checks. Why did I think I'd turn out any different than him?

When we hit the ice I was determined to show that I could still play. I had to overcome two dislocated shoulders and four seasons spent mostly off the ice. I had been given another chance, and I was making the most of it. Even better, Bernie, who had torn up the Metropolitan Toronto League, turned down offers from Michigan, Boston University, and Harvard so he could join me at Western. We were looking forward to spending some real time together.

When the games started I was still in the stands, watching. But this time, instead of letting it get me down, I practiced harder, my confidence soared, and I was sure that soon I'd get my chance.

At the same time my relationship with Delia was approaching a crossroads, and I was torn. I finally had someone to turn to, someone who'd listen to my problems and help ease my pain, but

I wasn't sure I was ready for marriage. I wanted to get my degree first and see how far hockey could take me.

When I returned to Kalamazoo for the second semester the team was getting ready for a big weekend series against rival Ohio State. Two of our starting defensemen had flunked out, which meant I would get my chance—until I learned I had an incomplete grade in an acting class, of all things. My afternoon naps had caught up with me.

While I was getting that sorted out, I missed the trip to Ohio State, so I got ready to make my debut the following weekend. But during a midweek practice my future changed in an instant. In the middle of a drill my skates got tangled up with a teammates', my arms ended up pinned behind me, and I came crashing down on the ice, face first. The ice cracked my cheekbone and knocked my teeth out, scattering them across the ice. I also dislocated my right shoulder—my "good" one.

I was done. To remove any doubt, I quit going to classes altogether, making it impossible for me to return to Western. Instead of admitting defeat and going home, I hid out in my dorm room for the rest of the semester because I wasn't ready to return to Canada as a failure—again.

CHAPTER 13

Getting Married

THE FOLLOWING SUMMER, 1976, I RETURNED TO TO-ronto, leaving Bernie at Western. I got a summer job working for the Government of Ontario's Public Transportation's GO trains. Our duties included painting the shelters and cutting the grass at each station. On the devilishly steep hills we dragged the mower with two long ropes from the bottom of the hill to the top. We had a four-man crew consisting of two skilled lifers and a fellow college student, Jim MacLeese.

Jim and I hit it off. Purely out of boredom, after work we created a television show on cable public access which was every bit as professional as *Wayne's World*. I was just screwing around, but Jim wanted to break into show business. A local AM country music station soon hired him, but he kept his day job mowing train station lawns.

It might seem surprising that I was having a good time mowing lawns after returning to Canada feeling like a failure. But my depression has never been solely based on my life circumstances; sometimes things could be going along very well on the surface, and I'd feel horrible. Other times my life could look like it was falling apart, as it was that summer, and I'd feel okay, even good.

But I couldn't ignore that my options were narrowing. Having flunked out of Western, I couldn't go back. But I still had a few possibilities: I could transfer to a school in Toronto or find some kind of job, or try to make one of the local semi-pro hockey teams that paid players by the game. One option Delia and I didn't consider was moving back in with my family, which was already on its fourth home in two years in Ajax, or hers, because they weren't very excited about their daughter dating me.

I decided to transfer to Ryerson Polytechnical Institute, now called Ryerson University, in downtown Toronto, and take out a loan. I hoped to play hockey for their school team too, with Delia generously agreeing to support me financially for a year. With the various credits I had somehow managed to pick up along the way I could graduate in just one year if I stayed focused.

After my lawn-mowing colleague, Jim MacLeese, got off to a good start on CHOO-1400 AM, the country music station in Ajax, he got me a regular six-hour shift on Sunday mornings. It sounded like fun, good for a few bucks.

My future, almost despite my efforts, once again looked bright.

◆ ◆ ◆

With Delia my early introduction to sex came back to haunt me, preventing me from building the kind of intimacy and trust couples should have. Delia and I might be alone, simply cuddling in the bedroom, but when we became amorous, I'd start asking her pointed questions. "Did you enjoy having sex with your first husband? How often did you have sex?" She naturally became upset, and my paranoia became self-fulfilling, as if I was denigrating myself, her, and our relationship all at the same time.

Thanks to my early sex education, relationships for me were not simple things, where an emotional bond turns physical. These were unconnected for me, which created problems years later. Delia was everything I thought I wanted, but because on some level I thought sex was dirty, it bothered me that she'd had sex before we met. That, coupled with my own feelings of worthlessness—which made me wonder how anyone could really love me—prompted me to sabotage our relationship.

Ignoring these signs, Delia and I set our wedding date for July 17, 1976. Delia did all the planning, but as usual my father was the wild card. Four days before our wedding he resurfaced to talk me out of it.

"What would you know about marriage?" I asked.

"You go through with this wedding, and you can forget about me being in your life. I won't bail you out of any more of your messes."

I probably should have let it go. But I couldn't resist pointing out how often his promised checks hadn't come through. That got him. He grabbed me by the throat and shoved my head into the wall.

"Why are you so stupid?" he yelled. He tightened his grip on my throat. "In a year you'll be selling pencils on a street corner! That girl is going to ruin your life!"

This confrontation drew a circle of people around us, urging him to let me go. But instead of sparking an outburst in me, his charade had the opposite effect. Suddenly the rage I had bottled up for years started leaking away. One thought took over: *This man will never be my father. I will never be his son.* It gave me a surprising measure of peace to know that his power over me was dwindling. I looked him dead in the eye and slowly pried his hand from my throat.

"I don't know where you've been my whole life or what you've been doing," I said, "but you haven't been around enough to involve yourself in any decision I make. As far as I'm concerned, don't come to my wedding, and don't show your face to me ever again."

My father showed up for our wedding, a humbled man—or at least a quiet one. He did not perform the usual fatherly duties and he did not interact with the guests, but there were no incidents, which is all I cared about. Delia's family was there, as were my beloved grandparents and my mother, Bernie, Gail, my aunt Yve, and my cousin Loretta. Our wedding went off without a hitch.

I wasn't sure where my life was headed, but in Delia I had found a woman who loved me enough to call me her husband, and this infused me with a welcome shot of self-worth.

CHAPTER 14

Country John Saunders

I THOUGHT RADIO WOULD BE A FUN, EASY WAY TO MAKE a few bucks, but it came with a catch: I had to start the morning after our wedding, working on about two hours of sleep.

I spun a Baptist sermon at eight o'clock, followed by a little Tammy Wynette, then I played the Episcopal service at nine, followed by some Conway Twitty, then I popped in the Anglicans at ten, followed by Willie Nelson and Charlie Pride—all for $46 a week. A good gig, but not the kind of work that makes you think, *Yes, this is my future!*

They called me "Country John Saunders," if you can believe it, but I liked it immediately. I have no problem finding great music in just about any genre, and country was no exception. On my first day I learned that Tanya Tucker had a little rock-and-roll in her country, for example, and Charlie Pride knew how to tell a story. Because he was a black guy trying to make it in a white industry, I gave him a little extra play.

As soon as I finished my first shift we put a "JUST MARRIED" sign in the back window of Delia's little Rambler and took off for Niagara Falls for our honeymoon. We stayed only one night because that's all we could afford.

For the first year of our marriage we lived in a one-bedroom basement apartment. After Delia left for work I often slipped back down the rabbit hole of depression. Some days it took all I had to get out of bed in our dark, dank apartment. Once I did, I had to drag myself to class and face the fact that I seemed more likely to vindicate my parents' predictions of failure than fulfill my vague vision of becoming somebody. But two endeavors proved very helpful in keeping me going: radio and hockey.

A year into my Sunday shift on the radio, mixing sermons and country songs, CHOO posted an opening for a morning newscaster's job. Perhaps to everyone's surprise, including mine, I landed it—but I'm not sure how many people actually wanted it. My shift began every weekday morning at six, with newscasts continuing every half-hour until nine, followed by hourly newscasts until noon. It paid $9,000 a year, the most I'd ever made, and rattling off newsreels certainly beat toiling in an electronics factory, mowing lawns, or digging for worms.

So I woke up at five and drove ten minutes to CHOO, delivered the news until noon, then drove a half-hour to Ryerson for a full day of classes, which I liked, followed by hockey practice. Afterward some of us would go to a bar near campus for a few beers. Being on a team again felt like reuniting with family, and those hours joking around together were gold.

I liked our coach, Brian Jones, who was just six years my senior. Ryerson had been a perennial loser, but Coach Jones brought in eight good players our first year, and we jumped from worst to first in a single season. My shoulders felt fine, for once, and I finally proved I could play at a decent level.

After years of failing to play more than a few games each season—if that—it felt good to play a regular role, and the exercise helped keep my depression at bay. As long as I didn't get hurt, there wasn't much harm in it, as it required just a few more hours away from home each day.

My finesse game was long gone, and with it my dreams of playing in the NHL. But I had transformed myself into a steady defenseman and an occasional enforcer—and I was pretty good at it. Maybe, I thought, I might still make a few bucks playing this game in the minors.

I paid just enough attention to my schoolwork to pass my classes. If I stuck it out, by the end of my second year at Ryerson, 1977–1978, I'd have only three courses remaining to graduate with a degree in psychology.

That year Delia and I rented a new apartment on the second floor of a clean new building with fresh white paint and large windows that let the sunshine in, a big improvement over our basement bungalow. I was working a full-time job, going to school full time, and playing varsity hockey full time. I was usually too busy to be depressed.

It was becoming clear early in our marriage, however, that I was no one's idea of a model husband. Because I wasn't ready to give up on hockey or college, we both had to keep working, which naturally put more stress on our marriage.

My physical desire for Delia had cooled shortly after we were married, too—another aftereffect of my too-early introduction to sex. Given my low self-worth, subconsciously I concluded that if a woman would have me, there must be something wrong with her. Even though I knew better, when that's hardwired into your mindset from an early age, it's hard to shake.

Not surprisingly, as my touches and kisses faded, Delia grew insecure and jealous. She couldn't stand it if I so much as glanced at a good-looking woman. When we watched TV together and an attractive woman appeared onscreen, I would leave the room just to avoid an argument—and there are a lot of attractive women on TV.

◆　◆　◆

Our team had slipped a bit my second season while the rest of the league had gotten tougher. The exception was the Royal Military College, a school that rolled Canada's army, navy, and air force cadets into one campus. The team was the worst in the league, and they played the dirtiest.

In our first meeting that season we were already ahead by a dozen goals when they started going after us. Before a face-off late in the game I told our center to hold the stick of the other center, one of their dirtiest players. He did as I'd instructed, allowing me to jam the shaft of my stick under the opposing center's chin, splitting it wide open. Amazingly, the referee didn't call it. Either he didn't see it—which seemed impossible, as he was about two feet away—or he thought the guy deserved it.

After the game, in the handshaking line one of their guys mumbled "nigger" as he passed me, then took off. I chased him into his own locker room—generally not the smartest move, where you're certain to be badly outnumbered by his teammates—while shouting at his buddies that this was none of their business, so they should stay out of it. I proceeded to beat the crap out of this guy and finished by jamming a trash can in his ribs.

When I was done I looked around and saw the stunned expressions on his teammates' faces: *This fool's crazy.* I turned my back and walked out, confident that no one would dare jump me. I can't say I regret my response, but I can say I was showing no signs of shaking my violent streak.

My defense partner, Frank Sheffield, was also a black guy, making us the only all-black blue line pair in the league—and probably in the world. Our coach grew accustomed to seeing us scrap over someone using the "n-word"—not that he liked it. Once, after Frank and I were both ejected for fighting because our opponents had used the "n-word," our coach all but begged us, "C'mon, guys! Can't you ignore them *just once?*"

I had gotten into the habit of playing close to the edge, getting away with as much dirty play and bullying as I could, which earned me a reputation among opponents and officials. But because the NHL had entered its nastiest era of hockey, with Philadelphia's Broad Street Bullies leading the way, I thought that might work in my favor.

Our parents rarely came to our games, but Bernie and Gail always believed my parents loved me. Years later Gail told me Dad had hung a picture of me in my Ryerson uniform. He was a hard man to understand.

My mother and Delia forged a solid friendship, which made life easier for Delia when I wasn't around. I even believed their friendship might help me improve my relationship with my mother.

But my biggest fan, by far, was Bernie, even though he'd long since surpassed me as a player and was tearing up his new league at Western Michigan. On those rare weekend nights when we didn't both have a game, Bernie would make the six-hour drive from Kalamazoo to Toronto just to see me play. When Bernie was in the stands, which were otherwise occupied only by a few friends, girlfriends, and winos trying to warm up, I always played my heart out. After one game Bernie attended, my coach asked if Bernie could come to every game because I played so much better when he was there.

One night Bernie braved a merciless blizzard that turned into a dangerous twelve-hour haul across icy roads to see Ryerson play Guelph University. Bernie managed to slip inside our rink just in time for the opening face-off. He was standing behind the glass at center ice, shaking the snow off his Western Michigan letter jacket and giving me a big smile right before the opening drop. I loved it and felt pumped up.

Right off the draw a Guelph player dumped the puck into my corner. I turned to get it, with a Guelph forward on my tail. As we approached the boards he hit me hard from behind, slamming me into the glass—a dangerous play that is now illegal. But it wasn't then, so I turned to elbow him in the face, then dropped my gloves and started a fight—definitely against the rules, then and now. I managed to land a couple of rights before he tied up my arms with my jersey and the refs pinned us both down.

Unlike the NHL at the time, in college hockey fighting meant an automatic ejection from the game. When we got up from the ice the referee motioned for both of us to leave, with one ref escorting each of us off the ice to make sure we didn't start fighting again. A few folks in the stands cheered for me, but Bernie was not among them. He had just risked his life driving through a snowstorm to watch me play, and I'd remained on the ice for a grand total of twenty-two seconds. When I skated off I could see him mouth the words, "YOU FUCKING ASSHOLE!"

He had a point.

A couple of months later we were playing Brock University on their home ice in St. Catherines, Ontario, near Niagara Falls. Early in the game one of their players told me they were plotting to take me out because a month earlier I had jammed my stick into their star player's ribs. When I heard our opponent's warning, I just laughed.

In the third period we were ahead by a couple goals when I picked up the puck in the corner. An opposing player chased me in hot pursuit. I glanced back at him for a second, and when I turned back to see where I was going, I met my fate.

To understand a cross-check, imagine gripping a broomstick with your hands about three feet apart, then using the middle portion to smash someone's face while he's skating toward you. It's a brutal and effective means to take out an opponent—and also illegal. That's what this guy did, and he did it well. His cross-check knocked me on my back, out cold. When I came to, I tried to stand, but my left leg gave way.

An hour later, lying in yet another hospital bed, I took inventory of my injuries. I'd suffered a broken ankle, probably when we all collapsed in a heap, a broken nose, a busted orbital bone, and more missing teeth. I watched the doctor stitching me back together, a familiar experience. She told me my ankle was shattered, and if she placed it in a cast right away it would swell and not heal properly. So we left that for another day.

On the hour-and-a-half bus ride back to Toronto I sat in the front seat, my leg raised. My teammates didn't utter a word to me. Either they didn't know what to say, they figured I had it coming, or both.

By the time I reached the hospital in Toronto my ankle was the size of a prize-winning grapefruit. The doctors said I'd have to remain in traction until the swelling subsided, and then they could reset the broken bones. It turned out they would have to break it again, twice, to get it to set properly.

My season was over, and so was any chance at a professional hockey career. What would replace my dream?

◆　◆　◆

Unable to get to my job at the radio station or to my classes, I slumped deeper into our couch, my leg raised in a huge cast. I would spend each day watching TV, wallowing in self-pity, and worrying about my future. *With no degree, no skills, and no goals, what the hell am I going to do with the rest of my life?* When I finished pondering those problems, I would dwell on the growing distance between Delia and me.

Even good news seemed to carry an edge. That spring Ryerson faced the University of Toronto in the first round of the playoffs. My teammate Rick Darling picked me up so I could watch the big game.

"Congratulations," he said as he helped me get into his car.

"About what?"

Rick opened the sports section of the *Toronto Sun* to reveal that I had been named an Ontario Universities Athletic Association All-Star. This was quite a surprise, especially as I'd missed a big chunk of the season. The award came with an invitation to play on the Canadian College All-Star Team against the top-tier junior players—the very players the NHL most coveted, making it the perfect chance to show the scouts what I could do. Or it would have been, if I wasn't still recovering from my ankle injury.

Before that night's game the University of Toronto's players skated over to the bench to congratulate me right before the most storied college hockey team in Canada blew us out. Ryerson's season was over too.

The flood of bad news overwhelmed me. With no hockey, no degree, no career goals, and a marriage that was losing steam by the day, I didn't have much to look forward to. I fell into a vortex, with no means of stopping it.

When I got home that night I was alone. I would have done anything to escape seeing my face in the mirrors around our apartment, showing me someone I couldn't stand. Then there were the voices—not the kind a psychotic killer hears but my own inner voice, telling me to harm myself.

I crutched my way into the bathroom and opened a box of razor blades, the old-fashioned Gillette Super Blues. I stared at the shiny blades.

Would I do it? *Could* I do it? My brother and sister would be grief stricken, but because they knew what I had gone through, I thought they'd understand, the kind of convenient lie depressed people like to tell themselves. I also thought about my parents. Unlike the others, whom I wished I could spare, I wanted to inflict as much pain upon them as possible.

I sat down to write a short note. Instead of thinking about the things my parents had done for me and the things they'd done to me, what stood out were the times they simply weren't there. To me their neglect meant that there was something wrong with me, some inherent evil that wouldn't allow them to care for me—or anyone else to really love me. I wrote,

> *Sorry and goodbye to those I love and who love me. This act is solely the responsibility of Bernard and Jacqueline Saunders. May they burn in hell.*

I can't say my note was fair, but I can say it's how I felt at that moment. I returned to the bathroom and ran a hot bath, the way I'd seen it done in a movie. I took off my clothes and slid into the water, a fresh blade in my hand. This would be painful, but I was already on so many painkillers for my ankle, I figured doubling the dosage would take care of that.

I rubbed the blade between my thumb and first two fingers. Then I readied it against my wrist, holding it steady. The feeling was familiar, reminding me of the hot wire hangers I used on my thighs as a teenager. I breathed in, exhaled, then sank the sharp blade into my flesh. A trickle of blood hit the water.

This is it. This is the end.

I dug the blade further into my skin but stopped short of hitting a vein. The act required more courage than I thought it would and more determination than I could muster—and that made me feel even worse. I had already failed at everything else in life, and now I was failing at ending it too.

I held my wrist up to stop the bleeding and slowly got out of the tub. I took two more painkillers and polished off a glass of whiskey. I was still wet and in need of a bath, so I climbed back into the tub, let my head rest on the back rim, and fell asleep.

I heard the phone ringing. I woke up in a tub of cold water. I got out of the bathtub and crutched my way to the phone, dripping wet.

It was Bernie. He had been driving all the way from Kalamazoo just to cheer me up and would be at our apartment in half an hour. I had to pull myself together. I wrapped my wrists in ordinary bandages and put on a long-sleeved shirt.

When Bernie arrived with a case of beer, I concluded he must have sensed my despair and wanted to kick my ass back into gear. I confessed to Bernie that I was depressed because I had no career prospects and no idea what to do next.

"John, you're in a business most people would kill to be in," Bernie said, referring to my nascent radio work. "Why not see how far you can take this broadcasting thing?"

It was the first time anyone, including me, had taken that idea very seriously. It was particularly powerful coming from my brother. No one knew me like he did. He often told me not to worry about the things my father said, forget the past, and take control of my life, because with my natural talent I could do whatever I wanted. His encouraging words made me feel there was hope for me yet.

As soon as Bernie left, I pulled out a tape recorder and started making copies of my radio newscasts, then set up an assembly line to mail them to every English-speaking radio station in Ontario and Quebec. I also sent letters to several hockey clubs in Europe that routinely signed North American college players. It felt good to be doing something about my future instead of just dreading it—and it certainly was an improvement over what I'd been doing an hour earlier in the bathtub. Bernie's visit was just what I needed.

Over the next two months I received rejections from station after station and hockey team after hockey team. But one day a letter arrived from a third-tier hockey club in Belgium that was searching for a player-coach. I called them at once, and the owner told me that the job paid $11,000 for a six-month season—more than twice what my radio gig at CHOO was paying. The job was mine, he said, if I wanted it.

I was thrilled, but things got even better a few days later when I came home to see a note Delia had left on the kitchen counter, with a phone number next to the call letters, "CKNS. Ask for Mr. Hillary."

CHAPTER 15

Chasing a New Dream

I WASTED NO TIME CALLING MR. HILLARY—WHOEVER HE was. Someone at the station picked up right away, and before I knew it I was speaking to the station owner. He explained that CKNS was a small station in Espanola, Ontario, an industrial town of about five thousand people a few miles north of Lake Huron. They needed a news director, which paid $10,000 a year, a thousand more than I was making at CHOO.

I initially thought moving to the middle of nowhere for a thousand dollars more wasn't a very good trade, but the station owner told me the news director I would replace had just landed a job in television, and CKNS was becoming a launching pad for up-and-comers. The station would also pay for housing if I would share an apartment they owned with two of their disc jockeys. That meant Delia would have to stay behind until I could find an apartment for us, but it was something to think about.

When Delia returned later that night I shared my news. She wasn't thrilled about the idea of me going ahead without her, but she agreed to stay in our Toronto apartment until I found a decent place for us in Espanola.

But I knew in my heart of hearts I was one step closer to being my father, always stepping out on his family. I thought, because I wouldn't know anyone in Espanola, it'd be great if my old Western Michigan hockey buddy Neil Smith could join me. He was game, so I talked the station manager into giving Neil a job as a disc jockey. This could work out!

A week later, still unable to drive due to my broken ankle, I boarded a bus to take me to my new home. As we pulled out of Toronto I looked out the window to see the great city's skyline shrinking behind us, and I took a deep breath. I was going to a town I'd never heard of to see if I could make a living talking into a microphone. It was strange, but I was starting over, and that felt good.

Five hours later we pulled into Espanola. What I hoped would be a breath of fresh air was filled with the heavy stink of sulfur. Yellow dust from a pulp and paper plant draped the buildings, the houses, and the cars. It was everywhere—including inside your nose the minute you stepped off the bus.

Even though I didn't have much to fall back on, the whole idea still seemed like a lark. But just three months into the gig a TV station in Sudbury, an hour east, offered me $12,000 a year and my own apartment: a bigger town, a bigger salary, and a home. I took it.

Although Canada had generally good race relations, growing up I had never seen a black face on TV, so it never occurred to me that I could get a job talking into a TV camera. This would be a big step.

When I called Delia to tell her the news, she was thrilled, but before she quit her job she wanted to be sure I wanted her to join me. "You have not included me in your life much while you've been in Espanola, so I wasn't sure if you still wanted to be with me," she said.

I said, "Absolutely, I want you with me. I'm sorry I made you feel this way." But the truth was that my two sides were still battling: my need to be loved and my tendency to run away.

Delia quit her job, I drove back to Toronto to help her pack, and we loaded up the U-Haul. We headed up to Sudbury and unloaded our boxes. But no sooner had we started unpacking, the phone rang. My new boss told me I'd be moving not to Sudbury, but ninety minutes farther east to their TV station in North Bay, some two hundred miles north of Toronto, to replace their sportscaster.

We packed it all back up again and headed up the road to North Bay, where they set us up in a Howard Johnson's for a couple of weeks. I was very nervous about my TV debut the next night. You could only prep so much with twenty-four hours' notice, while you're also moving to a new place. But after the show, when I got back to our motel room Delia said I was a natural, and I felt great.

After our two weeks at the Howard Johnson's was up, all I could find was a glorified shack on Lake Nipissing, a popular fishing spot. I didn't want Delia living in a place like that, so I told her she should go back to Ajax until I could find something better. In hindsight I'm not sure whether I was being chivalrous or chicken, but it was probably some combination of both.

Working on TV in North Bay—an attractive lakeside town of about fifty thousand people—made me look at things a little differently. With my hockey career over, the TV business was starting to look pretty good. When I took it seriously I discovered the TV game could replace the excitement of drugs and hockey. A good night in the studio could lift my mood just like a good night on the ice. On TV your mind can't be anywhere else or else you'll screw up. Such all-consuming focus took my mind off my problems for a few hours each day. I was getting hooked on broadcasting—my healthiest addiction to date.

◆　◆　◆

About a month into my stay in North Bay I found a better place and called for Delia to come back. It didn't take her long to get a job modeling for a dress store. She changed her look, cutting her long hair to her shoulders and dropping the bleach-blonde dye. Although her new look was lovely, it did little to dispel our lack of intimacy. Our trials had brought us closer emotionally, but we still rarely had sex.

Delia thought I was avoiding intimacy to ensure that I wouldn't get her pregnant, but my sexual hang-ups were the real reason. I couldn't explain this, though, because I hadn't yet pieced it together myself.

As the months went by my confidence soared on the set. I became more popular off-screen as well, while I grew farther from Delia.

One weekend we went back to Ajax to see family and friends. When it was time to return to North Bay, Delia wasn't feeling well so she stayed behind to see her doctor that Monday. When I called Delia later that day she told me she was in the hospital because she'd just learned she was pregnant, and it wasn't going well. Delia desperately wanted to have the baby.

I raced back to Ajax, where Delia suffered a miscarriage the next morning. I sat beside Delia's hospital bed, stroking her long hair. I felt like a fraud. I hated that she was in pain, but I still had no interest in being a father.

A week later, when we were both back in North Bay, I made a mistake that would doom our marriage.

"Delia, maybe it's for the best," I said, "because we're not ready to have a baby." The truth is that she might have been ready, but I certainly wasn't. I still had no interest in becoming a father and repeating my dad's mistakes.

Delia became hysterical. I tried to stammer an explanation and an apology, but it was becoming obvious we did not want the same things.

◆　◆　◆

In my spare time I began sending my tapes to any station bigger than ours—which was just about all of them—in hopes of eventually landing a job in Toronto. For Canadians, that's like making it in New York City.

I got a few nibbles, but nothing solid until I got a call from Dave Reynolds, the sports director of citytv in Toronto. Reynolds said he liked my work, although he didn't think I was quite ready for Toronto. But, he asked, would I consider working at their sister station in Moncton, New Brunswick, a thousand miles east of Toronto? He said he'd pay me $16,000 a year, and after a year of learning the business I could have a shot at the big time in Toronto.

I felt like I'd hit the lottery. I couldn't say "yes" fast enough—so fast, in fact, that I didn't even consult Delia first.

I knew that the career I had chosen was going to be a gypsy's life. To climb the media ladder you've got to move constantly, like a military officer. That wasn't a problem for me because I'd spent my boyhood hopping from house to house, but I didn't want to go through all that while being married.

When I left North Bay I told Delia I wanted to go it alone. Not long after I got to Moncton, a cute little town of about sixty thousand people, Delia visited me. We talked about everything. We cried, we hugged, but there was just no getting around the fact that I simply wasn't ready to be married. We held each other in silence that night, and I took her to the airport the next day. We kissed and said goodbye.

My last season of college hockey showed me I could be just as violent as my father. The last year of my marriage showed me I was no better at commitment either.

CHAPTER 16

Making It in Moncton

THAT SPRING OF 1979 BERNIE HAD JUST FINISHED HIS career at Western Michigan in spectacular style, leading the Broncos in scoring three times, being named their MVP twice, serving as their captain his senior year, and earning all-league honors. In other words, he did everything I'd hoped to do.

When he graduated he signed a contract with the Quebec Nordiques, who had just joined the NHL, with a $5,000 signing bonus. That summer he figured he could afford to spend a couple of weeks in Moncton, and he probably sensed how badly I needed him, so he offered to drive me to Moncton in the Datsun 280Z my father had bought him with the money he'd saved for Bernie's college, thanks to Bernie's scholarship.

We stopped in Quebec City to see the old coliseum, Le Colisée, where the Nordiques played. It wasn't much to look at except for the photos of players who had starred in that building, legends like Jean Béliveau, Guy LaFleur, J. C. Tremblay, Marc Tardif, and others we grew up idolizing. If Bernie got called up to the big club, this is where he'd play.

"You know," he told me, looking at those photos, "I couldn't have made it this far without you."

That was a very generous assessment, but it was good to hear—good enough for me to remember the rest of my life.

Not long after we pulled out of Quebec City Bernie told me a story that would answer one of our family's great mysteries.

The previous summer Bernie and his best friend, Gary, had worked with my father on construction sites in Cleveland, not far from Oberlin, where our father had been living most of the past fifteen years. When Bernie and Gary arrived at our father's home he was surprised to find Dad had bought three houses next to each other and was single-handedly renovating them while we had been getting evicted from home after home back in Montreal.

Our father lived in the nicest of the three, renting out the second house and using the third for a single mother and two teenage boys, who often played basketball in their driveway with Bernie and Gary.

One weekend Bernie drove all the way to Espanola for the wedding of our old buddy, Neil Smith, who married a local girl. When Bernie returned to Oberlin Gary had a troubled expression. Gary told him that Mary, the woman who lived next door, invited Gary over for dinner with her two boys. After the boys retreated to their rooms Mary told Gary she didn't live in the house where she'd just served him dinner but the one next door—with my father. They had been together for about eight years. Her boys called our father "Dad," although he wasn't their biological father. Mary knew about Dad's children back in Canada, but my father had told her he was divorced. He'd never introduced us to her, he explained to her, because he felt that we weren't ready to meet her and that we wouldn't understand his relationship with her boys.

While she's telling Gary all this, our dad showed up, unannounced, looking angry and jealous—which effectively confirmed her story. Gary wisely got out of there.

A year later, when Bernie told me this on our way to Moncton, I was in shock. My mind started running over the many nights we went to bed hungry, the evictions, and the cold mornings spent waiting for the Western Union office to open, only to discover he hadn't wired any money. Now I knew why: he was spending his money on another family.

"But if you think about it," Bernie told me, "We're luckier than those two teenage kids. We didn't have to put up with him all that much." We both started laughing hysterically.

I asked Bernie if he had talked with Mary's sons. I was secretly hoping he'd say they reviled our dad for his cutting remarks and bruising fists, just like I did. But he told me that their "dad"—*our* dad—spent his days teaching them football and baseball. He went to all their games and was always there for them.

I couldn't believe what I was hearing. "Bernie, stop the car."

He pulled over, and I stumbled out onto the shoulder of the highway, cars whipping past. Bernie led me away from the road. "That *sonuvabitch!*" I howled. After all these years here was proof that somewhere in that man was a loving, gentle father. We had seen those sides occasionally, but they were often eclipsed by his other sides and, more often, his absence.

The self-blaming thoughts came crowding in: *If only I didn't talk back, if only I'd worked harder, if only I was smarter or nicer or more obedient, maybe then he wouldn't have hauled off and hit me so often.* Objectively I knew this wasn't true, but it was hard to convince myself of that when he apparently treated someone else's kids so well.

Bernie advised me to put it away and move on, but I couldn't do it.

"I'll move on," I told Bernie, "when that man is dead."

◆　◆　◆

After I got settled in Moncton I was pleased to discover a surprising number of beautiful women in town, thanks to the government offices where many of them worked. I'd already tried alcohol, drugs, self-mutilation, and work to dull my pain, which now left sex. I can't say it made me forget my problems, but it didn't hurt.

Bernie generously paid for our nights on the town, but after two weeks it was time for him to head back to Toronto. When he stopped by a bank on his way out of town to get some cash, the teller informed him he had only $800 remaining. He told her there must be some kind of mistake because he had just deposited his $5,000 signing bonus, and we'd burned through a couple thousand, max. No, she said, $800 was all he had left.

When Bernie told me the news, we both had the same thought. Sure enough, a few days later Bernie phoned me from Toronto to tell me our mom had forged his signature on a few checks, draining him of three thousand dollars. That was still pretty good money in those days, enough to buy a new car.

In these situations Bernie and Gail were a whole lot nicer than I was. I told Bernie to put her on the phone. When she got on the line I asked her how could she rob her own son.

She started stammering something about almost losing her condo and a few outfits she had to buy Gail to start her modeling career. And, she added, she deserved something in return for raising three kids single-handedly.

I couldn't believe it. "You've stolen from Bernie," I told her, "someone who's been loyal to you. You no longer have three children, understand me? You have *two*."

She wouldn't give up so easily, countering that Bernie had stayed with her rent-free and was eating free too. I had to laugh. I concluded she just didn't understand what it meant to be a mother. That was the end of our conversation and what remained of our relationship. Characteristically, Bernie never displayed any anger. He accepted our mother for who she was. I couldn't claim to be that noble.

◆　◆　◆

As soon as Bernie left Moncton Gail showed up, which meant the world to me. Despite my warm welcome to Moncton, attractive women still intimidated me. As soon as Gail made some friends, she introduced me to them, helped me pick out clothes for dates, and built up my confidence, which I desperately needed. She was a godsend.

Moncton had a sizeable modeling agency, so Gail decided to audition for them. I took her on a shopping spree and kept telling her how great she looked. She had poise and style but little self-esteem. As the only girl in our family, she felt devalued. She didn't play sports—almost no girls did back then—and our parents didn't talk to her about college or careers, so she thought her only choice was to take advantage of her looks.

When I picked Gail up from her audition she walked out of the agency with the widest smile I'd ever seen and threw her arms around me.

"I've got a fashion show in just three days!"

"Gail, I'm so proud."

We went out for a celebratory drink. She wasn't too far into her glass of wine, though, when her expression changed. She told me that five years earlier, after they'd moved from Montreal to Ajax, our mom began to frequent a small bar, where she met a series of boyfriends. Because our parents had essentially separated years ago, this didn't come as a shock.

"Mom kept telling me: 'Stay away from black men. They're good for nothing. Just take the prime example—your father.'"

Our mother eventually fell for a butcher who was in the throes of a bitter divorce. Driving to work one day he noticed his soon-to-be ex-wife waiting at a bus stop. He reached into his glove compartment, pulled out one of his butcher knives, and jumped out of his car and attacked her. By the time bystanders pulled him off, she lay dead on the sidewalk.

A court convicted him of first-degree murder and sentenced him to twenty years in the federal penitentiary in Kingston,

Ontario. That's pretty severe for a country that doesn't have the death penalty.

You'd think most women watching this tragedy unfold would count their blessings that it wasn't them and let the man rot in prison. But not our mother. She made the four-hour round-trip to Kingston a few times, dragging Gail along each time. In the prison visitors' room Gail watched Mom apply her lipstick, then trot off to see her butcher.

Even I was shocked by this. I asked Gail if she was okay.

"I'm okay. I promise," Gail assured me. "I haven't told anyone else. I needed to get it off my mind."

"Stay here with me," I urged her. "Get your career started. We've made it this far, but we've got to stick together."

That night, after Gail went to sleep, I called my mother at about 2 A.M., when she had just come home. My voice was eerily calm.

"Gail told me about those trips to Kingston."

My mother was silent. Barely above a whisper I said the cruelest words I could think of. "Don't call her, or I'll be back to ruin your life." Anger management was still not a strength of mine.

When I watched Gail's debut in a fashion show three nights later I lit up like a proud father. Her modeling career took off in Moncton, but she was also burning up my long-distance bill calling her boyfriend back in Toronto, a nice guy named Paul. During a break in her modeling schedule she went back to see him—a good sign, I thought.

◆ ◆ ◆

Meanwhile I was trying to work my way up the minor leagues of broadcasting. Being a sportscaster in Moncton, New Brunswick, didn't exactly put me on the Toronto Maple Leafs beat, but we did cover Toronto's top minor league affiliate, the Moncton Hawks. The biggest event I covered that year was a tournament called the

Silver Broom, also known as the World Curling Championships. Never heard of it? Neither had I.

The Maritime Provinces, consisting of Nova Scotia, Prince Edward Island, and New Brunswick, were also home to a semiprofessional hockey league composed of guys who'd played for Canadian Junior teams, American and Canadian colleges, and even a few former NHLers who had no illusions they were heading back to the NHL but weren't quite ready to give up the game. The pay matched the quality of play at $75 a game. But they played three games a week, which came to about a thousand dollars a month—pretty close to the $16,000 salary I was making that year from my "day job." I decided I could use the extra cash, so I tried out for the Moncton Beavers, and I made it. When I discovered that each team was allowed to carry a couple of non-Canadians and paid them $300 a game, I called my old Western Michigan teammates, Bob Gardner and Steve Smith, and told them to "Get your asses out to New Brunswick. You'll make some money, and we'll have some fun."

That was all they needed to hear. They showed up two days later. I took them to the Cosmo, the best club in town, and introduced them to Linda Boyle, a reporter from our TV station who was having drinks with her sister, Diane. Smitty hadn't even sat down before he asked Diane, "Do you wanna dance?" She did, and they started dating.

Smitty, Gardner, and I moved into a house that cost $250 a month, split among the three of us. Suddenly my $16,000 salary, plus a few bucks playing for the Beavers, made me wealthier than I'd ever been and led to the most hedonistic phase of my life. We'd play a hockey game on Saturday night, head to the Cosmo, then bring back everyone in the club to our place—maybe 150 people, 100 of them women. The same man who only months earlier had clung to the wall of the Cosmo like a scared cat was now running the Playboy Mansion East—and loving it.

Sleeping around didn't make me a great person, of course. It didn't resolve my issues with sex either. In fact, it seemed to reinforce what I'd learned at a young age, which was not a healthy introduction to sex. But my year in Moncton was one of the happiest of my life. It started with long visits from my brother and sister and kept rolling with TV, hockey, and women.

But like all parties, this one had to end. The Beavers traded us in a three-man swap to a team in Chatham, New Brunswick, three hours to the north. It wasn't hard for me to conclude that my broadcasting prospects were a better bet than my dying hockey career. I stayed in Moncton while Gardner and Smitty went to Chatham. When that team went bankrupt, Gardner went to play in Belgium and Smitty came back to Moncton with Diane. Two years later they were married, and have been ever since.

Gail returned to stay with me that fall, but as Christmas approached, she asked me if it would be all right for her to return to her boyfriend, Paul.

"You have a real shot at happiness with Paul," I said. "Go back and make it work."

She worried about me constantly. She saw through my womanizing, realizing that I was still a lonely guy who couldn't forge a real relationship. Before she left, we went for a walk on the beach. She looked at me with pity.

"Do you ever think about getting married again?" she asked me. "Maybe start a family?"

"I'm not sure about another marriage," I said, "but I do know one thing: I'm never having kids. I'm scared I'll be a terrible father."

My eyes welled up, and she reached for my hand.

"Well, I want to have lots of kids. Maybe five or six. That way I'll always have someone to love me—other than you and Bernie."

We decided to call him. Bernie was playing for Cincinnati in the Central League, which was just one step from the NHL. He had arrived as an unknown and became the league's leading scorer by December. We reached him right before practice and caught up. We were family.

Bernie's team, the Cincinnati Stingers, folded that week, so their players scattered. But Quebec didn't want to lose him, so they reassigned him to the Syracuse Firebirds, in the American Hockey League, where he debuted on December 22, 1979.

I figured Bernie's game would be over around ten-thirty, so I waited until just before midnight to call. Bernie told me he notched two goals and one assist—a really big night. I screamed so loudly I must have scared him. Bernie was living our dream, and it honestly felt better than if it had been me.

Two days later, on Christmas Eve, 1979, I wasn't too eager to return to my mom's place in Toronto, Gail was with Paul, my brother was in Syracuse, and Gardner and Smitty were visiting their families in Ontario. I had successfully kept at arm's length the women I'd dated in Moncton, so no holiday invitations were coming from them.

I woke up on Christmas morning in our empty bachelor bungalow. A small storm drifted over Moncton, dropping a half-foot of snow. The streets were empty. I have lots of good memories of Moncton and lots more of Christmas, but none of that Christmas in Moncton.

My only companion was a case of beer. I tried to drink my way out of my misery, but because alcohol is a depressive, it just makes everything worse. Now deeply depressed, once again I considered killing myself, but circumstances were working against the idea. I had no drugs, no guns, and not even a garage to gas myself. So I just kept drinking. By noon I had knocked off a couple of six-packs and fell into a deep sleep.

Around four o' clock the phone woke me up. It was Gail. She was with Paul's family, and she was in a great mood. I told her I had a house full of friends from work and the modeling agency. I was having a ball, I said, and asked her to wish everyone well for me.

Then I went back to my chair and crawled inside another beer bottle. I drank one after another while staring at the TV—and the

TV wasn't even on. I'd have to mark 1979 as the most depressing Christmas of my life.

◆　◆　◆

Later that winter, in early 1980, I started a platonic relationship with Anne, a great looking woman with short brown hair and a sexy French Canadian accent. As winter faded into spring I started to fall for her.

One night, when Anne and I were sitting on my couch watching a TV show about an abusive father, I took one of the biggest chances of my life. I whispered, "I know just how that kid feels."

Anne turned to me. "What did you say?"

Hesitantly, I repeated my statement.

"What do you mean?" she asked, shifting her body to face me.

I started telling her my story—some of it, anyway. I had been in denial for years. Whenever people asked me about my father, even in my twenties, I continued to make up a character that didn't exist—a great teacher, a successful businessman, and a role model. Even my best friends in high school thought my dad was a hardworking family man. I'd almost come to believe that fictitious creation was a real person.

But not that night. For the first time I came clean about my father—and about me too. The real me, without any lies. It also marked the first time I'd openly admitted to myself what had happened to me. It was one of the most cathartic nights of my life. That moment also opened the possibility that maybe, just maybe, I was okay, and hiding from the truth all those years hadn't been necessary.

I was lucky that Anne was the first person I told. She couldn't have been more caring and concerned, understanding and sympathetic. If she hadn't been, I'm not sure I would have ever tried trusting anyone with my story again.

◆　◆　◆

I hadn't given much thought to the promises made to me a year earlier by citytv's sports director, Dave Reynolds. But in early May, with one year in Moncton under my belt, he called to say they liked my work and wanted me to join them in Toronto, starting July 1. This was great news, but it also meant my days in Moncton were numbered.

I took Anne out to a restaurant and told her. She was quiet, then finally said, "You don't know how much I'm going to miss you."

"Aw, we've got a couple months left," I said, trying to play it cool, "and you guys can always come visit me."

"No, John. I really care for you."

I didn't have the guts to admit I had feelings for her too. I had already risked enough by telling her about my childhood. I reached across the table, squeezed her hand, then leaned over and kissed her—our first. Walking back to her apartment, we talked like giddy kids.

"How long have you felt this way?" I asked.

"At least a few weeks," Anne said.

"Same here."

"Guess we wasted a month," she said. "And now we only have two more left."

That night we made love, but there didn't seem to be much of a future for us. Anne came from a large French Canadian family that had lived in Moncton for years, and I didn't think she would ever leave. I'd already had a long-distance relationship, and I wasn't eager to try it again.

The night before my going-away party Anne and I had a final dinner together. We sat in a dark restaurant and held hands across the table. Anne looked troubled.

Finally, she whispered, "I love you."

"I—I—think I love you too," I stuttered.

She started to cry. I wanted to call Toronto and tell them, "Sorry, but I'm not coming." Instead, I said, "Come with me."

"And do what in Toronto?" she asked.

"You're ready to model in a big city. All the top agencies are there."

But Anne didn't feel her English was good enough, she felt at home in Moncton, and she wasn't going to leave. When she took me to the airport we said we'd see each other soon and hugged tightly, but we both knew it was over.

CHAPTER 17

Bright Lights, Big City

AFTER JUST FOUR YEARS IN THE BUSINESS, AT THE RIPE age of twenty-five, it looked like I had achieved my dream job in Toronto. But it came with a few catches.

First, despite all the history between us, I had to stay at my mother's condo until I found an apartment. My welcome-home gift was an eviction notice my mother waved at me. She was behind on her rent.

"How could that be?" I asked.

"Gail has some sort of blood disorder," she said.

What?!? I ran to Gail's room in a panic. Both Gail and my mother were vague, suggesting she might be suffering from leukemia. Immediately I applied for a loan, with my new job as collateral. I figured I'd pay off my mother's debt, and the rest could help Gail. My loan was approved. To speed up the process I made the check out to my mother.

When I got home I called Bernie to find out what he knew of Gail's condition. He had just found out himself and planned to head home as soon as his hockey season ended in three days. When Bernie arrived, the four of us sat around the kitchen table and cried. Our mother did the talking.

"The diagnosis isn't good," Mom said. "Gail might only have two years left."

Bernie and I were so torn up that we pledged to do whatever we could.

"Well, the money helps," Mom said.

A month later my mother was evicted from her condo anyway, and the money I had given her was long gone. Gail apparently recovered from her blood disorder. It wasn't long after my initial relief that Gail would survive had worn off that Bernie and I figured out we'd been duped—again.

Our mom was many things, but stupid wasn't one of them. She knew Bernie and I were done giving her money, but she also knew we could never say no to our sister. I would love to tell you we were never suckered by my mom's tricks again, but she knew how to tug on our heartstrings for our sister.

◆ ◆ ◆

I'd been hired to be the third member of Toronto's citytv's sports team, the roving reporter who would fill in when the top weekday and weekend sportscasters were out. But within a week of my arrival the top newsman left. The top sportscaster replaced him, then they jumped me ahead of the weekend sportscaster for the top sports spot. It was a gigantic break for me, but it didn't feel like it. They paid me $17,000 a year, just a thousand more than I'd been making in Moncton, which is a much cheaper place to live.

I moved out of my mother's apartment as soon as I could, but that created another problem: I was broke. For an apartment with no roommates in the middle-class suburb of Scarborough Junction, rent ran $600 a month, which took a good chunk out of my $1,417 monthly check, minus taxes.

One morning I left my apartment with just 40 cents, a dime short of a subway ride. I figured if I just started walking, I'd come across a dime somewhere. But I never found one, and I ended up walking all the way to Toronto, almost three hours! Lesson learned: carry at least two quarters in your pocket!

After a month of this I gathered the nerve to ask my boss, a guy named Fred Klinkhammer, for a raise. I walked down to his office in the basement, where I saw a huge man with a giant head sitting behind a desk.

I knocked on his open door. He waved me in without looking up. Finally he spoke. "I heard you wanted to talk to me."

"Sir, I was brought here to be a reporter and the third man on the sports team," I stammered. "But for the last month I've been the number-one anchor on sports at 6 P.M., our most-watched show, and yet I'm being paid as the third reporter. I don't think that's fair."

"You're right, John," Klinkhammer said. "We're taking advantage of you, and it isn't fair."

I was stunned that my complaint had worked, and worked so quickly. It was that easy! But the punch line came next.

"So as of tomorrow," Klinkhammer said, "you're off the air."

As you can imagine, I backpedaled pretty quickly. I accepted the $17,000 for the top sports spot and kept my mouth shut after that!

But I couldn't dismiss the disparity between the lowly sports anchor and the station's big stars. On my first day on the job I was walking into the lobby when I heard the purr of a new Porsche 911. I turned to watch a beautiful blonde emerge from the passenger's side. When the driver's door opened, out stepped Gord Martineau, our lead newscaster, a dashing man of about thirty.

Gord and I soon forged a friendship. We'd work the same 6 P.M. newscast, then head out for dinner and drinks. Gord never let me reach into my pocket, and whenever he didn't pick up the tab, his friends did. I was a few years younger than most of them, so they nicknamed me "Cubby."

It seemed like everyone in Gord's gang was rich, either through business or family money. They flashed lots of cash and surrounded themselves with beautiful women.

Gord took me to a party in Forest Hill, Toronto's answer to Beverly Hills, hosted by a wealthy couple in their forties. We walked in the front door—the first mansion I'd ever been in—and I understood: *so this is how the rich live.*

While the couple gave us the tour I couldn't get over the sheer amount of money they possessed. In the front drive they'd parked a Porsche and three Mercedes. Their house was bigger than every one of the two dozen places I'd lived in my entire life, combined. And just like Beverly Hills, Toronto had found cocaine. Although I had been offered it a few times, I'd never tried it—but it was getting harder to avoid. That night there was a bowl of it in the bathroom, and various guests had it as well.

I sat down next to a few of them, looking over my shoulder to make sure Gord didn't see me because I didn't want this getting back to the station. With the coast clear, I raised the coke spoon to my nose and inhaled deeply. A few more hits, and I knew this was a drug I wanted to have around.

After a few months of this I'd love to say that I woke up, realized how dangerous and stupid cocaine was, and stopped snorting it. But the truth is I got out due to pure economics. I simply couldn't afford it.

Not long after that party the news director called me into his office.

"We want to offer you a new two-year contract," he said. "How much do you want?"

My mind raced, but I didn't skip a beat. "Thirty thousand in the first year," I blurted out, "and forty in the second."

"How about thirty and thirty-eight?" he countered just as quickly.

"Perfect," I said.

I had just jumped from $17,000 to $30,000 in one minute, with $38,000 promised the next year. But I didn't want to be one of those guys who snorts all his money up his nose. I was getting a huge break, and I didn't want to waste it.

With that salary I could also move into the city, ending my daily half-hour commute. I started looking for a house, which I would share with a citytv producer, Jim Shutsa. We found a four-story townhouse in a neighborhood called Cabbage Town, with a suite on the top floor. We flipped a coin to see who would get to use the suite for their bedroom, and I won. It seemed like everything was going my way.

At about the same time the *Toronto Sun* included me in a story titled, "Toronto's Terrific Men." I even dated a sexy club singer named Carlene for a little while. I never had it so good.

I was partying late and going home with a different woman every night. I spent the next year going from one girl to the next, with nothing in common except that I couldn't stay faithful to any of them. I spent more time creating alibis than building trust.

There was one exception. Early in 1981 I met a twenty-one-year-old named Lyndsay who worked in a bar near our studio. She dressed in the funky style of Madonna in *Desperately Seeking Susan* four years before the movie came out. She liked to party and didn't seem to have a care in the world. She also fed my fragile ego by latching on early and strongly. She was serious about me, and I hadn't let that happen in a while.

◆　◆　◆

After applying for my first job in Espanola in 1978, I never applied for a job again. It always happened the same way: someone heard me, liked me, and called me with a job offer, which is a lot more common in TV than in the "real world," I'm sure, because your work can be seen by anyone, every day. I admit: I've never thought twice about it—which shows how you can take your good fortune for granted. I'm filled with insecurities, but not when it comes to work. It's the one place I always feel completely at home, entirely comfortable and confident. Well, almost always.

A few months after I got my big raise in Toronto a headhunter from Stamford, Connecticut, called to ask me, "You ever consider working in the States?"

"Not really," I replied. Toronto was my dream, and I'd achieved it.

"How much are they paying you in Canada?"

"Thirty thousand," I said. "But I'll be up to thirty-eight in six months or so."

"What if I said you could make three times that in the States?"

He had my attention. "I'd say I'd have to listen," I replied.

He phoned again the next day. He said he'd sent my tapes around and got solid offers from stations in Denver, Oklahoma City, and Baltimore. I immediately turned down Oklahoma City. I didn't want to go as far west as Denver either, but I said I might consider Baltimore. That surprised him, as Baltimore was a no-torious crime capital at the time, but I'd read it was changing quickly with a revitalized waterfront. More important, I didn't want to live too far from Bernie, Gail, and my friends in Canada.

A few days later I took a tour of Baltimore and met the folks who ran WMAR-TV. At the end of my visit the station's general manager offered me a three-year contract: $80,000 the first year, $90,000 for the second, and $100,000 for the third. Because the Canadian dollar was worth about eighty cents to the US dollar, his offer would nearly triple my Toronto salary.

By the time my return flight descended over the lights of To-ronto, I knew I was going to leave my favorite city.

◆ ◆ ◆

During my last two weeks in Toronto I had one of the greatest thrills of my broadcasting career. On March 19, 1980, the NHL's Quebec Nordiques called Bernie up from Syracuse, making him just the fifth black guy to make it that far, starting with the great Willie O'Ree in 1958. Bernie's coach? None other than our old friend, Jacques Demers.

I hunted down a clip from a recent minor league game of Bernie's in Halifax—no small trick before computers. After I'd run through that day's sports headlines, I ended the show by saying, "Big news today. The Quebec Nordiques have called up Bernie Saunders—my brother!" I then rolled the tape of Bernie on the ice, scoring a goal. "Let's take another look," I said with a grin, "from that exact same angle." When I rolled it again my co-anchors and I were laughing, and I hope the viewers were too.

The following fall I drove to Buffalo, where the Nordiques were going to take on the Sabres. Whenever Bernie got on the ice, I jumped and hollered in the stands like a teenager.

After the game I met Bernie in the locker room. He took off his new uniform among some of the players we'd grown up watching on TV, guys like Marc Tardif and Andre Dupont and new stars like the Stastny brothers, Peter and Anton.

"You were fantastic out there," I said. "I'm so proud."

"I wish you were out there with me," he said.

"You know I was."

CHAPTER 18

Big Man in Baltimore

IN 1980 TORONTO HAD ABOUT 3 MILLION PEOPLE, AL-most four times more than Baltimore. But I knew that working in a major American market could open doors that even Canada's biggest city couldn't. After stumbling into this career as a lark, I was now playing chess with it, looking two moves down the board to set up a position at a national network.

It was also clear that the people at WMAR-TV in Baltimore were serious about getting me, and they proved it when they worked so hard with US Immigration to get me a work visa. Aside from the other sportscaster who was understandably a little frosty about getting passed over for the number-one spot on the sports desk, the people at the station were very welcoming, helping me get an apartment and settle in to my new hometown. Lyndsay followed me to Baltimore to see if we were for real.

My desk was about thirty feet from the men's room and about sixty feet from a soda machine. My routine consisted of walking to the soda machine, dying of thirst, drinking a soda, and then walk-ing to the men's room—then repeating this ritual a few times a day.

Once I got in bed I couldn't sleep for more than an hour without having to go to the bathroom. Lyndsay urged me to go to the doctor, but I stubbornly refused—a classic hockey player's response. Then one day she cleverly asked me to take her to her doctor's appointment. It wasn't until we got there that she confessed the appointment wasn't for her but for me.

When I told the doctor my symptoms he immediately tested my blood sugar. A normal blood sugar level runs between 80 and 120 milligrams; mine came in at a staggering 694. When Lyndsay left the room the doctor told me, "If your girlfriend hadn't forced you to come see me, you'd have been in a diabetic coma within a couple of days. After that, anything could have happened, including death."

The doctor admitted me into the hospital with a diagnosis of juvenile type 1 diabetes. I asked, "How can an adult get juvenile diabetes?"

He explained that sometimes it hits in adulthood. There are 29 million people with diabetes in the United States, and only about 1 million have type 1: I was one of the "lucky" ones. He said I'd have to take insulin injections for the rest of my life.

I've had a few serious incidents along the way, like most diabetics, but I've managed quite well with the disease, and it hasn't stopped me from doing much.

I will always be grateful for Lyndsay's intervention, which might have saved my life. But after a few months together she wanted to return to Canada to pursue college. I have to admit I didn't like the looks we got in Baltimore as an interracial couple—as often from black people as from white.

Single again, I quickly gained a bad-boy reputation at a disco called Martinique's. It didn't hurt that my career was taking off— even faster than I'd hoped. Despite the differences between Canadian and American sports, for the most part the transition was pretty easy. Both the Toronto Blue Jays and the Baltimore Orioles play in the American League. I didn't have far to go to see the NHL's Washington Capitals, who play in Toronto's conference, and even college football and basketball, which are largely foreign subjects to a Canadian who grew up in the sixties, were not hard to figure out. They quickly became two of my favorite sports.

I also got some extra help from a couple of future Hall of Famers. Eddie Murray, the Orioles' star first baseman, had been burned by a writer early in his career and vowed it wouldn't happen twice, so he refused to talk with the media—ever. He wouldn't talk to me on the record either, but he and I somehow became very good friends.

After the Orioles won the World Series in 1983 I felt comfortable enough to ask him if we could do an extensive interview. After teasing me about how lucky I'd be to get that, he agreed, and our two-part sit-down interview became a big hit for our sports department—and a big controversy in town. Predictably, the other reporters were jealous and claimed Eddie only talked to me because he was prejudiced against white journalists. They overlooked the fact that he agreed to talk to me because we'd become friends, so he felt he could trust me. After all, he wasn't talking to other black reporters either. But Eddie was right: I was very lucky to get that interview, which helped establish my credibility in town.

About an hour away, in downtown DC, Georgetown University basketball coach John Thompson had built the Hoyas into a national power. The team's "us against the world" attitude rubbed many the wrong way, but it worked for them.

I got to know the Georgetown staff while they were scouting practices at Baltimore's Dunbar High School, a national power in its own right. I had become friends with Dunbar's head coach, Bob Wade, and often stopped by to say hello and watch practice. The Georgetown coaches often visited their gym, too, to recruit stars like David Wingate and Reggie Williams. So when Williams signed his national letter of intent in 1983 to play for Thompson at Georgetown, I had the scoop, which resulted in my first network story on NBC.

On the air that night I boldly predicted that "the Georgetown Hoyas will win the national championship next year." That season, 1983–1984, Coach Thompson allowed me to watch his closed practices on occasion, which gave me an edge on the competition. Sure enough, the Hoyas beat Houston that year for their first national title.

I was thrilled to see Eddie Murray inducted into the Baseball Hall of Fame in 2003 and Big John elected to the College Basketball Hall of Fame three years later—both very well deserved. I owe Eddie and Big John a great debt.

◆ ◆ ◆

When I wasn't working, I confess I spent most of my free time drinking, getting high, and chasing women, but I also coached a hockey team of twelve-year-old kids with former Baltimore Colt star Tom Matte. I kept my waking hours filled with as much activity as possible—good or bad—to avoid facing my thoughts, in a vain attempt to keep my depression at bay.

Working remained my best distraction, although sometimes it came with its own distractions. I still had to handle comments from my dad like, "This Toronto and Baltimore stuff isn't anything to be proud of," and "When are you going to be on a network so I can see you?" My personal favorite: "You look like you've put on a few pounds. No wonder you can't get on network TV. Who wants a fat guy on their network?"

It was easier to brush aside those shots through self-medication than to deal directly with my father and all the insecurities he stirred in me.

By 1984, my fourth year in Baltimore, I had saved enough money to buy a townhouse in Ellicott City on the outskirts of Baltimore. Walking through that door as the owner was one of my proudest moments, a deep feeling of satisfaction. I even got a cocker spaniel named Angie.

My father had managed to weasel his way back into my life by doing me a few favors and odd jobs over the years. He really was an expert handyman too, so when I got my new place I asked him to come down and hang some curtains and blinds. I welcomed him when he arrived—no point in digging up ancient history—and he set to work hanging blinds in the basement family room. When I heard the drilling and hammering stop so he could cuss up a storm, I went downstairs to see what the problem was.

He wiped the sweat off his arm and said, "There's no beam above this damned door. Could you have bought a bigger piece of shit? You really got taken, you know. Those contractors must've seen you coming a mile off."

Just like that, I felt like I had been reduced from a TV journalist on the rise in the States to an incompetent ten-year-old kid back in Chateauguay. For a split-second I even feared he might hit me. My father had a knack for bringing me down when I was at my highest—whether it was winning a Little League title or moving into the kind of home he could only have dreamed of. But I didn't recognize the pattern until we started writing this book.

When I got a job in Moncton, he asked when I would make it to Toronto. When I moved to Toronto, he asked when I would make it in the States. When I made it to Baltimore, he asked when I would get to the network. When I moved into the home I'd worked hard to buy, he reduced it to garbage.

After his comment about my new house, I ran outside and kept running until I reached a pasture. I sat beneath a tree and cried. *I'll never be good enough*, I thought. But then I asked a better question: *Why did his opinion mean so much to me?* Even then, on some level I realized that this was his problem. It was only my problem if I wanted to make it my problem.

I wiped my tears and walked back, resolving not to let him put me down in my own home ever again. I walked downstairs and yelled at him, "Get out!"

When he tried to backtrack I ran upstairs, fetched his suitcase, and threw it down the steps. That was the day I decided I'd had enough of my father's bullshit.

He loaded his tools in his truck and left.

◆　◆　◆

Even when my career was going great, my problems were never far behind. If you don't admit you're depressed and get help, you tend to self-medicate. My drinking was getting out of control. That was horrible for my diabetes, but less because of alcohol's effect on my blood sugar level than the bad habits drinking encourages, like eating the wrong things at the wrong time. If you're alone, with no one looking after you, that can be deadly.

The "good" news, if you will, was that Baltimore's police officers had a reputation for protecting their local celebrities. Orioles manager Earl Weaver, for example, had allegedly been stopped while driving drunk many times, but they apparently let him go every time. The bad news was the same: celebrities could do virtually anything they wanted, and that wasn't what I needed.

One night I was driving about ninety miles per hour with my old Western Michigan buddy Neil Smith in the passenger seat and two girls in the back. We were passing around a bottle of whiskey, and Neil and I had a couple of beers going as well— being about as stupid as you could be. When we heard the siren of a squad car bearing down on us, I thought, *There goes my career.*

The officer approached my door and motioned me to roll down the window. He could clearly see the beer and smell the whiskey. He looked at my driver's license, then at me, and said, "Have a nice night, Mr. Saunders." That probably saved my career.

You'd think that encounter with the police would have woken me up, but it didn't. When I think back on those days I can only shake my head. I'm just lucky no one died while I was driving like that.

◆　◆　◆

That spring I visited Bernie at his place in Kalamazoo. He had grown tired of being shuffled between the minors and the NHL and decided to wind down his career. He could have played for a lot of teams in Europe or the minors, but he picked the Detroit Red

Wings' minor league team, the K-Wings, because he wanted to set up a career with the Kalamazoo-based pharmaceutical giant, Upjohn. Unlike so many athletes who never prepare for life after their careers end, Bernie had already earned a business degree and established a good reputation in Kalamazoo, and he was in demand.

He had gotten married, bought a small house, and had two sons: Jonathan—who, I'm proud to say, was named after me—and Shawn. Eventually they would have one more boy, Andrew. I was just as proud of Bernie's success after hockey—and maybe more impressed.

Back in Canada Gail had married her longtime boyfriend, Paul, and started a family. But she was often sick, suffering from an eating disorder one month, an obsessive-compulsive disorder the next, followed by a bout of agoraphobia. She had already begun to sequester herself in her home with her kids. Paul was concerned, but because he was at work all day, he had no idea just how sick she was.

I hated the distance between us, with me in Baltimore, Bernie in Kalamazoo, and Gail just outside Toronto. But we did a decent job visiting each other and staying in touch. I was probably doing a better job of being a brother as an adult than I had when we were growing up.

◆　◆　◆

My maternal grandparents had moved to a small retirement town northwest of Toronto, where they had recently celebrated their fiftieth wedding anniversary. I was working in Baltimore when I learned that my beloved Nanny, who had battled diabetes and heart disease for years, had been hospitalized. The next morning I drove from Baltimore and arrived in Toronto that evening. My plan was to have dinner with friends and then head north to see Nanny in the morning. I met up with Gord Martineau, my former news anchor at citytv, and we hit our old stomping grounds. After a night that ended too late I woke up and drove to my see my grandmother in the hospital.

When I walked into her room, she said, "John, you look terrible! Do you feel okay?" I couldn't tell her I was hungover, so I blamed it on my diabetes. That was the wrong thing to say, because when Nanny's doctor walked in to check on her, she said, "Doctor, can you look at my grandson? He's not feeling well." The next thing I knew, he had checked my blood pressure and blood sugar and found both to be high. I was on my way to the ICU. Instead of cheering up my Nanny, I just made her worry about my self-inflicted illness. When I reached the ICU I looked up to see Nanny being wheeled in to take care of me. I didn't have the heart to tell her I was just really, really hungover.

A year later I got the call I'd long dreaded. Nanny had passed away quietly in her sleep. Her funeral was a celebration of everything she had meant to so many people in her community, at her job, and especially in her church. But this was *my* Nanny, the first bright light I saw in a dark childhood. I wouldn't let anyone console me or even talk to me.

After the pallbearers lowered her into the grave, I dropped to my knees in the dirt and wept like a little boy. Bernie and my cousin Loretta pulled me away from the grave.

Two years later my grandfather joined Nanny, and I felt a deep loss again. The night we buried him my mother made plans to sing at a local pub. Growing up, I didn't understand her relationship with her parents, and I still don't.

◆　◆　◆

One night in Baltimore I had the enviable job of judging a Hawaiian Tropic Bikini Contest. I'd judged similar events, and the women were generally the same: amazing bodies and smiles but not too bright. This particular evening I brought along two friends from work, who shared a mutual interest in drinking.

When the contest was over, one of my friends headed directly for the contestants. I spotted my other friend in the back of the club, talking to two gorgeous women, so I went over. One of them simply floored me—and I had just judged a bikini contest. She was more attractive than any of the contestants. I could only muster an utterly lame line, but I said it with utmost sincerity, which might have been my saving grace: "You are the most beautiful girl I have ever met." I meant every word.

I liked the sound of her name: Wanda Burton. I took her out to the dance floor, then invited her to the afterparty held on a yacht. To my delight she said yes, so we hopped into my car and drove to the harbor. Although we'd only known each other an hour, I was already convinced this was the woman I was meant to marry.

When I drove Wanda home I was burning to ask her out the next day. But I'd become leery of women trying to get with someone who looked like he had a dollar—and when you're on local TV they always think you're a lot richer than you are. So I thought, *Let's just see how down to earth she is.* I conjured up the least sexy date I could think of.

"I've got to pick up a new lawnmower tomorrow," I said. "Want to come with me?"

She didn't miss a beat. "Only if I can watch you cut your grass."

Man, she was good!

"Well, I don't usually go that far on the first date," I said, "but for you I'll make an exception."

Wanda's parents had split up when she was eight or nine, and her father lived in Philadelphia. Although twenty-five, Wanda was close to her mother, Dolores, and still lived at home. That's where I picked her up the next day for our lawnmower date.

Dolores answered the door and invited me in. "Come on back to the kitchen with me. She'll be down in a minute."

Once we sat down I noticed that Dolores had a picture cube on the table. I picked it up, looking at every facet. All six of them were filled with action photos of Reggie Jackson—Mr. October.

"Big fan?" I asked.

She nodded and then asked if I'd ever met Reggie. I hesitated. Finally I said, as diplomatically as I could, "I don't want to burst your bubble, because you clearly like him a lot. But he can be . . ." I was searching for the right words but could only come up with, "a bit difficult."

"Oh?" she said, encouraging me to elaborate.

This put me in a tough spot. I was trying to decide how much to tell her of an exchange I'd had with Reggie about a year earlier at the batting cage. I had asked my news director if I could go down to the Orioles' Memorial Stadium when Jackson's California Angels were in town and try to get an interview.

"You're not going to get an interview with him," my news director told me. "He's under contract with ABC, so he only talks with ABC affiliates."

Our station, WMAR, was an NBC affiliate, but I figured, why not? If you're too afraid to ask for an interview, you're probably not going to make it in journalism. Heck, I had already befriended Eddie Murray and John Thompson, so I decided to take my chances. I approached the batting cage just as Jackson stepped out, which I figured was perfect timing.

"Mr. Jackson, may I have an interview?"

"No!"

"Oh, is it because of your contract?"

"It's got nothing to do with my contract," he snapped. In hindsight he might have thought I was asking about his contract with the Angels, not ABC, but that didn't stop him from dressing me down in front of the players and the press. "I don't like you guys! You're all a bunch of assholes."

As I slunk away, tail between my legs, the future Hall of Famer, Rod Carew, pulled me aside and said, "Don't take it personally, kid. He's like that with everybody."

So when Dolores seemed to be coaxing the story out of me, I tried to balance honesty and diplomacy. "Well, I tried to interview him once, and he kind of brushed me off." I left it at that.

Wanda's mother looked at me for a moment, smiled, and said, "I just wondered because he's my brother."

My eyes grew large. *Oh, crap!* I stammered an apology, but Dolores just chuckled. "Don't worry—we know how he can be sometimes."

"A great ball player," I kept saying, unable to stop. "Just a really great ball player."

While I struggled to extract my foot from my mouth, Wanda appeared at the kitchen door, looking radiant—with a giant pink curler still clinging to the top of her head. I did not think that was a new trend, but I didn't want to say anything. I didn't need to stick my other foot in my mouth too.

Her mother reached over and swiped the curler out of her hair. Wanda let out an embarrassed laugh and got over it quickly, which made me like her even more.

At the hardware store I picked out an electric mower.

"Why not a gas mower?" Wanda asked. "It'll be a hassle slinging that cord all around the yard."

I informed her, a bit haughtily, that I'd grown up hauling an electric mower across the yard—I had been a lawn mowing *professional*, after all—and I would manage just fine.

Once we got back to my place I showed Wanda to the TV room, got her an iced tea, told her I'd only be a few minutes, then headed out to wrestle with the yard. My living room windows looked out to the backyard, where I hoped she'd glimpse me sweating behind the mower, looking like the man of the house.

But not long after I'd started, sure enough, I proceeded to run over the electrical cord, slicing it in half, literally cutting the power to the lawnmower. When I went back inside and saw Wanda in the living room, she seemed to be drawn to her TV show, not looking out the window as I'd originally hoped. Lucky break. So I slipped back inside the kitchen, as if I had come back solely to get a drink and mop up what little sweat I'd produced.

She looked at me and said, "You cut the cord, didn't you?"

This woman already had me figured out.

I sat down on the couch next to her to watch TV, and just as I started to cozy up to her, my cocker spaniel, Angie, pushed her way between us with an ill-humored growl.

"Let me guess," Wanda said. "Your ex-girlfriend's dog?"

She didn't miss a thing. I was smitten beyond hope.

Wanda and I quickly became a couple. But whenever I'd pull her close, she cooled me off and kept me in check. I'd have to pay my dues before she'd let me get too close to her.

In Wanda I found a partner who was sensitive to my mood swings, even my dark spells. Where friends and the police failed to get me to straighten up, Wanda succeeded. She was the best incentive I had.

I was reveling in the thrill of this new love—someone completely different from all the other women I had dated—when I got a call that put me on the move again.

◆　◆　◆

Since our news anchor, Sally Thorner, and I had joined WMAR, our station had jumped from the bottom to one of the top stations in the Baltimore market, which turned out to be a great launching pad for talent. My years there happened to overlap with those of a young woman from Mississippi named Oprah Winfrey, who anchored the local news. She wasn't there long before Chicago came calling, and you know the rest.

In the summer of 1986 my agent, Chuck Bennett, phoned to tell me that a cable network called ESPN was interested in talking to me. You'd think I'd be jumping up and down, but I didn't even have cable then, and being from Canada, I actually had no idea what ESPN was. In my defense, ESPN had only been on the air for seven years and specialized in the America's Cup, Australian Rules Football, and other relatively obscure events. No one called it the Worldwide Leader in 1986.

Besides, I had just signed a new four-year contract with WMAR, and I was set to make $150,000 a year—more money than I'd ever imagined I could make playing hockey, let alone broadcasting. I'd done a few things with the NBC network, and they'd liked it. I was in the running to host their national baseball coverage, so I thought NBC would be my next stop. It seemed like the safer bet by far.

For all these reasons, not to mention my growing relationship with Wanda, I told my agent that I wasn't interested. Chuck called me back two days later and said that ESPN wasn't taking no for an answer.

"They want you to fly to Connecticut to see their facilities."

The job still didn't interest me, but I'd never seen Connecticut, and the trip was free, so I figured, *why not?* If they were trying to impress me with the tour, however, they failed. In 1986 ESPN was a two-room operation with a single antiquated studio. They told me they wanted me to be one of the lead anchors for their signature show, something called *SportsCenter*. I was polite throughout the visit, but I wasn't even tempted.

Chuck passed on to ESPN my decision to decline. Then in October Chuck called again to tell me they were offering me a four-year contract for a good chunk more than I was making in Baltimore. This fledgling cable network now had my attention.

But I still didn't say yes. There were too many hurdles. For starters I'd have to talk my way out of the contract I'd just signed with WMAR and gamble that I could talk my new love into coming along for the ride. I was certain the only way I could convince Wanda to leave her job and her family would be to marry her. The problem was that we were just five months into our relationship and were still moving slowly, so I sensed it was too soon to ask her to marry me. I needed to proceed very carefully with her.

Eventually I told ESPN I was intrigued, which meant I had to tell WMAR about ESPN's offer. But WMAR wasn't going to give up without a fight. When the general manager took me out to dinner I listened while he tried to play the guilt card, but he knew he couldn't in good conscience keep me from making more money and working for a national network—no matter how small. He finally agreed to let me out of my contract if I promised to stay through the Christmas season, or the fall ratings period. We made a deal, and we parted with no hard feelings. Baltimore had been very good to me.

Now for the tricky part: Could I convince Wanda to come with me?

CHAPTER 19

A Family of My Own

WHEN I FLEW TO CONNECTICUT TO LOOK FOR A HOME I brought Wanda with me, hoping to include her in the decision. I thought I could buy a home similar to what I had in Baltimore for about the same price. We were looking in the middle of Connecticut, after all, not New York. That's when I suffered my first real estate sticker shock. For the price of my home in Baltimore I could get a house in a run-down area of Hartford or a double-wide trailer. After some searching we found a townhouse under construction for $160,000 and I took it.

On the flight home I said something to Wanda I'd never said to anyone before: "It's clear where we're headed, and I want you to come here with me."

As usual, Wanda was no pushover. She said she had to talk about it with her mother and father before she could make such a big move. I understood, but after committing to leave WMAR for ESPN in late December, I could only pray that she'd come with me.

After talking it over with her parents, Wanda told me what I wanted to hear: she had decided to come with me. If she hadn't, I'm not sure I would have stayed at ESPN very long or even followed through with the agreement—which is not the approach I took with my early offers in Espanola, North Bay, Moncton, or

Baltimore, when my job always came first. My priorities were changing.

Soon after we moved to Connecticut we got married. Everything looked perfect from the outside. We had a nice home, a nice car, and a loving, committed marriage. But Wanda is pretty sharp, so it didn't take long for her to start seeing signs that all was not well with me.

For example, occasionally I would say something critical about my parents that Wanda couldn't understand. "You shouldn't say that about people who've taken care of you your whole life," she'd say.

"I *wouldn't* say that," I'd reply, "about people who had taken care of me my whole life."

Before Wanda and I were married I stood firm: *no kids*. I didn't want to repeat my father's mistakes, and I was still afraid I would. I hadn't been violent since I quit playing semi-pro hockey, and I was certain I would never abandon Wanda, but I was afraid the anger and violence were still inside me and could come out if I became a father. Besides, I was much too busy with my career to give children the time and attention they deserved.

But one morning I woke up beside Wanda and the words just sprang up from someplace deep within me. "When are we going to have a baby?" I asked. I hadn't planned on saying anything like that, but even as I looked at her shocked face, it felt right. Betting on myself was the risky wager. Betting on Wanda—this loving, caring soul—that was the easy one.

But it wasn't going to be that simple for us. In the early years of our marriage I usually kept my childhood to myself or, worse, would continue to fabricate the ideal parents I never had. I had become so accustomed to the fantasy version of my family that keeping up the façade had become a reflex. I would also pull away from Wanda emotionally, refusing to share my problems with her, and sometimes I retreated physically too.

After we decided to have children, Wanda visited her doctor and told her how often we were having sex. The doctor said,

"That's not going to work." I was spending long hours at ESPN, but the real problem was that I was still screwed up. Pushing her away was all I knew how to do.

Wanda finally gave me an ultimatum: "If we're going to have children, you have to come to grips with what went on in your past."

And that was how she persuaded me to see a therapist. I was definitely reluctant. It's difficult for anyone to tell people about their secrets, and it seems to be more difficult for men who grew up playing sports. We respond to pain with phrases like, "Suck it up," "Walk it off," and "Rub a little dirt in it." Those have their place, but they're not much help when you're dealing with childhood trauma, and the depression that often follows. Adding to the usual stigmas, black people seem to be especially reluctant to seek help. In all the therapists' offices I've visited over the years I've never seen another black person in the waiting room—ever.

But when Wanda makes up her mind, her mind is made up—and that's a good thing. She has the right kind of stubbornness. So when she said I had to see a therapist before we had children, that was all I needed to hear.

Dr. Sandy was in her forties, with an office in midtown Manhattan. I started seeing her in the early 1990s on Fridays before my ABC College Football broadcast. I barely said anything during our first few sessions—this was strange and scary to me—but gradually I warmed up. She really wanted to help, and she was a good listener.

Eventually we talked more about my childhood than I ever had before. With only a few exceptions I had kept my past to myself, so I didn't think it was that big a deal. By talking with her, though, I realized that so many things I had taken for granted as normal were far from it. When I opened up enough to tell her my stories, *she'd* be in tears—and she was a seasoned professional. It was the first time I truly saw how unhealthy my childhood had been. It was cathartic to learn I was not abnormal—as I had always

We probably looked like a model family, but life behind closed doors was far from picture perfect. Bernie and Gail (with our younger cousin Loretta) were my two biggest supporters, a real blessing. I can't imagine making it through childhood without them. (*Courtesy of the Saunders Family*)

In Chateauguay, a suburb of Montreal, I was a top hockey player and the class vice-president. I was also fighting my father, getting into Jimi Hendrix, and eventually, "self-medicating." Turbulent times, indeed. (*Courtesy of the Saunders Family*)

Bernie and I fought like brothers do, but I was thrilled when he joined me at Western Michigan. When he made it to the NHL, I was so proud I ran the tape on Toronto TV—twice! He's my best friend. (*Courtesy of Western Michigan University Athletics*)

When I met Wanda I said, "You are the most beautiful girl I have ever met," and I was right. When we talked, I was convinced she was the woman I was meant to marry. I was right about that, too. (*Courtesy of the Saunders Family*)

I'm filled with insecurities, but not when it comes to work. It's the one place I always feel completely comfortable and confident. Well, almost always! Recovering from my brain injury, on national TV, wasn't easy. (*Courtesy of ESPN*)

I didn't know how to spell ESPN before I accepted their offer in 1986, but my timing couldn't have been better. We were adding the NFL, the NBA, and MLB, and I was starting lifelong friendships with Boomer and Bob. (*Courtesy of ESPN*)

When Jim and I shared a ride to Philly, I knew I'd found a kindred spirit, a father figure, and a best friend, who would never betray me. He even taught me how to hug. (*Courtesy of ESPN*)

I was afraid to repeat my father's mistakes. But when we had Aleah, I found a deeper love that day for my new daughter, for my wife, and even a little for myself. When Jenna came along, it just multiplied. (*Courtesy of the Saunders Family*)

Wanda, Aleah, and Jenna are my life. They've given me far more than I could have imagined. The girls started calling me "Daddy" from the start. They still do, and it melts me every time. (*Courtesy of the Saunders Family*)

Of all the shows I've done, *The Sports Reporters* might be my favorite. It's fast-and-furious, fun, and often funny. Our panelists know their stuff, especially these three—Mitch Albom, Bob Ryan, and Mike Lupica—who also happen to be great friends. (*Courtesy of ESPN*)

I never tell Wanda to watch me, except after the college football title game: "Did you see me?" But not in 2012. Once I stepped off the stage, I was right back to where I was before: down in the dumps. (*Courtesy of ESPN*)

In 2013, the White House invited me to the first National Conference on Mental Health, along with Glenn Close, Bradley Cooper, and others. When President Obama asked what had brought me there, I mentioned my sister, because I was still too afraid to talk about my own struggles. (*Official White House Photo by Pete Souza*)

My love for my daughters is so strong, it's often helped keep me going. So it's ironic that my fear of losing them can sometimes eclipse the fun we're having. (*Courtesy of the Saunders Family*)

After my heart attack in 2012, I realized I've got too many people who care about me, and I've got too many years left, to stop now. I decided to enjoy the rest of my life. And that's what I'm doing. (*Courtesy of the Saunders Family*)

My surprise 60th birthday party. "Thanks to all of you, it's getting easier for me to enjoy life. I can't begin to tell you how much you mean to me." That included Robin Roberts, a loyal friend, and a fighter. (*Courtesy of the Saunders Family*)

There's nothing I love more than seeing old friends, playing golf with Bernie, and being with Wanda and our girls. I still have bad days and bad weeks. But bit by bit, day by day, I'm getting better and better. Imagine that. (*Courtesy of the Saunders Family*)

believed. But my childhood was, and I learned that was why I was so incredibly sad so often.

With Dr. Sandy's help I started learning how to live in the moment instead of constantly dwelling on the past or worrying about the future. This isn't easy for me, but it was essential if Wanda and I were going to start a new family. I couldn't bring all my baggage to a new family and expect things to turn out better for my kids.

I was making real progress, taking steps I'd never thought I would. Wanda saw this too, and agreed we were ready to have kids. When she became pregnant we were thrilled, but I still didn't want to have a boy. It would be too easy to fall into my father's horrible habits if I had a son. I feared I'd find myself pushing and confronting my son the way my father had with me.

But as silly as it sounds, Wanda promised me she would have a girl, and damned if she didn't deliver—literally. In the summer of 1989 I held Wanda's hand while she gave birth naturally, with no epidural for the pain. At that moment I wished the doctor had given *me* the epidural because Wanda was crushing my hand— but when your wife is giving birth, it's probably best not to complain about that! I thought I was a pretty tough hockey player, but Wanda showed me something that day. She was amazing.

I found a deeper love that day for my new daughter, for my wife, and even a little more for myself, than I ever thought possible. I knew I'd need more self-esteem to give all the love I could to this beautiful girl.

I'd heard the name Aleah only once or twice, and this was before the singer Aaliyah had made the scene. For some reason I absolutely loved that name. I was convinced no other name would have fit her, so in my mind there was never any doubt about our daughter's name: Aleah. Wanda agreed.

Aleah Noelle Saunders was six pounds, six ounces of pure angel. As she entered the world, my life changed forever. I was a father, but I was determined not to be the type who thinks his job is done when he pays the bills and puts food on the table. I wanted to be the kind of dad who'd always feel love for his child, even if she angered or disappointed me.

With Aleah's arrival, love leaped into the burnt-out hole in my heart. When she was still very small she liked to spend quiet time just lying on my chest. On Sunday mornings I'd place her on my chest, and she'd happily stay there through the afternoon. When the NFL games started, she got excited, as if she could understand what was happening. I think she was more enthralled by the flashing colors than the actual game, but I pretended we were watching the game together.

Aleah was a quiet baby, but she was very vocal about wanting to be with me. Seeing me walking into a room, she'd squeal and giggle with delight, and that thrilled me. When Aleah was old enough to walk she would reach up for my hand, and when her fingers touched mine, she'd beam. Holding her little hand did more to keep my depression away than anything else could.

I never imagined that the love I felt for Aleah could be duplicated. I didn't think I had enough to go around. But when we had Jenna four years later in 1993, it just multiplied. Jenna did almost everything early, and she became my rough-and-tumble little girl, always digging into something for her own amusement. Sometimes I'd just stand outside her room and watch her play and talk gibberish to herself. I wish those early years had lasted forever, but with each milestone reached, I learned to appreciate the present.

My girls thought I walked on water. Like most dads, I could make them laugh by being silly, like when I'd sing the Spinners' classic "Rubber Band Man," with all the pantomime stretching motions. They loved it, and I did too. One time, when Wanda was driving them somewhere, the song came on the car radio and they shouted, "Mommy, they stole Daddy's song!" When they got home I had some confessing to do.

The love I have for my children is greater than any I can imagine. That may sound like a given, but for someone who feared he had no love and could never raise children, it's a bit of a miracle.

When Aleah was only six we learned she also had diabetes. I blamed myself for passing the disease on to her. I sat by her bedside every night she spent in the hospital and hated myself for it until I realized she'd gotten some of my strength, too. I could see she was scared, but she wasn't defeated. I saw her withdraw every time the nurse wanted to give her a shot of insulin, but I soon learned that it was partly because she felt her daddy could do it better than anyone else and was confident I'd teach her, which I did. She's never let it stop her from doing what she wants to do, and that's something I could only hope for.

◆　◆　◆

Our daughters have given me a thousand life-changing gifts, but they've also given me one new fear. It surfaced years ago, when we spent Aleah's seventh birthday in Key West, and we both got our ears pierced at the same time. When we were walking back to the hotel, she said, "Daddy, why do you look so sad?"

"Because," I said, "you're growing up so fast." I should have stopped there, but I couldn't help but add, "and I don't want to lose you."

Each passing year filled me with both pride and fear. I was proud to see the girls learn to read so well, to compete in sports, and even to pick up lyrics to a song. But each new step forward reminds me they are one step closer to leaving me. Facing this fear has been a constant challenge for me.

But as they've grown older I've been relieved to see we've not drifted apart but become closer. They're thick as thieves with their mom, which is not a given in mother-daughter relationships. But they've always told me everything, and no topic is off-limits. I was the one they came to when they'd been hurt by a cruel classmate. I was the shoulder they cried on when they first got their periods. Wanda tells me that many girls barely talk to their fathers and don't even want to be seen with them, but that's not the case with us.

A girl's father is in some ways a daughter's first boyfriend, the first man to love them, to cherish them, to take them through good times and stand by them during bad times, setting a pattern I hope they will duplicate when they meet someone special down the road. I can't guarantee that my girls will never do anything wrong, and I can't prevent bad things from happening to them even if they don't, but they've earned my confidence that they'll make good decisions.

Aleah refused to follow the high school crowd that was drinking and partying in the woods. She once confessed to me that she felt left out, but at the same time she had no interest in what they were doing. I told her she'd spend much more of her life as an adult than as a child and that the decisions she made now were ones she'd deal with later. As always, our talk ended in a hug and telling each other "I love you."

Jenna recently came home in tears because one of her close friends had begun to drift from her circle. I explained that sometimes life's most painful disappointments often lead to our most exciting new stages and that her best friends would probably come along a little later in life. She might even reunite with her friend down the road. I held her for a long time, and when we were finished, she was laughing again.

I am grateful beyond words for my daughters—and so glad that, with Wanda's help, I overcame my fears to take the biggest chance of my life.

CHAPTER 20

The Worldwide Leader

I MIGHT NOT HAVE KNOWN HOW TO SPELL ESPN BEFORE I started working there, but I didn't need much time to figure out I had arrived at the right spot at exactly the right time. I immediately started hosting *SportsCenter*, ESPN's main franchise at the time. The next year ESPN got the rights to cover NFL games, so I joined that studio show. The year after that, 1988, ESPN added *Major League Baseball*, so I did that too. And in 1990 I became the first on-air talent to cross over from ESPN to ABC to host ABC's *College Football Saturday*, which they wanted to restore to its previous luster.

ESPN in the early days provided the perfect environment to welcome a newcomer. The company was still small enough to have a family feeling, an intimate operation compared to the giant it is now. Most of us were pretty young, just starting families, and learning to behave like sensible adults. I never sensed much jealousy or competitiveness among the staffers. We all just wanted to put out a quality product and prove that we were working for a serious outfit—and that wasn't a given in the late eighties, when the old guard saw us as little more than a toy store. Our main goal was to make sure ESPN looked as good on the air as the three-letter networks.

In 1988 ESPN's executives put me on the Calgary Winter Olympics, ESPN's first, and we got lucky: Calgary gave us the Jamaican bobsled team and Eddie the Eagle, the ski jumper who seemed to crash as often as he landed safely. Everything we did over those two weeks was new to us, and we shared in each other's success. It was a great time to be at ESPN.

I was also forging lifelong friendships. I got to know Bob Ley when we hosted the NCAA basketball tournament together. Chris "Boomer" Berman and I partnered on the NFL studio show and NFL *Primetime*, and Tom Mees and I worked on the NHL telecasts. All three became close, trusted friends. We lost Tom in a drowning accident in 1996, which I still think about. Bob and Boomer remain two of my best friends to this day.

I have never been paired with a TV partner I couldn't work with. I've been lucky to have formed some terrific teams in my thirty years at ESPN—Chris Berman on *SportsCenter*; Barry Melrose on hockey; Dick Vitale on college basketball; Leo Rautins on Toronto Raptors games; Tim Legler, Steven A. Smith, and Greg Anthony in our NBA studio; and Craig James, Jesse Palmer, Mack Brown, and Mark May on college football, to name a few.

All good friends, but no one was more important to me than James Thomas Valvano. America fell in love with Jimmy V. in 1983 when he led NC State past Houston for the NCAA title, one of the biggest upsets in NCAA history. Then he ran around the court frantically looking for players to hug. On ESPN and ABC he proved to be a natural entertainer and became an instant star.

He debuted on ABC at the Big Four Classic in Indianapolis in 1990. Before the broadcast had even begun, I knew I'd found a kindred spirit. We had the same sense of humor, except he was funnier. I could whisper an observation to Jimmy off the air, and he'd convert it a few seconds later into instant comedy on air. Jimmy just had it.

After telecasts around the bar or in a restaurant, he'd hold court like Johnny Carson or David Letterman, always the funniest guy in the room. People were drawn to him, and he made them feel like the stars. When we started working together in the studio at ESPN, after every show we'd go to Art Secondo's Hall of Fame Sports Lounge and talk about politics, the news of the day, or whatever made us laugh. We started taking golf trips together, and during road trips to basketball games on the East Coast we'd drink expensive scotch and tell cheap stories. We'd be back in the studio Wednesday night and then fly out to games on Thursday.

One Wednesday night we took a limo together for the two-hundred-mile trip from Bristol to Philadelphia. We asked the driver to stock the car with snacks, some club soda, a bottle of scotch, ice, and two whiskey glasses. We had barely pulled out of ESPN's parking lot when we were on our second drink. By the time we'd reached the highway I had begun to tell Jim stories I hadn't told anyone: about my father's beatings, my mother's transgressions, my drug use, my hospital stays, and, most of all, the recurring depression. Our limo had become a therapy couch on wheels.

Just by listening, Jim made my stories seem acceptable, almost normal, and that in itself was a huge help, as liberating as the first time I confessed to Anne in Moncton about my dad beating me. Jim didn't once look as if he were shocked, amazed, or critical. Perhaps I shouldn't have been surprised: this was a guy, after all, who had made his living listening to high school kids, often from tough neighborhoods, tell their stories.

In an instant, it seemed, I had discovered the father figure I needed—but he was also like a best friend who would never betray me. Then, as if to seal our blood bond, he told me a couple of his secrets, which made me feel as important to him as he had become to me.

We spent the rest of the ride to Philly laughing harder than I can ever remember. Having already unburdened ourselves, it was pure catharsis. We told jokes, we told stories, we compared our likes and dislikes. Jim loved Sinatra while I loved Public Enemy. Jim loved Martin Scorsese, while I loved Spike Lee. But most importantly we respected whatever the other guy admired. The fact that one of us enjoyed something automatically gave it legitimacy to the other.

When we arrived at our hotel in Philadelphia, I knew that I was a much richer person than the man who had left Connecticut just three hours earlier.

Among the many gifts Jim Valvano gave me was the ability to hug. Growing up, I limited my hugs for my Nanny and Aunt Yve, but Jim refused to greet or part without giving me a great big bear hug. When he hugged me the first time, I wasn't expecting it and probably looked like I was afraid of catching something. But he persisted until I understood that hugging someone is more than a meaningless way to say "howdy." It's confirmation that someone actually cares about you and isn't afraid to show it.

Jimmy also became a close friend of the family. He started coming to our house when Aleah was just a little girl. She'd always take his hand and haul him around the house, but Jim didn't just play along. He *loved* it, laughing and joking with Aleah the whole time.

Aleah would always pronounce his name as one word. "Jim-Valvano! Come see my room JimValvano! Come watch TV, JimValvano!"

I had to ask. "Aleah, why do you always call him, JimValvano?"

"Because, Daddy, on TV you always say, 'I'm John Saunders, and this is JimValvano.'"

Well, there you go. That's how close we were.

◆ ◆ ◆

In the early nineties Jim contracted bone cancer, and I was heartbroken. When Jim was in New York for his initial chemotherapy at Memorial Sloane Kettering Hospital, Jerry Seinfeld sent over videotapes of his show to cheer him up. Jim and I sat in his room, binging on Seinfeld's sitcom, laughing as hard as we had in the limo. Even in the throes of a cruel disease, his love of life never left him.

One morning Jim's wife, Pam, asked me to stay with him during his ritual recovery from the chemicals designed to kill the tumors that ravaged his body. It's a rough process, so Pam didn't want their three girls to see what their dad was going through. I was happy to spare them that, but afterward, when I saw his wife and daughters in the hallway outside his room, I couldn't help but admire how Nicole, Jamie, and Lee Anne leaned on each other and drew strength from each other. At this time Aleah was still an only child. Seeing Jim's girls like that really made an impression on me.

On the way home that night I called Wanda to say I would never want Aleah to have to go through something like that alone, so we should have another baby. Without missing a beat Wanda said, "I'm glad you feel that way, because I'm pregnant."

Wanda gave birth to a beautiful baby girl on my birthday, February 2, 1993: Jenna Tiana Vanessa Saunders, named in honor of James Thomas Valvano.

Just a few months later, on April 28, 1993, Jim left us.

CHAPTER 21

Our Sister

FROM THE START I'VE ALSO BEEN VERY CLOSE TO MY nieces and nephews.

Bernie has three sons, two of whom became college hockey players, just like their dad. When Gail visited me in Moncton, she told me she wanted to have "a bunch of kids," and she did. In October of 1991 Gail gave birth to her fifth child, Joshua.

So now she was raising five children, all under the age of nine, which would be a handful for anyone, but for my sister it became an overwhelming task. After she had Joshua she sank further into depression and began to distance herself from her husband, Paul. Her family time was reduced to sitting on the couch in her pajamas and holding the little ones while her oldest daughter, Stephanie, took over cooking and cleaning for the family. Paul tried everything he could, shuttling her from doctor to doctor while working two jobs to pay the bills for his big family.

Our father stilled lived in Ohio, so he didn't know what was happening with Gail. Our mother often presented herself as the sympathetic one, but it seemed to me she was doing more for herself than our sister.

During this tough time Bernie and I became flat-out scared for Gail and her family. We talked with her on the phone a lot and visited her whenever we could. For me that meant covering as many NBA games in Toronto as possible. I reminded her of fun times we'd had together and spoke of better times to come. Bernie was great with her, as always. We could only hope it would be enough, but we feared the worst.

◆　◆　◆

My faith in my ability to raise my daughters the right way grew year by year. In 1999, when the girls were ten and six, we moved into our current house in Hastings-on-Hudson, just north of New York City.

Or, rather, we tried to. I hunted long and hard to find an African American architect to build our dream home. His work was great, but he kept extending the deadline—an occupational hazard, it seems. When it became clear the builders wouldn't be able to finish our house in time, we put a trailer on our property and lived there, with four people and two dogs stuffed into two bedrooms. What was supposed to be a four-week stay stretched to seven months, straight through the winter, which often resulted in frozen toilets. The experience gave me flashbacks to my teen years when our father was usually gone, we lived in a cramped apartment, and I resented every minute of it.

I didn't fare much better as an adult living in a similarly cramped space. I felt like I wasn't taking care of my wife and daughters. I still feared becoming my father—just like my mother warned me I would.

My dark moods made me retreat from family and friends. Sometimes when I closed the door of the trailer I sat as far away from the girls as I could and just sobbed. Wanda had grown accustomed to the roller-coaster ride that was her husband, but the girls hadn't. One day I heard Aleah call to Wanda, "Mommy, he's doing it again!" I felt horrible affecting them that way, but I couldn't pretend to be happy or explain what was wrong.

I didn't answer the phone very often either, or talk much when I did. So when Gail called one day in the spring of 2000 sounding incoherent, I had no patience. I asked what was wrong, and she stumbled and slurred on her answer as if she'd been drinking. My sister didn't drink or do drugs, so I knew she was probably over-medicated. I barked, "Call me later when you feel better!"

Not long after I received that call, my mother called to tell me Gail was in the hospital, and she didn't think she would get out. When I pressed her for more information she said Gail had taken too much of her medication. She added that Gail had been staying with her, which made me wonder how such a thing could have happened.

Gail had been in the hospital a few times, and you could never be sure if Mom was exaggerating, so I admit I didn't understand the gravity of the situation until Gail's daughter Stephanie told Bernie and me that we really needed to get to Canada as soon as possible. Bernie felt we should call our father, who was now living near Bernie, and ask him to come with us, so I booked three tickets to fly from Newark to Toronto that night. On the way to the airport the rain came down in buckets. After we had waited a few hours at our gate, our flight was canceled, so we returned to my house in complete silence.

The next morning, May 10, 2000, when we were preparing to return to the airport, my mother called to tell me Gail had died. She was gone. I couldn't believe it. I cried all the way to the airport and during the entire flight to Toronto. Bernie and I tried to figure out what could have happened, while our father sat in silence.

When we reached my sister's house in Oshawa, a Toronto suburb, my mother answered the door. My grief was quickly ambushed by anger. There stood my mother with a brand-new hairdo and fresh makeup. She had just returned from the beauty salon, as if she were preparing to entertain guests.

Later that night, after we'd finalized plans for the funeral, Gail's oldest daughter, Stephanie, passed on to me what my mother had just told her. Apparently about a month earlier Paul was concerned that Gail's behavior was affecting their kids, so Gail checked herself into Oshawa General Hospital. A few days later she checked herself out and took the bus to my mother's apartment in Guelph, ninety minutes away.

According to my mom's account to Stephanie, Gail lived with our mom for three weeks or so. One morning she asked mom for a cup of tea and waited at the kitchen table. She had a few bottles of antidepressants with her and began to drop the pills into her mouth, one after the other—certainly not the way they'd been prescribed. My mother questioned why she was doing that, but apparently accepted Gail's answer, whatever it was. Before long Gail passed out and remained that way most of the day, while my mother decided to run some errands.

Only when Mom returned did my she realize she needed to call the paramedics. By the time they arrived, Gail's organs had failed. A few hours later she died at the hospital.

The day of Gail's funeral Bernie and I tried our best to help Paul with their five kids who'd just lost their mom. At the same time, I tried to avoid my parents. I had nothing to say to them.

I didn't want to see Gail, but when Bernie headed upstairs to see her open casket, I couldn't let him go alone. So I grabbed his hand and climbed the stairs to say goodbye to our sister. When we first saw Gail, looking much older than her forty-one years, I'd wished I hadn't. But I was glad Bernie and I were there for each other. Looking at my sister in her casket, I promised her I would do everything I could to make sure her children never suffered as she had.

During my sister's burial I couldn't believe it when my mother draped herself over Gail's casket and screamed, "Oh, my God, she was my best friend!"

Gail's death only deepened my depression. When we returned to our temporary trailer, there was no hiding my condition from the girls. This was especially hard for me, because after our marriage and the birth of our beautiful daughters, I naively thought nothing could get to me anymore. This downturn brought with it the cruel realization that nothing—not wealth, fame, nor even a loving family—could protect me from depression.

I thought about Gail's tragedy almost every day. I avoided seeing my mother except at holiday gatherings, when my dutiful brother would bring her along. I waited until the spring of 2000, almost ten years after Gail had died, before I told my mother I wanted to see her. I wanted to get some answers.

When I was preparing to go, Wanda sensed my apprehension, so she and the girls packed and hopped into the car with me, and we all headed to Guelph. It was a good thing she did, because after we sat down in my mom's apartment I suddenly had nothing to say, so Wanda carried the conversation with small talk.

When Wanda and the girls left to pick up lunch I was finally alone with my mother. I was sitting at the same table where my sister had started popping her pills. I felt Gail's presence, which gave me the strength to ask our mother the question I came to ask: "What happened?"

I was prepared for her to deny the story my niece had told me ten years earlier and make up a new one. So before she could start spinning a different version, I began recounting the events exactly as I had heard them from Stephanie: how Gail had arrived from the hospital in Oshawa, sat at my mother's table, and started popping pill after pill until she passed out. Then I told her I had heard that she'd left my sister unconscious while she ran errands, and called 911 only after she had returned.

As I laid out Stephanie's account of my mom's confession, more calmly than I thought I could, my mother's face didn't reveal anything, so I expected her to repudiate everything I said. But when I finished, her reply shocked me: she told me that's what happened.

I was speechless. I leaned back in my chair, overwhelmed by what I'd just heard. I felt the life slip out of me.

When Wanda and the girls returned I could only sit silently as the small talk started up. When we finished our lunch I stood up and said, "Well, it's time for us to leave."

On the drive home I told Wanda what had happened. She was as amazed as I was, but she told me she knew I was not going to get the answers I'd ached for. Wanda thought I was still hoping there would be an answer to all this that made sense, that would allow me to think of my mother as a loving, caring person. I realized Wanda was right: that's what I had secretly wanted. Instead, I'd received confirmation of the opposite. But at least I knew the truth, and there was some cold comfort in that.

It's sad for anyone to lose a little sister, of course, but to lose her that way—with five kids counting on her—it's more than I can describe.

◆　◆　◆

Much to our relief the builder finally finished our home in the summer of 2000. The wait had been tough, but ultimately worth it. We now live in the home I'd always dreamed of.

My home is so important to me. It has nothing to do with how big it is, or how much it cost, or the neighborhood we live in. It's about finally having the security, the stability, and the safe place that I longed for growing up.

My attachment to this home was underscored a few years ago when Jenna was sitting in the living room with Wanda, watching me walk around the driveway picking up some paper scraps that had blown out of our trash cans.

Jenna asked, "Why is the house so important to Daddy?"

"Because," Wanda told her, "he never had one."

CHAPTER 22

Livin' in America

FROM THE TIME I SIGNED ON AT ESPN JUST ABOUT EVERY aspect of my life was about to change dramatically, but one transition was already well underway: re-adapting to America. Raised in Canada but living in the United States, I feel more acutely than most how radically different the two countries can be.

When I moved to Baltimore I was shocked when I first saw American police officers. In Canada the police keep their guns holstered, with a large leather flap covering the handle, making it look less like a holster and more like a gun purse. The idea is to downplay it, though no one seems too worried that a Canadian officer couldn't get to his weapon quickly enough. It was much less likely that a Canadian police officer would actually need his gun than an American officer because Canadian citizens need a special permit to carry a handgun, and very few receive it.

The police officers I saw in Baltimore had their guns holstered, but with the butt end exposed. To me they looked like Wild West gunslingers, and it sent another message: American police had a greater fear of armed criminals because that's the reality here. Unfortunately, the need to respond faster sometimes means that someone who is perfectly innocent gets shot. That is extremely rare in Canada—and when you're black and you move to the States, you have to think about such things.

I was rarely a victim of racism in Canada, and what I did experience—usually in a hockey rink—wasn't much. But when I arrived in the United States I quickly learned that many people saw me as a threat simply because I was a black man. As every New Yorker knows, it's not easy for a black man in Manhattan to get a taxi to stop for him. I've even proved it to some of my white friends by having them stand a hundred feet behind me and watch me try to wave down a cab while wearing the same business suits I wear on the ESPN set. The taxi invariably passes me by and picks them up. Then they understand.

Sometimes it can get ugly. One time in New York my cabbie was of Middle Eastern descent. When I asked him to open his trunk so I could put my suitcase in, he started yelling at me. When I told him he went to the wrong address, he called me a liar. I was so irate that I copied his license number down. When he saw me doing this, he grabbed me by the arm.

"Get your hands off me," I said, and jumped out of the cab. After retrieving my belongings from the trunk, I left it open to make him get out to close it—which he would have done for most customers. He leaped from the cab to shut the trunk, then yelled at me as I walked toward ABC's studio: "You may have a suit and tie, but you're still just a fucking NIGGER!"

I turned to confront him—this is where my hockey background might have come in handy, for better or worse—but he jumped back into his cab and peeled off. Walking into the studio, my anger turned to sorrow. To a lot of people it didn't matter how I was dressed, how much money I earned, or how big my house was. I would always be "just a nigger."

The cabbies can be a problem, but they only have so much power. That's why the police can be much scarier. When Wanda and I were driving from her mother's home in Baltimore to our new home in Connecticut one Sunday afternoon, a New Jersey

State Trooper pulled us over. Wanda was asleep, but I quickly dismissed the fear that I might have been speeding because we were rolling calmly along with the flow of traffic, which barely reached the speed limit.

"License, registration, and insurance," the trooper asked. I gave him the items. He returned to his squad car, where he spent about twenty minutes, probably running every check possible to find something to ticket me for. He finally walked back to my car.

"You're free to go," he said, then he tossed my cards and papers in my face. "Know why I stopped you?"

I shrugged.

"Because you're a nigger in a Porsche."

He turned and walked back to his car. I felt completely helpless, but I was grateful Wanda was still asleep.

Being a black man in this country keeps me on edge in ways that aren't always easy to explain or understand. There's a veiled layer of institutional racism that can affect us every day—something I don't feel when I'm in Canada. My suspicions of racism are not always accurate—it's worth remembering the Baltimore police officer who refused to give me a ticket when I richly deserved one—but those suspicions are correct often enough that I feel I always need to be vigilant, and this takes a toll.

When you grow up feeling as insecure as I did, always wondering if you're worth anything, throwing racism on top of it doesn't help. Anxiety over racism is one thing I'm grateful I wasn't burdened with growing up.

At ESPN I soon found I was able to use my new position to show my support of the black community and my belief in lifting each other up. (You'll notice that I refer to my race as "black" and not "African American." Being Canadian, I never felt the latter term applied to me.)

I can't separate my passionate belief in racial equality from my work, and I don't try. In one of my ESPN/ABC contracts I was asked to be a spokesman on racial issues. In another I was named a diversity recruiter to help increase the black profile at both networks. You may see many black faces on the screen, but you'll find far fewer working behind the scenes, holding positions of power.

I have spoken out many times on racial issues, on camera and off, taking advantage of the pulpit that comes with national TV. Yes, I occasionally get some backlash, but I figure, if I can't speak up, who can?

For everything I've been given, it is a very small price to pay, and one I pay happily.

PART THREE

◆　◆　◆

The Façade Cracks

CHAPTER 23

The Psych Ward

DR. SANDY, MY FIRST THERAPIST, HAD BEEN GREAT, GIV-
ing me a crucial, welcoming introduction to therapy. If she had
been cold, indifferent, or ineffective, I would not have come back
for a second visit, let alone become a convert.

But in 1999, in the midst of our "trailer winter," I decided I
needed deeper, more comprehensive help, so I started seeing a
psychiatrist named Diana Horne. Her approach included medications like Wellbutrin and cognitive therapy, which is based on
logical reasoning. For example, although most people would consider it absurd that a child would be responsible for his father's
abuse, I had believed all my life that I was at fault for the beatings
my father had given me, thanks to my big mouth and drug use.
Cognitive therapy makes the patient aware of his irrational be-
liefs, and then you start revising them.

I responded so well, in fact, that by 2006 I felt like I'd learned
all that therapy had to teach me. That spring I walked into Dr.
Horne's office, beaming, and said half-joking, "You've cured me!"
Thinking I was finally good to go, I stopped seeing any therapists
for three years.

On the outside everything seemed like it was getting better
and better. In addition to a great family, my career was booming.

In 2006 *USA Today* reported that the Davie-Brown Index ranked me as the nation's most likeable sportscaster.

At last I seemed to have reconciled the two sides of my personality: the part of me that was prone to risk taking, violence, and fleeing at the first sign of trouble, and the part that was safe, stable, and successful. I still had a few drinks each day, but I was responsible and hard working. I never felt any impulse to hurt my wife or my daughters, and I could never imagine abandoning them. So I was defying my greatest fear: I wasn't my father after all.

My emotional state, however, was eroding. I have an intense fear of losing my daughters—either suddenly, through a tragic accident, or slowly, as they grow up and go away, leaving me behind. I could cry right now just thinking about it. They both know I suffer from depression and that they need to hold me up sometimes. Every Father's Day my daughters buy me the same thing: beer mugs with a personal engraving. Recently Jenna gave me one that reads, *I will love my daddy for always and always and always.* You can guess what that means to me. When we hug, it's for me as much as for them.

My love for them has often helped keep me going, so it's ironic that my fear of losing them sometimes can replace my happiness with sadness. Even our best moments can turn into dread because I fear *losing* those moments.

❖   ❖   ❖

In 2007 my father was diagnosed with colon cancer. We put him into a nursing home in upstate New York, then moved him to a hospital in Ossining, New York, where his condition worsened. Some friends, who knew about our relationship with him, asked why we paid for his care. As for Bernie, he knew our father's childhood probably wasn't any easier than mine, and he loved him despite his flaws. As for me, I think I secretly hoped that at the eleventh hour he'd become the man I had pretended he was when I was growing up.

In May of 2009 the doctors told us he was near the end, so Bernie and I went to see him. I'm not sure what I was hoping for—a final reconciliation, perhaps, or a simple apology, or an unconditional expression of love—but none of that happened. By then he was too sick to communicate much. I shouldn't have expected it, of course, but the heart can be stubbornly irrational.

After Dad died, Bernie and I arranged to have him cremated. We weren't sure how many people might attend a funeral for him, so Bernie and I decided we would simply get together, raise a glass and pour out a little liquor, as the Tupac song states, which is the custom in the black community.

My father's death didn't affect me the way I thought it might. I didn't feel relief or sadness or even happiness. I felt nothing. Not numbness, but simply nothing at all. But in hindsight I might have been fooling myself, ignoring the pain his death really caused me. Our last chance to make things right had passed, forever, which might have affected me far more than I let on to anyone, including myself.

I continued to blame myself for our dysfunctional relationship—and the one man who might have convinced me otherwise was now gone. As my depression deepened, my long-dormant impulse to cut or burn myself resurfaced. Freud used to say depression was anger turned inward against yourself, and my response to my dad's death might have been proof.

I also had suicidal thoughts pop up again while I was driving. I could hit a tree or a lamp, I thought, or drown myself in a roadside lake, and that would be it. What made things progressively worse was that I wasn't doing anything to address these issues: no therapy, no medication, no acknowledgment that I was doing anything but gliding along, leading a perfect life.

By December of 2009, a few weeks before Christmas, my façade finally cracked under its own weight. I went to see our family doctor, Dr. Michael Gerdis, for a checkup. He'd known me for almost two decades, so as soon as he saw me he didn't need medical tests to know something was off.

"John, you don't look right."

I didn't pull any punches. "To be honest," I said, "I'm feeling kinda down."

"In what way?"

I thought about it for a moment, then decided to tell the truth. "I really don't feel like going on." Even I was a bit surprised to hear those words come out of my mouth.

He looked at me carefully. "You realize that when you say that, I should send you directly to the hospital."

"No, I'm fine."

"You promise me you're fine?"

"Yeah," I said. "I'm fine."

He wasn't satisfied. He left the room and returned with a slip of paper. "I can tell something isn't right, so I want you to visit this place, Westchester Medical Center, that has a psychiatric unit. Promise me you'll go."

I promised I would. As soon as I left his office I went directly to the WMC, met with a social worker, and told her the same thing: "I don't feel like going on anymore."

I wasn't saying I wanted to kill myself. I was saying I was worn out. I didn't want to keep doing this: waking up every day, already tired, constantly struggling to keep going, with little hope I'd ever get much better. It was exhausting, with no end in sight.

Hearing me say this, she summoned a psychiatrist, who asked me a lot of the same questions. Then he asked a new one: "Do you feel like you're a threat to yourself?"

"No."

"But you've just told two professionals that you don't feel like going on."

"I just don't feel like doing this anymore," I repeated. "I'm tired of this."

While the doctors stepped outside to consult with each other, Wanda arrived to see me. We sat by ourselves for about an hour, not only talking about why I felt so sad but also discussing the normal husband and wife subjects: the kids, their school, all their activities.

Like many spouses of depressed people, for years Wanda had understandably tried to fix my problems with many approaches, including cheerleading: "Go out and tell yourself today is going to be a good day!" or "Think of all of the wonderful things you have to be thankful for!" She had all the best intentions, of course, but with depressed people this approach rarely helps, and sometimes it can magnify the problem. Not only do you still feel horrible, but you also feel guilty about feeling horrible. You think, "It sounds so easy. Why can't I do it?" When Wanda realized that didn't work, she learned to ask what I wanted, which was usually not much more than to be listened to or held. She is great at both.

When the psychiatrist came back he said, "I want you to go to the Westchester Medical Psychiatric Ward at Mt. Sinai and check in."

"Why?" I asked.

"We want to have you under observation for a while."

"Why?" I asked again. I wasn't going without a fight. "I feel fine."

With that, the psychiatrist turned a little tough. "John, all I need is two doctors' signatures to have you admitted: mine, and the admitting physician's. If we do that, then you're committed, and you can't be released without my say-so. Or you can admit yourself and sign yourself out whenever you like. So you have a choice: I can admit you, or you can do it."

You might think, given those choices, that I'd jump at the latter and admit myself. But I wasn't so sure. I sat in silence for a while, wondering if perhaps it might be best to have the doctor admit me so I couldn't sign myself out until they thought I was no longer a danger to myself. After mulling it over I finally concluded it was best for me to admit myself.

Wanda remained extremely calm throughout, one of her many strengths. She knew that overreacting only made things worse.

We drove straight to Mt. Sinai and started filling out reams of paperwork at the front desk. By the time I headed to my assigned room it was almost midnight.

Along the way I encountered some interesting hallmates. One guy on our floor was constantly screaming at the nurses, who kept telling him to get back in his room. Some guys were walking around like zombies. Other guys were just screaming at who knows what. I also heard a lot of strange sounds, things I couldn't even identify.

I was thinking I'd be getting a nice private room. But when I opened the door I discovered I had a roommate. It was so dark that I never got a good look at him, and I had no idea what he was "in for," if you will. I knew he couldn't be an axe murderer because they had a different place for dangerous felons. But I imagined he could be a *potential* axe murderer, and I could be his first victim. All night I was thinking, "This guy is gonna kill me." I've been in a lot of tough situations, but my first night in the psych ward was an altogether different kind of challenge. I didn't sleep a wink.

The next morning I saw the guy who had been screaming at the nurses. He was now standing in his doorway, because they didn't allow him to go any farther. So there he was, leaning against the door jam, glaring at the world and cursing any nurse who walked by. And that's when I was hit with the scariest thought of all: in the eyes of the doctors, these were now my peers.

◆ ◆ ◆

Bernie came to visit me my first day. He's seen me in a few hospitals and tends to take it in stride, but his expression that day told me he was almost as unsettled by what he saw as I was. After a good look around he whispered to Wanda, "What the hell is John doing in here?" He knew my doctors thought I needed to be observed, but he was convinced this was not the place.

After two days on the floor—which had only served to make me more anxious, not less—Wanda discovered a special wing.

For $1,200 a day, on top of our coverage, I could get a private room in a wing with only a dozen patients and as many nurses and doctors. I was grateful we were able to afford it. I also thought about those who couldn't afford it and were stuck on the original floor—not to mention the thousands more with no coverage at all who are probably living on the street.

The private room was a big improvement, but I was still in a psych ward. When my girls came to see me it was very disturbing for all of us.

My depression quickly got worse. I used my laptop to read online, do my homework for the coming weekend's games, and write down whatever was on my mind. But they wouldn't let the patients use a power cord because they were afraid we'd hang ourselves with it, so I could use my laptop only as long as the battery lasted.

I wanted to shut my door and be alone, but they didn't let you do that either. They hung a towel over all the patients' doors so we couldn't shut them.

The floor had lots of rules too, such as mandatory group therapy meetings four times a day and no eating your meals by yourself. You had to sit at least two to a table, with nurses joining in to encourage conversation.

I wanted no part of any of this. The first two days the nurses had to come to my room and make me get out of bed for every meeting—and they were relentless. After being dragged out of my room the first couple of days, I started cooperating. I realized that if I was going to be depressed, I'd have to be depressed sitting with a bunch of other depressed people.

During our group therapy sessions about a dozen of us sat in a circle of chairs. The doctors started the morning session by asking, "Is today a good day?"

Then we'd go around the circle and give our answers. "No, it's not," someone would say, followed by things like,

"I only slept two hours last night."

"I'm worried about my kids."

"I want to get out of here."

Others would say, "Today's a pretty good day. I got a good night's sleep." Simple stuff, but it made you open up, bit by bit, even if you didn't want to.

For my first two days in these sessions I said the bare minimum. I simply didn't want to be there. I didn't think I was in the same boat as everyone else, and I wasn't comfortable telling my story in front of strangers. I was also afraid that people would recognize me, betray my trust, and publicize my problems, and then the world would think I was nuts. That could make my work—and my life—that much harder.

I consider my bosses at ESPN to be enlightened, caring people. If I told them what I was going through, I'm confident they would have protected my privacy and done everything they could to help me. But I still was too embarrassed to let them know I was dealing with serious depression. So I told my supervisors at ESPN that I was in the hospital for my diabetes, which gave me more incentive to get out soon before I had to blow my cover.

For all these reasons I was content to listen to everyone else, some of whom had been there far longer than I ever planned to be. When I heard them tell their stories, and all the difficulties they'd had, it was hard not to be moved by their struggles.

One guy, probably in his seventies, was trying to quit smoking so he took some medicine a doctor had given him, but it turned out to have the unfortunate side effect of throwing him into suicidal rages. He seemed like a gruff, good-hearted guy who loved his grandkids, but now he had some serious issues he'd have to work through to get back in their lives.

Another guy, in his midthirties, had just had a baby. He seemed like a simple, nice guy but completely docile, as if he'd quit fighting. When you talked to him it was like no one was inside. I soon learned why: he was there to receive electroshock therapy—one of the last resorts for people suffering from depression.

At my lowest points some doctors had suggested shock therapy to me, and I'd always said, "No, I don't want that." It raised a lot of fears in me, some rational, some less so. I was afraid I would never be the same person, and my family wouldn't be able to connect with me. I also feared I would not be able to do my work, and that the difference in me would be obvious on camera.

The experience of another patient, a woman in her sixties, confirmed my fears. On my second day she told us she was about to go for her first electroshock therapy the next morning, and she was scared. *So* scared. She wasn't in tears, but you could tell she was on the verge.

The next morning when we joined our group she was just coming back from her first treatment, and she had that same glassy look the young father did. During our afternoon session she just kept repeating, "I have a terrible headache. A terrible headache." That settled it for me.

Even when you think you've hit rock bottom, that your situation is as bad as can be, you don't have to look very far to find someone who has it worse. And if you can't, you need only visit your local psychiatric hospital.

◆　◆　◆

On my third day the doctors determined that my medications weren't working for me, and changed my prescription. That was a little scary, but the results from the new medication were encouraging.

By that day the psych ward had finally worn down my resistance. You had to say *something* in each session, and you had to eat with each other too. Unless you were completely antisocial, it would be pretty hard not to open up eventually. That morning, a few of the folks in our group who knew who I was asked me how I ended up there. Unlike other people, however, they didn't ask why I wasn't happy "with all I had." They knew what depression could do.

With this prompt I began talking in the meetings, starting with my childhood. After I spelled it out—the verbal and physical abuse and the lasting effects—they understood.

There was a lot of give-and-take in these meetings, a place where no one dared mount a high horse, and celebrity status didn't count for anything. We became more comfortable talking with each other, sharing how we felt, and actually feeling some kinship. Maybe the rules kind of forced us to be friends, but after a while we really were. I was even willing to concede that we were all in very similar boats.

The next morning, my fourth on the floor, I met two new patients at breakfast. One was a young woman in her early twenties, whom I'll call Abby. She was a little heavyset, and she felt bad about her weight, among other things. Her parents had pushed her to go to the ward, and her doctors had committed her.

The second new patient was a lady in her late forties, whom I'll call Colleen, a very attractive, middle-aged mom with three adult children. In the course of our sessions she would tell us her children had given her a sense of purpose, and now that they were gone she was having a very difficult time figuring out what was she going to do. It sounded like her husband, a successful businessman consumed by his work, didn't understand what she was going through, and it wasn't clear if he was even trying.

The three of us bonded immediately, perhaps because we were the newest patients in the ward, starting our "sentences" at about the same time. But mere coincidence didn't explain all of it. All three of us had plenty going for us on paper, but we'd each hit a wall, and we were probably more open to each other than we'd normally be because of it. It shows you how little demographics actually matter when it comes to really connecting with another human being.

Colleen, the mother of three, was a talker! Just nonstop. If you didn't know she was in the psych ward, you'd would have never thought she was depressed. But if you understood depression, you could see it in her, something about the way she talked. Underneath all her extroverted energy, her heart was breaking—almost as if she feared that if she stopped talking, she'd start crying, so she drowned out her worries with words.

Colleen's children had all done well, and she was proud of them. But when someone tells you too many times how great things are, you know they can't be that great. Shakespeare got it right: she doth protested too much. When her kids moved out, Colleen lost a piece of herself—which perfectly described my greatest fear.

But Colleen was still funny in the meetings because she was so inquisitive. "What is *that* like?" "Really!" "How do they *do* that?" She was a spark plug in a place that could use one, and just a very likable person.

Abby, the twenty-two-year old, latched on to both of us, perhaps because she was looking for validation from some kind of parental figure. She was very sweet and very bright. With Colleen and me she could be funny too. But she was also hurting, and it wasn't hard to understand why.

Her room was right across the hall from mine. Because the towels kept our doors from closing all the way, I could hear her call her parents every night before our bedtime. You could tell from the way she was responding that her parents were arguing with her.

"Mom, Dad—I'm trying, I'm *trying*! I know, I *know*. Yes, you're right—you're right." The calls never went very long before she'd start crying.

After those calls she would walk out of her room and go to the computer station, which was just outside her door. After hearing these conversations two or three nights in a row, then watching her go to the computer station, I left my room to sit next to her and ask if she was all right.

"Yeah, I'm okay," she said.

"Okay," I said. "But if you want to talk, we can."

When the same thing happened the next night I spoke to her again.

"Yeah, I'm okay," she repeated. But perhaps because I have two daughters about her age, my instincts told me I could press her a bit this time.

"No, you're not," I said softly, not as a correction but as an invitation to talk. That's all it took to open the floodgates.

"I went to a good college," she told me through her tears. "I did very well. I've always done very well. But I don't like the way I look. I don't think I'm a good person."

Hearing her declaration was like sticking a dagger in my heart, as if someone was repeating my own thoughts, fears, and dark secrets, and shoving them right back in my face.

With Abby I knew exactly what to say because I felt the truth of it, and I probably wished someone had said it to me when I was younger. "There is absolutely nothing wrong with you," I told her, then I repeated it: "There is *absolutely nothing* wrong with you. I have only known you for three days. And I *know* that you're a good person, a caring person, a fun person, and you're somebody I'd like to have for a friend. I hope that when I get out of here we stay in contact."

She looked me in the eyes when I said this. This seemed to get to her. I knew how she felt. What I said probably couldn't counteract two decades of her parents' messages to her—intentional or otherwise—or what she had internalized all those years because of it. But I also know it can feel pretty good when someone you think might know something says, "You're okay."

She seemed to search her emotional memory for the appropriate response, as if she couldn't recall how to react when someone gave her a sincere compliment. She finally settled on, "Thank you," and she meant it.

I like to think I helped her in some small way, and I *know* that trying to help her helped me too. It was like I was talking to my younger self, giving her the support I wished I'd received. I suppose that was the point of our endless group therapy sessions: some of the best help we received came from each other.

Depression allows you to have incredible insights into other people souls yet still be incapable of transferring those insights to your own situation. That's true of everyone to some degree, of course, but I've often been struck that such serious problems can seem so easy to solve, so clear when they're not mine—and so stubborn and opaque when they are.

◆　◆　◆

After seven days in the psych ward I had missed hosting only one *ABC College Football* and one *Sports Reporters*, so I still didn't feel I needed to tell my bosses the real reason I'd called in sick. But the issue arose again when the psych ward's lead doctor told me he wanted to keep me there into the next week—and who knew how much longer after that?

I felt I had to take action. I met with the lead doctor and his assistant. They talked about the medication adjustments they were making and how they wanted me to stay a little longer to make sure the transition went well. If they were off, things could go very badly, very quickly.

But I insisted, "I'm ready to go home." Because I had taken my doctor's advice and admitted myself, I could leave when I wanted to. If I had needed two doctors' signatures, I'm not sure I would have gotten them anytime soon.

The psych ward doctor still had his doubts, until I told him how much I wanted to get back to work. I think he saw that as a positive sign, because people with severe depression usually aren't eager to do anything.

It was kind of funny: two weeks earlier, I'd told my doctors I didn't want to go on with my life. Now, I was telling them how badly I wanted to leave, and get back into the swing of things. You'd have to conclude my time in the psych ward did what it was supposed to do.

The doctor agreed to let me out the next day, a Friday. But before they let me go I had to do an "exit interview" in the group session. When we were back in our circle of chairs the doctor asked if I wanted to say anything.

"I want to thank everybody," I began, "for being so forthright in talking about your own issues, and allowing me to see so many different sides of this disease."

In addition to making me feel better, I told them, the sessions were almost like taking a crash course in depression. Hearing everybody discussing different medications and different treatments opened my eyes to the breadth and depth of the disease, and the many approaches available to address it.

"But more than that," I said, "I just want to thank you for being real people, dealing with real issues. Being with you went a long way toward helping me. If I can ever do anything for you, let me know."

CHAPTER 24

Dr. Dangerous

BEFORE THEY RELEASE YOU FROM THE PSYCH WARD THEY make sure you're seeing a psychiatrist on a regular basis. Because I had stopped seeing Dr. Horne three years earlier, they assigned me a new one.

When I walked into his office for the first time in early 2010 I met a psychiatrist in his late fifties with a world-weary, smug expression that never changed. He had diplomas on his wall from fancy schools and was listed as one of "America's Top Doctors" in airline magazines. I'll call him "Dr. Dangerous."

He started our first session by reviewing my hospital file, while rarely making eye contact. He asked me if I was thinking about hurting myself, or others. I wasn't. Then he asked how I was sleeping.

"Okay," I said. "But I wake up a lot."

He nodded, and then said he'd like to make some changes to my treatment—meaning, my medications. When I entered the psych ward I was already taking a small amount of a drug called Klonopin, maybe a quarter milligram, which reduces anxiety. I don't suffer from clinical anxiety, but they gave me a little more to ease the transition into the psych ward. Dr. Dangerous increased that dosage to 1 milligram a day. Of course, I had no idea what Klonopin was for or how powerful it was. Shame on me for not doing my homework—a mistake no patient should make.

Our following sessions all started with Dr. Dangerous sitting in his chair, looking bored. I would sit down, and he would say nothing, letting the silence grow for minutes before he'd finally ask me, "So how are you feeling?"

"Not good," I'd say. That was the reason I was there, right?

Dr. Dangerous would eventually reply, "So, you're not feeling good."

Then he stared at me in complete silence for a few more minutes until I'd say something, *anything*, just to end the staring contest. Sometimes I asked if he thought it might rain or whether he liked the Yankees. (He didn't like sports). He usually confined his answers to a grunt or occasionally a condescending smirk. Perhaps, I thought, this was a new technique: we're going to *stare* the depression out of you!

During one of the many pregnant pauses between us I wanted to shout: "*Do* something! You're not even *trying* to help me!" But I kept my mouth shut.

Just to mix things up, he might ask, "What are you thinking?" Sometimes I really wasn't thinking of anything, or maybe I was thinking about the hockey game I'd watched the night before. But because he wasn't a sports fan, I'd just make something up. "I'm thinking about my kids," I'd say.

"So you're thinking about your kids," he'd reply, and then I actually *would* start thinking about my kids—and my fear of losing them. This fear had been with me from the day my daughters were born but manifested itself in different ways over the years. When they were young I had the usual fears of something happening to them, like an accident or a kidnapping. As they got older, I feared losing them to friends or even hobbies and activities, anything that would reduce their desire to be with their dad. When they got to college I worried they'd be off on a new adventure, and they might move to California and never come back. And finally, of course, I worried that Mr. Right could turn out to be Mr. Wrong. I knew that once I ran through all these fears in front of Dr. Dangerous, I *would* get depressed. At the end of the session, during which we might have exchanged a dozen sentences, Dr. Dangerous would never forget to ask for his $200 check.

Sometimes I'd walk *into* Dr. Dangerous's office feeling pretty good, and I'd walk *out* feeling depressed. I'd be stewing the whole way home: *I just drove fifteen minutes to spend an hour and $200 on a guy who barely even talked to me, and all he wanted was his money at the end of the visit.* That didn't make me any happier! This man had less soul, and was less help, than my fellow psych ward "inmates." I got more out of them in seven days than I got out of him in six months.

It would have been bad enough if Dr. Dangerous just wasted my time and money. But he violated the Hippocratic Oath: Above all, do no harm. After I handed him his check at the end of each visit, he invariably asked, "Do you need a prescription?" After a few sessions he started increasing my Klonopin dosage. Six months later he had me taking 2 milligrams in the morning and two at night, but I had no idea if that was a lot or a little.

Another patient might have questioned his approach, and I certainly should have, but at that time I rarely second-guessed doctors. Besides, I was already on a smaller dose of Klonopin before I'd met Dr. Dangerous, so it didn't seem that radical to me.

I did know, however, that six months of these mind-numbing sessions hadn't done me any good. I kept waiting for something to happen, for something to change for the better, but nothing did. Finally, I'd had enough, and in mid-2010 I stopped going to see him. Afterward he didn't call to see how I was doing, or why I was stopping, or even to check on my medications, my referrals, or anything else. For all this guy knows I could have died a month after seeing him, perhaps by suicide. He did, however, send me a bill for $400, to cover the two visits I'd canceled.

I carried his legacy with me, however: I kept taking the Klonopin he'd prescribed for me—4 milligrams a day.

Since leaving the psych ward I had started walking a fine tight-rope. Thanks to the Klonopin, my sleep patterns were completely off. As a result, my moods swung wildly. One remedy was work, but that only lasted until I finished the eighty-seven-mile drive from ESPN's headquarters in Bristol to our home. By the time I pulled into our driveway I was already starting to feel awful—physically, emotionally, you name it.

I would feel the effects of Dr. Dangerous's work for several years.

Wisely, in the midst of the six months Dr. Dangerous spent hiking up my dosage of Klonopin, I stopped drinking. On February 22, 2011, I decided I would never drink another drop of alcohol, and I haven't. I didn't enter a twelve-step program such as Alcoholics Anonymous, which I know can be very effective. I just stopped cold—and I felt better almost immediately. Once I stopped, it didn't take long for me to recognize that, through all my ups and downs, alcohol had not been making my life any easier. If you're depressed, alcohol is not your friend.

Although I didn't know it at the time, if Klonopin is combined with even moderate drinking, it can lead to respiratory arrest and even death, so this simple decision might have saved my life.

CHAPTER 25

Falling Backward

SATURDAY, SEPTEMBER 10, 2011, WAS A BEAUTIFUL FALL day.

A car picked me up at my home for the drive to ESPN head-quarters in Bristol, Connecticut. When I joined the network in 1986 the entire ESPN "empire" consisted of a single building that could house all one hundred or so employees. That was all we needed to produce *SportsCenter* and NHL and CFL games—which is all we had. Today ESPN has deals with Major League Baseball, the NBA, and the NFL; more than five thousand employees; and offices in New York, Los Angeles, Chicago, Denver, Hong Kong, Toronto, and South America, not to mention the sprawling campus in Bristol, which now looks more like a contemporary college campus than a TV network.

I was entering my thirty-fifth season in broadcasting, my twenty-fifth at ESPN, my twentieth hosting *ABC College Football*, and my tenth season hosting *The Sports Reporters*, which might be my favorite show. It's a good job. Scratch that—it's a *dream* job.

Aleah had just graduated from Fordham University a few months earlier and was considering law school. Jenna had just enrolled at my alma mater, Ryerson University in Toronto. By any objective measure I had a pretty good life—particularly for a guy who had been raised by an abusive, deadbeat dad.

But I was just minutes away from almost losing it all.

◆　◆　◆

I walked into our studio, went to makeup, then finished my preparation for the 3 P.M. show, which was a summary of the entire day in college football. We would start by reviewing all the early games when they hit halftime, preview the handful of regional games that ABC would be covering at 3:30, then preview the best prime-time games. If all went according to plan, we'd be done by seven, which would make it the easiest game day of the season.

At three o'clock I started our second broadcast of the 2011 college football season by saying, "Welcome to *ABC College Football*. I'm John Saunders, alongside Jesse Palmer. We've got a great day of college football ahead, including Alabama at Penn State, which we'll be covering live here on ABC in just a few minutes. But first we've got an exciting game already underway between Virginia Tech and East Carolina."

Of course, there was no way to predict when each game would hit halftime. Fortunately we had a great producer, Rob Lemley. Now, producers aren't typically known for their bedside manner—it all happens so fast, there's no time to worry about people's feelings—but *College Football* has a great one in Lem, who's also a good friend.

I've always liked the people I work with, and I like the work too, though it's harder than it looks. When I'm on the air the producer delivers information about the ongoing games into my ear a mile a minute, just seconds before we go on the air. Then I start telling the TV audience what he just told me, while he continues telling me what I'll be talking about after that.

That's hard enough. Once we go live I add descriptions to the highlight tape. Ninety percent of the time I haven't seen it, and sometimes I can't see it when it's playing live either, even while

I'm describing it to the TV audience. If I'm lucky, the researcher standing nearby might hand me a card I can read while the re-play rolls. But more commonly I only get the producer barking in my earpiece, "So-and-so just ran for 44 yards and a touchdown," which I then say in my mic to the audience, as if I'd been re-hearsing it all day: "So-and-so just ran for *forty-four* yards—and a touchdown!" You're basically driving blindfolded while the guy in the backseat is telling you when to turn.

As I'm delivering the producer's highlight line, he's already telling me what's going to happen on the next highlight, so it's like having three records playing in my head at once: the first is what the producer has already told me, the second is me repeat-ing that on air, and the third is what he's telling me now, which I have to retain so I can repeat it after I've finished what I'm saying while he's talking to me. I'm basically converting a poundingly fast hip-hop song coming from my producer to a lovely waltz for the audience—while dancing to both of them simultaneously. Then I add a fourth record once I start talking with my cohost, Jesse Palmer.

The only way to handle all this without scratching the records is to master two very different approaches: preparation and spon-taneity. For each weekend I start doing my research on Monday to give myself every chance to get all the facts right that Saturday without stumbling. (I might have launched my career as a lark, but I take my homework very seriously now.) Then, once I'm on the air, I need to be able to think on my feet because all the prepa-ration in the world can't help me when the producer is talking in my ear at full speed while I'm talking to the nation like I'm cool as can be, apparently having a good time—and making the viewer *feel* like I'm having a good time.

Ultimately, my job is to make sure the audience can't sense any of the craziness pumping through my earpiece. It looks like fun—and it is—but it took me years to learn. If you do it right, everyone wants your job because they think it's easy. "You just sit up there, talking about sports!"

Many things that other people find simple I find difficult, but I've never struggled at this. Growing up there were always voices in my head. Now it's just a producer.

◆　◆　◆

On this day Lem said in my earpiece that we planned to start with a Fresno State–Nebraska score, but right before we went on the air he told me East Carolina had just scored against Virginia Tech, putting the heat on, so he thought we should lead with that instead. Then he cut in again, telling me Auburn had just slipped ahead of a ranked Mississippi State team, which could be an upset in the making, so we might put that ahead of the Virginia Tech game. And just for the heck of it, he broke in once more to say that the Texas Longhorns were in an unexpected battle with BYU, so heads-up.

When we finally got to our first segment that Saturday we decided to go with highlights from the East Carolina–Virginia Tech game, followed by the others. Then Jesse and I set up the rest of the day for the viewers, with me feeding him questions about Stanford versus Duke (the "Brainiac Bowl"), Wisconsin at Oregon State, and Notre Dame at Michigan, the first night game in Big House history.

Then we focused on our centerpiece, Alabama–Penn State, with Jesse breaking down Penn State's offense versus Alabama's defense, the keys to the matchup, and who had the advantage. I would try to put him in a position to articulate all that and do it in a way that's fun for both of us—and the audience. I have a good rapport with Jesse—a real pro, a true friend, and a fellow Canuck, to boot—and the first segment went smoothly, as it almost always does. So far, so good.

When ABC kicked off the 3:30 games we left the desk and walked across the studio to sit down in front of a bank of TVs to watch all the games. Our researchers stood nearby working their tails off, furiously writing down the stats and highlights coming in. While Jesse and I sat there, waiting to get back on the air at halftime, Lem started preparing a batting order for the rundown, but we knew that could change a half-dozen times in the ninety minutes it took to play a half of football.

Normally when there are a few minutes to go in whatever game is getting to halftime first, we walk back to the set, where we work live for about fifteen minutes, with three commercial breaks, then go back to the bank of TVs, wait for the games to end, then do the postgame wrap-ups.

On this day, however, I looked at the lower right corner of the Alabama–Penn State game and saw that there was a little over a minute left in the half. Then I stood up to walk to the set.

And that's the last thing I remember.

◆ ◆ ◆

The next thing I knew I was on the floor, looking up at Jesse Palmer. Apparently, after I stood up, I blacked out, then fell backward. I'm six-foot-one and 225 pounds, so falling like that with nothing to cushion the blow creates a lot of trauma when your head smacks against the hard tile floor. Jesse later told me I was out for about a minute.

When I came to I saw Jesse kneeling next to me, urging me, "Stay down. Stay down!"

Being a hockey guy, I said, "No, I gotta get up to do halftime!" As has been documented, we are tougher than we are smart.

Jesse convinced me otherwise, but I kept pleading with him to at least let me sit up, and he eventually relented. He put his hand behind my head to help me up, but when I sat up a stream of blood shot out from the back of my head through Jesse's fingers. I didn't know what was happening, but I could see Jesse's eyes grow big. Whatever it was, it was worse than I thought. A beat later my head started throbbing like never before.

Despite all this, I actually thought I could still do the halftime show—until my colleagues gently suggested that perhaps blood shooting out of the anchor's head on national TV might not make for the most professional broadcast. Once I heard the cut-in announcer, Robert Flores, taking over the halftime show without Jesse or me, I knew I was done for the day.

When the paramedics showed up they whisked me off to Bristol General Hospital. I was still thinking this would be a simple matter of getting checked out, maybe stitched up, then off to the Residence Inn, where I'd stay overnight and host *The Sports Reporters* the next morning. But that's not how it went.

In the emergency room they stapled my head shut, which wasn't much fun. I still prefer old-fashioned stitches. My head was pounding so bad that I had blurred vision and couldn't tolerate light, so they gave me a little morphine. It kicked in quickly, so I was pretty upbeat and figured I'd be getting out soon.

Aleah was at home, but Wanda was in Toronto helping Jenna move into Ryerson University. Bernie happened to be in Toronto on vacation, so the three of them went out for dinner that night. I didn't know that one of my best friends at ESPN, a senior producer named Gerry Matalon, called Wanda on her cell to give her an update. The problem was that he thought she already knew about my fall, so he started by telling her, "I'm on my way to see John in the hospital."

Wanda is pretty hard to rattle, but that scared her. When Gerry backed up and explained the situation, she calmed down, called me, and told me she'd fly back that instant. But this was September 10, 2011. The next day was the tenth anniversary of 9/11, and I didn't want any of my girls flying anywhere. Besides, I thought the worst was behind me. There was no reason to do anything rash, so I told her not to worry about it. I'd be fine.

After they put me in the intensive care unit, Jesse Palmer, Rob Lemley, and Bill Graff, the man in charge of the studio for college sports, along with another good friend, showed up to see me. The 7:30 P.M. Notre Dame–Michigan game had just started, so we decided to turn it on. To our amusement we couldn't get ESPN in Bristol—probably the only place in America you couldn't! Hell, if we had just opened the window we probably could have heard the broadcast coming out of the studios. We had to laugh at that. Nothing seemed too serious at this stage.

So I opened up my iPad, and the four of us gathered around my bed to watch it on the WatchESPN app. At halftime the nurses moved me from the ICU to a hospital room, a good sign. My friends followed, so we watched Michigan start the fourth quarter down 24–7 and come back to win 35–31 in the final seconds. After the thrilling finish my friends went home, and everything seemed okay. I assumed I'd be released the next day, shake off the headache, and get back to work, just like always.

I didn't have a clue.

I was not walking out of the woods. I was walking into them— as deeply as I ever had in my life.

CHAPTER 26

Scaling Mt. Sinai

WITH CONCUSSIONS, IT'S COMMON PRACTICE FOR THE nurses to wake you up every hour to make sure you're okay, then let you go home the next day. But the nurses at Bristol General hovered around me the entire night.

To stop my brain from swelling, the doctors had started me on intravenous steroids the night before. But it turns out that fluids actually *increase* the swelling, so by Sunday morning the pain in my head was unbearable. I still had blurred version, and I still couldn't tolerate light, but now I couldn't stand up and keep my balance. I'd slowly keel over. But my biggest problem was the least obvious: by swelling my already-bruised brain with liquid steroids, the damage was increasing by the minute—an issue I'd be dealing with for months afterward.

That afternoon Aleah, then twenty-two, drove up from our home to see her dad in another hospital bed. When she walked in she saw what I couldn't see, which was a crimson halo behind my head on the pillowcase from the blood oozing from the back of my head. She started crying. When she finally spoke she didn't say, "Daddy, are you okay?" but "Daddy, are you *going* to be okay?"

I got the message. In spite of the excruciating headache, I reassured her that I was going to be all right. But at that point I was starting to have real doubts myself. They had stepped up the morphine, but it wasn't working. My head was killing me.

After seeing me in this state Aleah took a few days off from work to stay with me, and Wanda joined her the next day. But as one day became two and then three, I still wasn't getting any better.

During the neurologist's one visit he told me I had suffered a traumatic injury to my brain, which wasn't very surprising. He also said they had found an abnormality in my brain scan, but he never told me what it was, and I never saw him again. The rest of my care at the hospital consisted largely of pain management—namely, more morphine.

By Thursday I called our family doctor, Michael Gerdis. He's normally a very calm guy, but when I told him what had happened and what the doctors were doing, he sounded genuinely alarmed.

"We've got to get you out of there."

◆　◆　◆

Just hours after we hung up, Dr. Gerdis had arranged for an ambulance to rush me a hundred miles to Mt. Sinai's brain injury ward.

"Your brain is swollen," the first doctor told me. "It's pressing right up against your skull."

They started immediately with intensive steroid therapy too—but with pills, not fluids, to get the swelling down. They also did an MRI, an echocardiogram, and a stress test. When they sent me to the brain injury ward with the top neurologists at Mt. Sinai, I knew they were concerned. I was slowly recalibrating the magnitude of what I was facing, and not for the last time.

The next day Bernie flew back from Toronto to see me. My poor wife has been visiting me in hospital beds for twenty-five years, but my brother has been doing it his entire life. All together I've spent more than a year of my life in hospitals, and my brother has visited every time, almost every day.

Bernie has seen it all, and he's a very even-keeled guy—far more so than I am. But when he walked in this time, from the change in his expression I could see how bad I must have looked. And when he had to help me walk to the bathroom, we both knew it was more serious than any of us had thought.

Near the end of my first week in Mt. Sinai they were able to take me off morphine and put me on Dilaudid—a small step down but still a very addictive narcotic. They had me on the highest dose I could take. Wanda started to get worried because whenever she saw me I was totally out of it. They decided to switch me from the Dilaudid IVs to the Dilaudid patches, which are time released, so they don't give you that loopy jolt that the IVs do. My situation wasn't getting much better, but I was always reassured to see Wanda by my side, looking out for me.

After a week in Mt. Sinai's brain injury ward I was moved to the testing ward so the doctors could study my brain for forty-eight hours straight. A nurse came in to hook up dozens electrodes to my skull, then wrapped my head like a mummy to keep them all in place. I could feel what she was doing, but she didn't tell me why she was doing it, and I couldn't see it. So when my brother saw me in this mummified state, with dozens of wires attached to my head, he said, "Whoa, where's my brother?" I didn't know what he was talking about.

That night when I went to sleep my head was pounding so hard it hurt to open my eyes. I buzzed the nurse for help, but she didn't realize I was already on the painkiller patch, so she gave me some painkiller pills and, later, still more. After all this kicked in I got up to go to the bathroom in the middle of the night. But I still had all those electrodes stuck to my skull and chest, with the wires attached to two different machines, which stood on the far side of the bed from the bathroom. When I started padding toward the bathroom I felt the pull of the wires on my head and torso attached to the machines. But I was so out of it that I started yanking off the electrodes, like the Incredible Hulk tearing off his shirt. Then I grabbed onto anything I could to steady myself on my way to the bathroom.

Once I got to the bathroom I was in for a bigger surprise: the mirror. When I saw this alien looking back at me, in my heavily drugged state, I wondered if I had been abducted by some mad scientists running bizarre experiments on the human brain. I managed to stay calm enough to pee, but when I got back into my bed I was in full freak-out mode, ripping off the wrapping around my head and pulling the electrodes off my skull.

I rang the nurse again.

"What is all this? What are you doing to me?"

Then I saw the little plastic cap they put on your finger to monitor your pulse, and for some reason it looked to me like it was homemade. So now I'm thinking none of this makes any sense—the electrodes, the mummy wrap, this homemade finger cap. I was right! I've been abducted! That's it!

The nurse got a doctor on the floor to explain what was going on, and I calmed down. Then the doctor sat at the foot of the bed and started asking me questions in a soothing voice:

"Do you know where you are?"

"Do you know why you're here?"

"Do you know what month it is?"

They asked me questions like that every day. At first the only one I could answer correctly was, "Who is the president?" With each day I got more questions right, but on this night, when I couldn't answer anything except "Barack Obama," she furrowed her brow and looked at the nurse for a moment—never a good sign.

If she had any doubts that I was not quite right, I erased them a moment later when I bolted upright, whipped my head to the side and asked, "Did you see that?!?"

Her eyebrows raised. "See what?"

"The *cats!* Did you see the *cats?*"

"You see . . . cats?"

"Yeah, they went right across the bed! And they go so fast, you just can't catch 'em!"

They looked at each other again, checked my chart, and discovered that I had inadvertently received a double medication of Dilaudid—the patches and the pills. But they knew that would likely have knocked me out, not created hallucinations. They concluded that the head trauma sparked the illusions, which told them my condition was worse than they thought, too.

They gave me something to put me to sleep. The next day the same nurse started reattaching all those electrodes all over again. In a much clearer state of mind I could tell she wasn't very happy with me, and I couldn't blame her.

❖ ❖ ❖

I'll always be grateful for the care I received at Mt. Sinai—but not the food! So my friends smuggled in all my favorites. Tim Brando snuck corned beef hash from the Carnegie Deli; Kelly Naqi slipped me some carrot cake, a personal favorite; and Rob Lemley, my producer, somehow got a dozen Heath bars to my room. I know I'm a diabetic, but I was happy. When the nurses came in to check my blood sugar, they found it was a little high— imagine that!—but they weren't going to give me any more insulin because they hadn't yet gotten approval to administer my daily medication.

Because Aleah and I have diabetes, my wife always keeps an insulin syringe in her purse. After the nurse left the room Wanda pulled it out and was an inch away from injecting the needle when the door burst open and the nurses started yelling, "WHAT ARE YOU DOING?! STOP!"

I've never seen my wife look so scared. She jumped back. "I'm just giving him his insulin!" she said, and they soon understood.

After they left the room I told her, "They probably thought you were trying to kill me. 'Dammit, if the fall doesn't kill him, this will!'"

Wanda started laughing, something we both needed, so I kept it up. "Uh, you *weren't* trying to kill me, were you?" This had her rolling. Despite everything we've gone through, we still manage to laugh a lot, but rarely had it felt so good than it did at that moment.

Before she left she slipped the insulin needle to me, and I gave myself an injection after everyone was gone.

◆　◆　◆

The data from the forty-eight hours with the 120 electrodes didn't turn up anything unusual. You might think that would be a relief, but it only left all the questions unanswered. Why did I black out? Why was I struggling to do even the most basic physical and mental tasks—like walking to the bathroom and remembering what day it was? And the scariest question of all: Would I ever be the same? That week the doctors could provide no clear answers to those questions.

I just wanted to find out what was going on, get it fixed, and get out of there—back home, back to work, and back to my life. Instead, they moved me back to the brain injury ward for more tests, but none of them explained what had caused the blackout and all that followed. That was a low point.

The days dragged on. After four weeks at Mt. Sinai they moved me to a new room in the rehab unit, just as the parents of my new roommate were getting ready to leave. He was maybe sixteen years old. He was in a wheel chair too, but he didn't look like he'd be getting out of it any time soon. He had a thick, fresh scar running from his left ear across his shaved head, all the way down to his chin on the right side of his face. His head was tilted to the left, as if his neck wasn't strong enough to hold up his head, and his speech was slurred. I didn't know what had happened—maybe a car accident—but you could tell he was in serious trouble.

After his parents left he started crying hysterically. The nurses gave him something to calm him down, but right before it was time for Wanda and Aleah to leave that night he went into hysterics again, crying that he needed his mother. The nurse got his mother on the phone and tried to persuade her to come down, but for whatever reason she couldn't—or wouldn't. When the nurse had to tell my roommate that his mom was not coming back, he started shouting, "Mommy!" to a mother who was not there. "Mommy, why did you leave me here?! I don't know where I am. I don't know where I am! Why did you leave me here? You don't love me!"

There was no calming him down. I have never heard anyone sound so desolate, so forlorn.

Aleah was distraught. She whispered, "Isn't there something we can do for him?"

"Not really," I said. "There isn't anything anyone can do for him."

There wasn't anything more that Wanda and Aleah could do for me that night either. They told me they loved me, kissed me, and hugged me, as they did every night, then headed out, promising to come back tomorrow.

After they left all I could do was listen to my roommate wail in the dark. I felt so heartbroken for him.

It brought me back to my first visit to the hospital as a ten-year-old after my explosives experiment went wrong, when I waited weeks for my father to show up, and he never did. My roommate's cries exhumed my feelings of being abandoned, unworthy, unloved, even unlovable.

Our room at Mt. Sinai was at the corner of Madison and 99th. From our window I could see the structure where Wanda had parked. That night, after they had said goodbye, a few minutes later I saw them walking to the car. I started crying quietly. I couldn't stop, and I couldn't sleep.

I've been depressed before, but I always had other things going on to distract me, including my duties as husband, father, and sportscaster. But this time there was nothing to stop all these horrible feelings from rushing up to me and weighing me down. That night was devastating.

The next morning the nurses wheeled me out for yet more tests, which took a couple of hours. On the way back they told me they were going to move me into a new room, I'm not sure why. But I had to ask, "What about that young boy?"

"He'll be going home soon." I was relieved to hear it, but when we came back to get my stuff—including a Western Michigan football helmet the guys at ESPN grabbed from the set and had everyone sign—the kid was still there. He was by himself again, eating his lunch—and crying while he ate. That has to get you.

Two days later I saw him leave with his parents. I still think about him. Even at my lowest point it was not hard to find someone who had it worse.

CHAPTER 27

Learning to Walk

WHEN YOU'RE IN THE REHAB UNIT, YOU'RE SURROUNDED by victims of aneurysms, tumors, severe car accidents, and strokes. You get a pretty clear sense of just how many ways your life can be turned upside down—often in just a few seconds.

While my brain injury was certainly serious, compared to the people around me, I knew how lucky I was. But these were now my peers, just like in the psych ward, and that was a chilling realization. I felt like I'd been sent to the cancer ward with a common cold.

After four weeks at Mt. Sinai they started me on a rehab program consisting of physical therapy, mental therapy, and walking therapy—literally learning how to walk again. And yes, I needed to learn how to walk again with complete balance. I could now go to the bathroom by myself, but they wouldn't let me walk down the hallway because the last thing I needed was to fall and suffer another concussion.

That might sound like we were being overly cautious, but one of the least talked about side effects of concussions is the loss of balance and spatial judgement. The victim of a serious concussion has a hard time just standing in place without tipping over, so walking through a doorway becomes a complicated task.

It feels like the doorway moves as you start walking through it, so even if you get through it safely, your judgment is off, so you end up banging into furniture on the other side. (You can see why neurologists don't call them concussions but rather "brain injuries"—because that's what they are.) Of course, we have to navigate more than bathrooms and doorways in this world, so maneuvering your body through all the obstacles your day presents becomes a constant challenge to avoid falling down, hitting your head—and starting all over.

On my first day of rehab at 10 A.M. sharp, a small, sweet, and feisty woman named Fanny Hernandez came to take me down to the physical therapy room. She started my session by instructing me to pick up a rubber ball and put it into a basket on the table. It wasn't difficult, but it was humiliating. I've spent my career covering world-class athletes who can put a ball in a basket while spinning through the air past a defender. And here I was, sitting down, picking up a rubber ball and placing it in a basket.

At the same time I was surrounded by people for whom it *was* very difficult, people who, just a year earlier—before their aneurysms and accidents and strokes—would have been just as embarrassed by this preschool exercise as I was. But when I looked around and saw people who had to be propped up by two nurses so they could lift a five-pound weight, you take a different view.

Besides, my winning streak didn't last long. I got my comeuppance on our next task, which required me to pick up a batch of plastic clothespins and clip them onto pegs. Yep, that was it—something a kindergartner can do without much trouble. When Fanny described it to me I rolled my eyes, but I soon discovered just how much I had lost.

I had a tough time just trying to pick up the clothespin and open it. Even after I gave the task real effort and focus, I accidentally knocked some of the clothespins across the table. When I finally managed to pick one up and open it, it snapped out of my hands, flying into the air. Once I managed to pick one up and open it successfully, I had trouble clipping it onto a peg. I missed my mark a few times, and sometimes I didn't put the peg on all the way, so it would snap back off, which was pretty jarring. For a former college athlete, this was tough to take.

Some exercises combined seemingly unrelated tasks. For example, in one I had to stand on one of those plastic bubbles—which I couldn't do, so the nurse had to hold me up—while she had me write ten words that started with the letter "b" on a white board. I quickly came up with three b-words: "bubble"—I was standing on one, after all—"bottle," and "bottom." And then . . . nothing. I make my living tossing sentences together off the top of my head, without making grammatical infractions, factual errors, or even saying "Um" or "Ah." But here I was, unable to think of seven more words that started with "b."

When I stalled, Fanny showed her sweet side and gave me hints. "A kind of fruit," she said. Banana, obviously. I kind of knew where she was leading me—I knew it was rattling around my brain somewhere—but I couldn't come up with it. Then I started staring at the board, which made me feel like the class dunce. I felt like I was trying to learn a second language—so incompetent and so helpless, I almost started crying. Instead, I stared at Fanny until she had mercy on me and stopped the drill.

Fanny didn't provide any more hints or ask any more questions. She knew my first physical therapy session was done.

But I couldn't go back to my room. Not yet. After I failed my way through physical therapy, it was time for mental therapy, where I hoped for a little redemption.

Fanny knew what I did for a living, so she said in a soft, encouraging voice, "I want you to write something. What would you like to write about?"

"Well," I said, "my job is to cover these incredibly gifted, talented people. But since I've been here in rehab, I realize *these* are the real athletes, and I want to write about them. It's not LeBron dunking over Tim Duncan. It's someone who could barely lift their heads and say their name a couple of months ago, and now they're speaking fluently and lifting five-pound weights."

"Okay," she said. "Write about that."

Fanny left me alone while I sat down to type for the first time since I had fallen a month ago. I was pleasantly surprised by how easily the words flowed from my mind to my fingers, and how smoothly my hands glided across the keyboard. This felt good, especially after the drubbing I'd just taken in physical therapy. When I finished I felt pretty good about what I had written. Having composed a few essays in my career, I'm pretty tough on my own writing, so when I feel good about it, that usually means I've written something decent.

When Fanny came back to see how I'd made out, I was looking forward to showing her that I hadn't lost everything.

"Okay," she said, "let's look at what you wrote."

But when I started reading it back to her, I knew immediately that my little essay didn't just have a few burrs in it, which you might expect. It was *awful*. I mean, *terrible*, filled with grammatical errors, spelling mistakes, even words reversed. You could barely understand what I was trying to say, as if I was just learning English.

But the scariest thing to me wasn't my horrible writing; it was the fact that I thought, when I'd finished, that I'd done pretty well, perhaps good enough to be a first draft for a "Parting Shot" on *The Sports Reporters*. I *rely* on my internal critic to make sure I don't humiliate myself on national TV. How could I be so unaware of what I was doing? Could I trust my brain to do good work again—and not embarrass myself in front of my bosses, my colleagues, and a few million viewers?

"John," Fanny said softly, "don't worry. You are only taking the first steps right now in a long process. We're going to get you back to where everything is just fine—I promise. Do you have a computer in your room?"

"Yes. Wanda brought my iPad."

"Great," she said. "I bet you've gotten a lot of emails from people to see how you're doing."

"Yes, I have."

"Have you started answering them?"

"No, I haven't."

"Well, go back and start doing that."

So I did. But when I read my first attempt at an email response, it was the same thing—riddled with embarrassing mistakes.

I had a long way to go.

◆　◆　◆

I wanted to crawl back into bed, throw the blankets over my head, and hide, but my first day of therapy still wasn't over.

I was allowed to go back to my room before my last session, walking therapy, to eat my lunch and enjoy a nice visit from Aaron Taylor, a former two-time All-American offensive lineman who played for Lou Holtz at Notre Dame and then went on to win a Super Bowl with Green Bay. He and I had worked together on *ABC College Football* for a few years and we'd stayed in touch.

We'd been catching up for twenty minutes or so when Fanny Hernandez came back to tell me it was time to start walking therapy.

"Can I see this big guy for a while?" I asked. I assumed it wouldn't be a problem.

"Nope, it's time for walking therapy." Fanny said, and when she turned tough, she meant it—but I didn't know that yet. So I kept chatting with Aaron until she interrupted us: "RIGHT NOW!"

We were both startled and stifled our laughs, but I got up and I got going. Aaron followed me and watched our exercises through a window. Unlike physical and mental therapy, walking therapy was conducted in a class with five or six of us in various stages of recovery.

Fanny started us off. "Mrs. Johnson, you'll go first. We're going to have you walk in a circle three times."

Mrs. Johnson did it. A day earlier I might have been tempted to chuckle at this, but I'd already gained a ton of respect for what these people were overcoming, and a good dose of humility about what I could and couldn't do.

"Okay, Mr. Jones," Fanny said, "we're going to have you climb up these three steps."

Mr. Jones climbed the three steps, as you'd expect. But when Fanny asked me to climb up three steps, I tilted to the right and was about to fall over when Fanny saw it coming and caught me. For a small woman she was amazingly strong. With some effort I made it up to the top step, then turned around and walked back down.

When I saw Aaron watching me through the window I was pleasantly surprised by his encouraging smile. This was an athlete who'd gone through many weeks of rehab, after all, and he understood the process. He gave me a thumbs-up, then went on his way.

After the session I went back to my room and did my best to text Aaron. "Had second-fastest time in 'Rehab 50 Foot Walk,' behind only the ninety-three-year old lady. Kickin' ass!"

The next day I texted Aaron: "Almost had her today. But not fair. She used a damn cane!"

He replied: "We'll put an asterisk next to her record, just like Sosa's and McGuire's."

A few days later he followed up: "How you doing, big guy? I've got some XXXL blue scrubs if you need me to pretend to be a doc and bust you out."

This was one of the hardest patches of my life, but you can see how valuable good friends can be, and the occasional good laugh.

◆　◆　◆

None of my problems we were addressing directly affected my depression, but when I realized just how much I had lost and how long it would take to recover—if I ever could—it made me sink again. It didn't help that I couldn't resist watching the shows I was supposed to be hosting, but it would have much harder if ESPN hadn't been so good about my recovery. They never doubted me or pushed me to come back too soon.

After watching an episode of *The Sports Reporters* one Sunday I sent an email to our producer, Joe Valerio, who is also one of the show's creators. "Great show, Joe," I wrote. "I wish I could be there!"

I got a call from him a few minutes later. "We miss you, John. Take care of yourself, and focus on getting better."

Because Joe has always been a good, caring friend, I felt I could be more candid. "Joe, I have to tell you, it's very difficult to sit here and watch my shows go on without me. In most jobs you don't have to watch a video of your replacement sitting at your desk, doing your work. And it's not just that someone's taking my job—it's that I'm no longer capable of doing it myself."

"I understand," Joe said. "But you'll be back. We're just keeping the seat warm for you."

Joe was being awfully nice. So were Jeremy Schaap and Mike Lupica when they guest-hosted *The Sports Reporters*, softening the blow each week by saying, "I'm just filling in for John Saunders, who'll be back soon."

Everyone needs to be reminded that people care, but because I'm prone to depression, I might need more reminders than most. My "emotional metabolism" seems to run a little faster than other people's. When I'm depressed, I burn through praise faster, and its positive effects wear off more quickly, which is pretty typical for depressed people.

Paradoxically, even hearing how much people cared could be a double-edged sword. Sometimes their support confused me because they seemed to care more about me than I did, which made me feel unworthy of their love and concern. My thought pattern went something like this: "Why do they care about me? Don't they know I'm not worth it? I'm scared they'll find out I'm not and stop caring about me."

I needed to know they cared, but it could also make me feel bad because I knew they were worried about me, and I didn't want to be a problem for them. Perhaps this helps explain one of the most common themes of suicide notes: the person no longer wants to be a burden to the people they love.

Those were deep issues that I wasn't going to resolve any time soon. But getting back to work was something I could focus on.

When you're depressed, any distraction can be a great savior, and work is one of my best. Focusing that intensely, with the cameras rolling, can push the depression into the background for a little while. You can go back home or to the hotel room and cry for the rest of the night if you like, but while you're in the studio you have no choice but to put it aside and focus on your job.

For me, fall weekends are the best. We prep during the week, but on Saturday I'm working at the studio all day. Then I stay in Bristol Saturday night and get up at 5:30 A.M. Sunday to tape *The Sports Reporters*. I walk back to my office at ESPN around 8 A.M. and take a nap until 11 A.M., when I watch my buddy Chris Berman host *NFL Countdown* until 1 P.M. After that I join Boomer and the NFL staff to start watching the games in one of the studio's war rooms. When the games are over I do our NFL show from 7 to 8:30. During the car ride home Sunday night I'm still riding a bit of a high, capping a forty-eight-hour break from depression.

It's a great drug, and I knew I never needed it more. So my motivation was doubled: I didn't just want to get better; I wanted to get back to work. To the doctors the two went hand in hand, as they should. But I was convinced that if I could just get back to work, I would get better. And I knew that if I couldn't, my depression would get worse. Each day I was away from my job I felt like my life raft was floating away.

◆　◆　◆

After about a week of rehab with Fanny I could do all the simple tasks fairly well. I could stick the clothespins on the pegs consistently, and I got good enough putting the ball in the basket that I started shooting it. I felt my form was pretty good, but from the line I wasn't much better than Shaq. Well, maybe a little better. It was only a few feet, after all.

Near the end of my second week of rehab I started going on regular walks down the corridors with one of the orderlies. We soon added a basketball, which we tossed back and forth during our walks. We didn't chat much because I was focused on following his instructions.

I could even walk up two flights of stairs—a far sight better than the set of three I struggled to climb when Aaron Taylor had visited. Still, Fanny Hernandez urged me to use the handrail.

"No!" I insisted. "I can do this!"

I actually freaked her out a little bit when I jogged up the steps. I'm sure she was afraid that if I stumbled, she couldn't help me.

Six weeks after my fall I was much better at the physical and walking therapy, but the mental therapy proved to be the most aggravating of the three. So even though I was getting better physically, I was getting more depressed.

The only times I wasn't crying was during rehab, because I didn't want to cry in front of strangers, and with my daughters, because I didn't want them to worry about me any more than they already were. Fortunately Jenna didn't have to experience this directly because she was away at Ryerson. As outgoing and vibrant as she is, she's very, very sensitive. After four weeks she called me in tears.

"Daddy, I didn't know you were going to be in there for so long!" If she were living in New York, I'm not sure she would have been able to handle this.

To be released I needed the approval of Fanny Hernandez and a team of three doctors. One of them, Dr. Greenwald, was the head of the rehab unit. Most of the nurses and doctors were very nurturing. Dr. Greenwald was not. He'd tell me, "You're not getting out of here until I know you're ready to get out of here." I was not going to charm him into letting me go.

After I'd been on the rehab floor for a couple of weeks he'd come into my room and say, "We're gonna get you out of here soon." But he would never give me a day or even an estimate. I was beginning to fear that I would never get out of there. I know that wasn't rational, but during this stretch rational thinking wasn't my strong suit.

When Wanda came to see me one day during my sixth week I was crying almost as hard as my sixteen-year old roommate was on my first night at Mt. Sinai.

"I've got to get out of here," I told her between sobs. "I can't stay here any longer. I can't take it anymore."

She tried to comfort me, but I was inconsolable. I had gone to the hospital seeking help for a head injury. But now that the injury was healing, ever so slowly, I was discovering something more dangerous underneath it.

CHAPTER 28

A High-Stakes Stroll
in the Park

A FEW DAYS LATER I WAS LYING IN MY BED, FEELING LIKE a man with two broken legs contemplating his first Boston Marathon. As desperately as I wanted to leave, I felt unprepared to return to the real world. And yet if I stayed in the hospital much longer, my depression would only deepen, which would make it even harder to get my life back. I felt trapped.

So there I was, crying quietly, when in walked two women from rehab: Fanny Hernandez and a new therapist, Helen, from Canada.

"John," Fanny asked, "how'd you like to go for a walk?"

"Where?"

"Outside," was all she said—but that was enough for me! I hadn't been outside in six weeks. Anywhere that wasn't my room sounded good.

I had fallen backward on Saturday, September 10, 2011, and now it was late October, two-thirds through the college football season. It was a beautiful fall day, but it could have been raining golf-ball-sized hail and I would have thought it was a fine time to go outside for a walk.

I got my shoes and a pair of jeans, but I had no belt, so they brought me a stretchy yellow band. I looked like Jethro on *The Beverly Hillbillies*. Once we got to the hospital entrance Fanny said, "First, we're going to walk two blocks ahead to a Starbucks."

Sounded like a fun little field trip. But when we got to the Starbucks Fanny said, "I want you to walk in, look at the menu, and find the prices for a pumpkin latte and a cappuccino, and add the two prices together."

That's when I realized this was no Sunday stroll. This was my test to get out, probably the most high-pressured exam I had ever taken. I simply could not take another week in that hospital. I *had* to pass.

After we walked through the Starbucks doors Fanny turned to me. "Do you remember what I asked you to order?

"Yes," I said, and I really did, which was not a given at that time.

"Okay, find them, add them up, and tell me what they cost."

I stared at the menu, and I stared and I stared—and I could not find those two items! I thought maybe the sun was hitting the menu at the perfect angle, creating a blind spot, so I walked around a bit, trying to see past it. Then I started thinking that maybe they weren't actually on the menu and that this was a trick question.

"They're not on there," I told her.

"John," she said, "they're on there. It's a classic . . . "

The other therapist, Helen, also started giving me hints. "A Halloween trick-or-treat?"

To my surprise, after I moved around a little more, the sunbeam hitting the menu was finally gone. "Ah, there we go," I said. "I can see it better now!"

Little Fanny gave me a look I won't forget, a look that told me she wasn't buying my BS. Regardless, I had a job to do, and now I could do it.

"I found them!" I said. I added up the items, and blurted the answer.

"That's right!" Fanny said.

I couldn't resist explaining my delay. "It must have been the sun."

She gave me the same look but added a wry smile. I found out later the reason why I couldn't see them is because when you have a brain injury, you often can't see things that are right in front of you. So moving around basically resets your brain, the same way you restart your computer when it's stuck. And that's what happened when I moved the last time: my brain restarted and I could see what I couldn't before. Now, Fanny knew this—but I didn't!

I was just relieved to get it right. I'm thinking, *I passed the test, and now we're going for a walk!* But Fanny wasn't done with me. Far from it. We left the store and headed uptown toward Central Park.

"We're going to make a left on 95th," Fanny told me, "and walk to Fifth Avenue, then make a right. Then I want you to stop at 101st and walk to the *northeast* side of the street and stop. And we'll go from there."

It's just five blocks, but by the time we had made the left—just ninety seconds later—I had already forgotten where I was supposed to stop. What street was it? I was in full panic. Convinced I wouldn't be able to remember, I racked my brain for a way to bluff my way through this one.

When we walked past a children's museum, I said, "Wow, my daughters would really love this!" Jenna was in college, and Aleah had already graduated. They were a little old for a children's museum! But I was just trying to build in an excuse for walking past the right street—"I was distracted by the museum!"—but Fanny didn't grin. She didn't ask any follow-up questions. She wasn't giving any hints.

A couple of blocks later she said, "John, do you remember what street you're supposed to stop at?"

I hesitated, trying to think of some way to bluff my way past this too, but then I just confessed, "No, I don't." I wasn't sure if that would disqualify me then and there, but I knew I wasn't going to fool Fanny Hernandez.

She said, "101st." A big break.

So we kept walking, but if you're not a New Yorker, identifying which is the northeast corner is not intuitive. There's no sign that says, "This is the northeast corner."

I started working the Google map in my head as we walked: we're heading to Harlem, so we're going north. The FDR Highway is over there, so that's the east.

As we approached 101st Street Fanny asked, "Do you remember where you're supposed to stop?"

I didn't hesitate. "The northeast corner of 101st."

She smiled. "You got it."

I smiled back at her—probably for the first time in days. After we got to 101st I led us right to the northeast corner. Success.

"Now we're going to Central Park." The way she said it didn't sound like I'd passed the test yet.

We crossed the street. To get into the park, you need to walk down four or five steps, with no handrail—something you'd never even think about unless you'd just spent a couple of weeks relearning how to navigate a staircase. Fanny had seen me struggle with those steps, so they walked backward down the steps in front of me. That's when I understood why Fanny had brought her Canadian helper—to catch me if I started to fall. But honestly, if I had started to fall, I'm not sure how much help they would have been trying to catch a man who was about the size of an NFL fullback.

Fortunately I made it down the steps, no problem—and I wasn't nervous doing it either, unlike my earlier challenges. My confidence was building.

We walked about twenty yards, past a bathroom, toward a small, circular garden, and then we went around it. Then we came to a fork, went right, and stopped. Fanny said, "Now, John, you need to go back the way we came." I would be walking in front of them, and there would be no helping me.

"The way we came?" I asked, trying to buy a little time to think.

"All the way back to the hospital," she said.

I hadn't paid attention to the first legs of our trip because I didn't think I'd have to. I was terrified—simply terrified. All my confidence was dashed. I wasn't sure I could even get out of the park—and we had only gone about three hundred feet into it.

I stood there, frozen, as if my feet were nailed to the asphalt. But I knew if I didn't start moving, I'd fail by default and be stuck in the hospital for another week—at least. So I started shuffling, uncertainly, toward the fork in the garden, in front of the circle. I had to go around the circle, either to the right, or the left—whichever way we had come. But the problem was, when you're going back the way you came, it doesn't look the same as it did when you're going the other way—and I wasn't paying attention getting there either because I had no idea I'd be tested going back. I was panicking, moving as slowly as I could, scanning the land-scape for any clue.

And that's when I saw the bathroom I'd seen before. Lifesaver! I remembered that it was directly in my line of sight when we came around the first time. I figured, for that bathroom to be di-rectly in my line of sight on the way here, we would have had to come from the right. So that's how I made my brilliant deduction: if we came from the right, I'd have to go back to the left—same path.

Feeling better, I picked up the pace and whisked past the bath-room. I *bounced* up the stairs, with Fanny and Helen rushing to keep up with me. I saw the "WALK" sign to cross the street, so I kept going across Park Avenue.

Fanny yelled, "John, we have to go back the same way!"

She didn't know it, but she'd just set me up for my major vic-tory. She thought I should cut right down 95th. But I was going to go back the *exact* same way we had come, which meant we had to go down *the eastern sidewalk* of Fifth.

I didn't break stride. I just turned back, smiled, and said, "But we have to go back the *exact* same way—and we came up *this* sidewalk!" I smiled—and she smiled too, probably relieved that I hadn't blown it. I waved, "Come on! Let's go!"

When they caught up to me Fanny asked, "How are you feeling?"

"I feel great! Now come on! You two are slowing me down!"

Now I'm cruising. I've got this thing, and I know it. We pass the children's museum that I'd tried to use as a distraction on the way there. I looked at it, but I wasn't making any comments this time. No need, man. I just kept walking about as fast as I could, back toward the hospital.

When we got to 98th, on our way to the entrance that we'd started from, Fanny told me to go ahead and take the 98th Street entrance—her concession that I had demonstrated mastery over the test.

I knew then that I'd passed. I all but skipped back to my room, with Fanny and Helen struggling to keep up.

Just an hour earlier I had been crying in my bed, without an ounce of hope—and now I was on top of the world!

I *knew* I was getting better.

I hoped I'd be going home soon.

◆　◆　◆

I returned to my room, feeling great. Now I'm thinking, *Going home is not a matter of if, just when.* And once I'm home, I'll be working again, right? Everything will be fine!

I had settled back into my room only for a few minutes when I received an unannounced visitor, a cardiologist named Dr. Sweeney.

"We've tested everything in your heart," he told me, which made me wonder what was coming next. "And everything looks fine," he said, which gave me a sigh of relief. "But the last thing we need to do is implant a heart monitor so you'll have a twenty-four-hour EKG. With that, they can get the data at the hospital or even by having you put a phone up to it and get the data we need that way. It's a really easy procedure. We just go under the skin, not under your ribcage."

Okay, I said. If it meant I was one step closer to going home, I'd do just about anything.

They didn't waste any time. A few minutes later they knocked on my door to tell me they had a gurney outside my room. I hopped on, and they pushed me to the operating room.

Now, I've been through enough surgeries to know the difference between out-patient surgery and in-patient surgery. When we got just outside the operating room I could see four doctors and nurses inside, prepping the same way they did to operate on my shoulder and my knee, which were obviously in-patient procedures. Soon enough they were shaving me and scrubbing me, and I realized, it's legit. This is a serious operation.

I asked, "What is going on?" No one answered.

The guy from MedTronics, which makes the heart monitor, took it out of a plastic package and laid it on my chest, then outlined it with a Sharpie pen on my skin for the doctor. It was about the size of an old-fashioned cigarette lighter.

The doctors shot my chest with a few injections of Novocain, then asked me to turn my head. They draped one of those paper sheets over my head, with a hole to breathe, so I wouldn't be able to see what they're doing.

Then, using the Sharpie-outline as his guide, the doctor started cutting my chest.

"Whoa!" I said.

"Still feel that?"

"Uh, yeah!"

They gave me more Novocain, but it still felt like their scalpels were tugging at my skin. At that point I didn't want to stop them again, and I've felt worse, so I didn't say anything, and they kept working on my chest.

One of the doctors said to the other, "Okay, there's going to be a lot of bleeding here."

I knew that meant they were not just cutting the skin—they were cutting deeper, into muscle tissue or maybe even an artery. I felt my flesh burning and saw smoke coming up from my chest.

I asked the technician near my head, "What the hell is going on?"

One of the doctors heard this and said, "We have to stop the bleeding, so we're going to cauterize this artery."

My eyes grew big. *Artery?* To smell burning flesh—a smell you cannot forget—is disturbing enough. To know that it's yours is another thing entirely. I assumed they were going to implant the monitor and I'd be out of there in a few minutes. But then they brought out the little blow torch again, and the barbecuing of John Saunders resumed.

I asked the technician, "*Now* what are they doing?"

"They have to make a 'pocket' in your chest cavity and seal it with the torch to put the monitor in."

Holy smokes! It was one of the most invasive procedures I've endured, and I wasn't getting anything more than you get for a couple of cavities—not even a Valium.

They formed the "skin pocket" in about ten minutes, implanted the monitor, then sewed me up. The surgeon took off his gloves and said, "I'll see you in a month for the first reading."

They told me they would take it out in three years, when the battery died, then wheeled me back to my room.

What a day! I started at the bottom, then enjoyed a great high in the middle, but the surgery brought me back down to earth. When the Novocain wore off I started to feel the effects of what they had done, and it was extremely painful. I'm used to pain, but what threw me off was getting another reminder that I wasn't getting better. I felt like I'd just taken a big step forward and two steps back.

When was I going to get better? When was I going to go home?

◆　◆　◆

That same afternoon Dr. Greenwald—the rehab unit's gate-keeper—stopped by my room to see how I was doing.

We started talking about the new iPhone that Apple was about to launch. "I'm not sure if I'm going to get it," he told me. "I'm going to watch the Apple press conference tomorrow on my iPhone and then decide."

So the next day I watched the press conference on my iPad, and I was sold. Later that day I was doing my new walking rehab, tossing the basketball back and forth with the orderlies. My newly installed "chest pocket" still hurt, but I wasn't going to let on. I'd do anything to get out and go home.

When we were passing by the orderlies' desk I saw Dr. Greenwald and asked him, "Did you see the press conference?"

"No, I couldn't. How was it?"

I told him all about the new features that were going to be on it, and he perked up.

"Well, I'm definitely going to buy it!" I think he was also pleased to see how much of the information I had retained and could deliver spontaneously—good signs. That, coupled with my performance on the walking trip to Central Park the day before, I hoped might improve my chances of getting out soon.

During my next lap around the orderlies' desk Dr. Greenwald stopped me. "John, how'd you like to get out of here?"

I could only stare at him and tear up. That's when he put his hand on my shoulder and said, "You've earned it. You're ready."

Dr. Greenwald was no pushover. I *had* earned it. They had *made* me earn it! I knew I wasn't 100 percent, physically or mentally, but I so needed to go home. I went straight to my room, grabbed my iPhone, and called Wanda.

"Please come and get me! They're gonna let me out—and I don't want them to change their minds!"

She was thrilled. "I'll be there in an hour."

I packed my bags. My roommate, a cranky investment banker, was getting out the next day. When his wife saw me getting ready to leave, she walked over to say, "I don't know you, but you've been very, very nice to my husband. Thank you, and I hope everything works out for you."

She was sweet from start to finish. He, of course, said nothing. I didn't care. I was too excited to get out.

Don't get me wrong: I knew I didn't have a clean bill of health. I still had an incredible, nonstop headache, which started the day I fell in the studio and hadn't let up, even six weeks later. I had to set up regular therapy sessions of all sorts to get back to where I'd been, physically and mentally, before my fall. I had doctors to see and a heart monitor to be tested.

But I thought the road would only be a few weeks longer. Once I got home and got back in the chair that Sunday morning to host *The Sports Reporters*, all would be well.

❖ ❖ ❖

I travel a lot, usually every week, but I'd never been away from home longer than I had been during my stay at Mt. Sinai. True, just about everybody I really cared about had come to see me in the hospital—dozens of friends and relatives—and that was a wonderful thing. But during all those weeks in Mt. Sinai I never stopped believing that being home again would give my recovery a much-needed boost.

It's always good to come home, but man, after all I'd been through, it never felt better to walk through the door of my home. I felt like I'd been rescued and returned to a safe and loving environment. Just to be able to sit on my spot on the couch was incredible.

I thought, *This is the answer. I'm good, and things are going to be great from now on. I cannot imagine anything getting in my way.*

Just three days earlier I'd been sobbing uncontrollably, convinced I would never get better. My last resort would be shock therapy, or worse. Now I was back at home, feeling great.

Depression made my highs higher and my lows lower. Worse, I believed that every high and every low would never end, no matter what side of the scale I was on. Now that I was on the right side of things, it was easy to believe my good fortune would never end.

CHAPTER 29

Ready for Prime Time?

THE NEXT DAY I CALLED UP JOE VALERIO—THE PRODUCER behind *The Sports Reporters*—and casually told him, "I think I can come back to work this Sunday."

I knew I couldn't handle the complexity of ABC's Saturday college football show, with scores and news coming into my ear constantly, requiring countless snap decisions. But *The Sports Reporters* was taped, it only ran thirty minutes, and my main job was to serve as a facilitator for the three sportswriters on the show. I thought I could handle that.

Joe is a great businessman, but he's also one of the most caring people I know. He congratulated me on returning home, but as for me returning to the show, he didn't hesitate.

"John, don't come back," he said. "You're not ready."

"Okay," I said. But I wasn't listening because I was convinced I was coming back anyway.

A couple of days later Wanda took me back to Mt. Sinai for my first outpatient visit to see a host of doctors. The most critical was Dr. Tanvir Choudhri, a skilled neurosurgeon who took the lead on a lot of my care. I had come to trust this guy, and I was hoping he'd say I was good to work that Sunday.

When Dr. Choudhri walked in he asked how I was doing. I said, "Great! I'm going back to work on *The Sports Reporters* this Sunday." Never mind that Joe Valerio had said no such thing. I was certain of it.

Dr. Choudhri is a big sports fan who watches my shows regularly. He would have liked nothing more than to see me back on the set, but he was a doctor first. He looked me in the eye and said, "John, you are not ready for that yet."

"Whaddya mean?" I said. "I feel great!"

"You're not *close* to being ready," he added, to dispel any illusions. He then asked me to rate my mental capacity, on a scale of one to ten.

"I think I'm about an eight and a half," I said. That was a hockey player talking.

He stared at me, then said, "You're about a five—at best."

Wanda chimed in. "I wasn't going to say anything, but I think that's right." I stared at both of them in disbelief.

"You don't realize what a traumatic brain injury you had," Dr. Choudhri explained. "To expect to get back to an eight and a half out of ten in six weeks is ridiculous. I can tell just by talking to you, you're no better than a five."

Hearing this was a kick in the gut. Seeing my dour expression, Dr. Choudhri tried to soften the blow.

"Let's do this," he proposed. "Let's target the first weekend in November for *The Sports Reporters*. If for any reason I think you can go sooner, you will. But let's target the first weekend."

Wanda was nodding in agreement while I sat there, feeling like a ten-year-old who's just been told he can't ride his bike that summer. I didn't think I could wait that long. That would mean I'd be out two full months without working—and during football season, normally the busiest time of year for me. But as much as I would have loved to, it wasn't like I could just sneak back on the set and not have Dr. Choudhri notice. I simply had to wait.

◆　◆　◆

The next phase in my treatment would entail two full days of cognitive testing to see where I stood, and to determine how to get back to where I'd been. Dr. Wayne Gordon, head of Mt. Sinai's brain trauma department, met with me and Dr. Emily D'Antonio, the woman who would be administering the tests a couple of weeks later. Dr. Gordon explained that the tests were quite rigorous, so much so that they wanted to be sure I was in good enough condition to fail the tests without being emotionally crushed. That got my attention.

When I told Dr. Gordon that Dr. Choudhri's target date to return to work was early November—naïvely hoping Dr. Gordon would move things up—he took a different tack. "Just from talking with you for an hour and looking at your chart, I would advise you not to go back for another six months."

Six months?!? To hear that was positively sickening. I couldn't believe it. Well, I thought, good thing I'd seen Dr. Choudhri first and not Dr. Gordon! The fact is that they were both right, and I believe they agreed on this: I needed to get back to work as soon as possible just to keep my depression at bay, but I wouldn't be able to do everything I could do before my fall for many months.

But I walked out of that meeting feeling defiant. I was tired of people telling me I wasn't ready. I *felt* like I was ready, so I must be!

Wanda and I met with Dr. Choudhri a few days later, on October 26. When I asked again about going back to *The Sports Reporters*, he said I could return the first Sunday in November, his original target date.

I said, rather boldly, "I think I'm ready to go now."

He looked at me for a moment, then said, "If you're feeling up to it, you've got my go-head to go back on October 30."

I was on top of the world! It was the best news I'd gotten since Dr. Greenwald told me I could go home. Now I felt validated. I was right all along!

I called Joe Valerio and told him I'd be there on Sunday. He was thrilled for me, too—this time with no hesitation about allowing me to come back. Wanda was happy for me because she knew how miserable I'd been sitting on the sidelines, which I'm sure didn't make her life any easier, either.

Now that I was going to return to the show, I was back in the game. Every week Joe sends out subject files to the panelists for that weekend's show. Because I hadn't been on the show, I hadn't been getting the files for a couple of months. But after our call I received Joe's email file and dug in immediately, studying the subjects even more intensely than usual. I had something to prove to the world, to my doctors, and to myself.

I was back on the team and ready to go. I called a lot of family, friends, and colleagues at ESPN, telling everyone I was coming back that Sunday. "Alert the media!"

◆ ◆ ◆

But that didn't mean all systems go. Both doctors had made it clear I was a long way from where I was before I hit the floor.

Then there was the more practical matter of being off the set for two months. Yes, *The Sports Reporters* is taped, but it's pretty fast and furious, and our panelists know their stuff. Was my sports knowledge up to the task? Would we have to do endless retakes? True, you don't see the outtakes, but when you have to repeat a segment, you can never duplicate the same energy and spontaneity. That's why we do the show "live to tape," which means we tape it as if it was live and accept the interruptions and everything that goes with it. To keep stopping the show and starting over would affect the feel—not to mention the mood of our guests, who usually have to catch a plane right afterward. But now I feared I'd get in front of that camera, introduce myself, then *freeze* and just stare blankly at Mitch Albom. Not good!

Still, worrying about that Sunday's show was a luxury. When I went to bed Saturday night I was anxious, but thrilled to go back the next morning.

Wouldn't you know it, Sunday morning brought a huge ice storm, the kind that coats the trees in crystal. That was beautiful, but the roads weren't. Some highways were closed. To get to Bristol we had to take a series of back streets, which got me in about forty-five minutes later than my usual 6 A.M. arrival.

When I walked into the green room Joe Valerio was already pacing around. Not because I was a few minutes late, as I first thought, but because Mike Lupica couldn't get out of his driveway. The ice storm knocked out the power at his house, so the electronic gate at the end of his driveway wouldn't move. He had called a car service, but he would be late, and we had no idea just how late.

Well, there wasn't much I could do about that, and it didn't throw me off that much. Just walking into the building again was a huge high for me. Then seeing the staffers I've worked with for years giving me hugs and well wishes, telling me, "It's great to have you back!" was a tonic no doctor could prescribe.

But when people asked, "How are you doing?" it created a dilemma for me. I wanted to tell them I was feeling great—and that was what they want to hear. But even though I was feeling better, I still had the nonstop migraine from the fall, and I was trying to recover from one of the deepest depressions of my life. I ended up telling them, "Thanks! I feel a lot better, and it feels great to be back."

With Lupica trying to get to the studio, we taped our "Parting Shots" first, even though they're the last thing you see on the show.

I wrote mine the day before. Often I debate writing about this topic or that, but this time there was no question what I'd be writing about, and it came to me clean. We only get 170 words to make our points—about half a page—so you need to be pretty economical. After I finished typing it came to 170 words exactly. Guess I hadn't completely lost it, after all.

I'd done the show depressed more times than I could count. That never stopped me, and it wasn't going to this time either. However, I'd spent the last two months learning what I had lost mentally, from the day I wrote my first incomprehensible emails to the time I struggled to see the items on a Starbucks menu. But when I sat in my chair on the set with my "Parting Shot" on a teleprompter in front of me, I was ready.

"Spending almost two months unable to be here taught me a lot," I said. "How great the people are that I share this set with each week. You find out who your friends are, and I am lucky to have many here at ESPN, and among you as well. And I was reminded how lucky we all are to have a friend in this world of sports.

"We just watched a glorious World Series, football and hockey seasons flourish, and even an NBA lockout gives us something new to obsess about. Even in tough times we can always turn on 'the game.' Cheering for our team can make the world's problems temporarily disappear. Your boss may be mad at you, your car might be out of gas, and your spouse could be telling you to take the trash out. But who cares when it's fourth-and-goal or you're one strike from winning the World Series?

"Sports doesn't solve our problems, but boy, does it make it easier to put them aside. And that's a medicine you can't bottle."

I felt that I'd delivered it okay, but I didn't know for sure. Before my fall I'd have had full confidence in my ability to judge objectively whether I had done a good job. But after overestimating my abilities for the past two months, it would no longer shock me if someone said, "Geez, John, you should've taken another week off."

I didn't have time to ask anyone, though, because just as I was finishing my "Parting Shot," Lupica came through the door. Once the show started I felt like I'd never missed one. It went smoothly, with an easy back-and-forth among the panelists, just like old times.

It felt great to do the show again, but once more I didn't trust my own barometer. My insecurities didn't creep in until we headed upstairs to the makeup room to take off all the powder and cream.

I pulled Valerio into a side room, without closing the door, and asked him point-blank: "How'd I do?"

He didn't blink. "John, you were great. Based on your performance, I never would have known you had been out."

Joe's a very nice man, as I've said, but he's no bullshitter. Besides, he cares too much about his show to allow anyone, even a close friend, to bring the standards down. More than that, he would protect me if I wasn't ready yet by gently suggesting I should take some more time off. So when he said that, I was inclined to believe him.

When Lupica walked by he stopped to chime in. He guessed what I had asked Joe and, more importantly, he knew why.

"John, if you have any doubts about how you did today," he said, "throw them away. You were fantastic. If I didn't know you'd just come back, I couldn't tell."

Then he showed a side that few get to see. "I was stuck in my driveway this morning," he told us. "It was impossible to get out or go anywhere. Under any other circumstances I'd have called Joe and said, 'I just can't make it. You'll have to grab someone.' But there was just no way I wasn't going to be here on your first day back."

That warmed my heart. I was feeling great about the show. I was one-for-one on my comeback. No, it didn't solve all my problems, but what if Dr. Gordon had been right and I simply couldn't write or deliver a coherent essay or handle the panel's back-and-forth? Even Joe would have hesitated to bring me back for weeks, and it would have set back my psychological recovery more than I'd like to imagine.

On the ride home my phone was flooded with texts and calls from friends congratulating me. All this made me incredibly happy—what a relief! But it also forced me to remember I still had a long way to go—even if I had no idea how far.

I was about to find out.

CHAPTER 30

Testing, Testing

THE WEEK AFTER THE SHOW MY DOCTORS HAD SCHED-
uled two consecutive days for cognitive testing.

I had just taped a nationally televised show without missing a
beat. What could they possibly throw at me? How hard could it
be? I didn't give it a second thought.

On Monday I took the train to see Dr. Emily D'Antonio, who's
probably in her midthirties, in a room in the basement to take
these tests. The sooner I got them out of the way, I thought, the
sooner I could return to working full time on all my shows.

Dr. D'Antonio explained the first test: "A letter is going to
come up on the screen. It could be any letter, but you only want
to press the button when the letter A comes up."

I looked at her, mildly insulted by the silliness of this exercise.
But when the letters started popping up, I kept pushing the button on almost all the letters—and not many were As. I can't tell
you how many times I pushed the button for W or V or even Q,
while sometimes *not* pushing it for A! I couldn't believe it—and
I couldn't seem to stop myself. Unlike previous tests, I had no
false hope that I was doing anything but bombing this. What was
happening to me?

Dr. D'Antonio explained later that what I was struggling with was one of the side effects of serious brain injuries: a loss of impulse control. You know you shouldn't say that or do this, but you just can't seem to stop yourself. This is one reason why some football players end up doing drugs or getting into crazy relationships with strippers or drinking and driving. The mental governors that regulate such behavior are gone. They don't have any brakes.

Next Dr. D'Antonio laid out a bunch of blocks on the table. She told me she was going to put a few of them together, then take them apart, and ask me to put them back together in the same manner. I nodded. Again, what could be easier?

She laid down a puck-shaped block, then put a rectangular block on top of that, then another puck-shaped block on top of that, then added a smaller rectangle block on the side. Then she took it apart and asked me to rebuild it, something my girls could have done in kindergarten.

I put the rectangular block down, which was my first mistake, then went completely blank. I started guessing, then I'd mumble some false logic, like, "Well, I remember the circle was on the other side of the rectangle," to make it seem like there was method to my madness, but I certainly wasn't fooling Dr. D'Antonio. I couldn't even get started correctly.

Oh-for-two.

For my next test Dr. D'Antonio would flash a geometric shape up on the screen—like a circle, square, or triangle—and ask me to draw each on a sheet of paper. I simply couldn't do it.

Then she brought out a wooden board with ten holes drilled into it and a bag of ten wooden pegs. My job was to put the ten pegs into the ten holes. If you were working slowly and carefully, you'd need about thirty seconds. It took me six minutes.

The drubbing went on, test after test, and lasted all day. I was failing miserably. It felt like I was taking the SAT and blowing it so badly that, by the time they announced, "Time's up!" I knew my dreams of college were dashed.

When I arrived for the second day I had no illusions. If it was anything like the first day, I knew I was in for another beat-down, and I was right. Test after test I simply could not complete the most basic tasks. What was more remarkable: the doctors felt they had to wait two months just to give me these tests, knowing I wouldn't even be able to attempt them until then. In other words, since my fall, this was the top of my game.

I knew I was failing, but I was still surprised just how badly. On many of the tests I finished in the bottom 1 percent—basically dead last. Now, years earlier I'd passed a Mensa test with an IQ score of 154, but on this IQ test I scored a 102. I felt like I was losing the one thing I could always count on, even when everything else was going wrong. Worse, I was convinced I would never get it back—and it might even get worse. My *confidence* in my intelligence was slipping too.

After seeing the results from this two-day disaster I was not surprised when Dr. Gordon told me, "You should not be doing live television for a while." He knew I could embarrass myself badly on national TV, and that could end my career.

This time I believed him.

My dramatically revised view of my situation affected how I related to others. Now that I was out and about more, I ran into a lot more people. Invariably, they'd say, "You look great!"

I wanted to say, "Yes, thank you! But I *feel* horrible—and I have the test scores to prove it!"

Of course, they're whizzing by, like we all are, so you can hardly burden them with such a bombshell. But this is one of the central problems, I think, people with depression have to face: the inability to explain your situation to people you meet who can't see what you're dealing with. If I had been in a car accident and left the hospital in a wheel chair, everyone could *see* the wheelchair, so no one would expect you to join them for a jog.

With depression no one sees your wheelchair. So they think you're fine, and if you try to tell them you're not, you come off as a whiner. So you learn to keep your mouth shut, which probably doesn't help things, either.

◆ ◆ ◆

Even after I failed the cognitive tests Dr. D'Antonio had just given me—or maybe because of my failure, which gave me a greater need to redeem myself—I was determined to dive back into my work. After I returned to *The Sports Reporters* and all went well, I figured, *Hey, I'm back! I can do all the shows I did before.*

So I decided to return to *ABC College Football* over Thanksgiving, a big weekend with games on both Friday and Saturday, and *The Sports Reporters* on Sunday. When Bill Graff, who is responsible for my schedule, saw I was doing three dates in a row, he threw up the caution flag. But I ignored his advice, and all three days went great. That convinced me that I was right and the tests were wrong.

Jesse Palmer was thrilled to have me back. The guys who had filled in for me on *ABC College Football*, John Anderson and Scott Van Pelt, were terrific, but Jesse and I have the kind of chemistry you develop only after years of working together. We also have a lot of fun, and it all went just like my return to *The Sports Reporters* did: without a hitch.

So the next week, figuring I was now completely good to go—or perhaps doubly determined to prove those tests wrong—I booked *ABC College Football* for Saturday, December 2, *The Sports Reporters* for Sunday morning, and a basketball game Monday night at the University of Detroit's old Calihan Hall, where they were going to honor their most famous coach and my good friend, Dick Vitale, by naming the court after him. Then I'd fly back to New York after the game to cover another special event the next night, the Jimmy V. Classic, a college basketball doubleheader at Madison Square Garden. I'd be working with Bob Knight and Digger Phelps, just like the old days.

I committed to five events in four days because I wanted the word to get out: Saunders is back! But when Graff saw my schedule he got a little tougher, warning me it was a bad idea and urging me to cut back.

"No, I'm all right," I told him, even more confident after Thanksgiving weekend had gone so well. "I can do this!"

I did okay through Saturday's *College Football*, Sunday's *Sports Reporters*, and Monday's basketball game in Detroit, but when I was flying back that night after the game I could tell my batteries were running low. By Tuesday night, when I was covering the Jimmy V. Classic at Madison Square Garden, it all caught up to me. The combination of the nonstop crowd noise, the bright lights on the court, and the even brighter TV lights in my face all conspired to make my nonstop headache much worse. I started to feel dizzy and queasy, almost like I'd turned back the clock to the day I fell backward on the studio floor. It was unbearable.

I got through the first game, but by the second game's intermission I was in bad shape. Knight turned to me and said—as only Knight can—"You look like shit. You need to go home."

"I can't," I protested. "We have a postgame show."

He wasn't hearing it. "No, you have to go home. *Now.*"

Digger chimed in: "Yeah, Bob's right: you gotta go."

Knight didn't wait for another word. He got on the talk-back to the producer, Eric Mosley, and made the call: "John's gotta go home." Then he put one hand on my shoulder and said, "John, you gotta start caring about yourself. There was no need for you to even come here tonight."

Knight has his critics, but don't tell me he doesn't have a heart.

Hearing this, Mosley came on my headset and asked if I was okay. With Knight glaring at me, I knew I couldn't lie. "I feel like my head is going to explode."

That was all Mosley needed to hear. "Okay, then you need to leave."

I called for the car service, and Digger walked me out of the Gardens, then waited with me at the curb to make sure I got safely inside the car. Slumped in the backseat, my head pounding, my stomach churning, I felt sick as a dog—and defeated. I'd done far tougher stretches than that in my career, countless times, but now four consecutive days were enough to overwhelm me. I thought I was ready, but clearly I wasn't close.

ESPN didn't wait for Dr. Choudhri's orders to force me to take more time off, cutting everything except *The Sports Reporters*.

It was another reminder of the damage done, and how far I had to go.

PART FOUR

◆ ◆ ◆

Collision Course

CHAPTER 31

The Damage of Doctor Dangerous Revealed

MY TEAM OF DOCTORS FOCUSED ON MY SEVERE BRAIN injury, which was clearly the most urgent concern. They knew that if they followed the proper rehabilitation protocols, I would be able to overcome the effects of the brain trauma over time. But most of them missed the bigger problem, depression, which would prove to be a far more stubborn foe.

The first person to recognize my underlying problem was not a doctor or a therapist but Hall of Fame slugger Reggie Jackson, Wanda's uncle. He had long since become a close friend, a trusted ally, and a welcome visitor in our home. When Reggie was recovering from shoulder surgery at Columbia University in December 2011, he stayed with us in "the Reggie Room" of our house.

During this visit, just a few months after my fall, he could see that my problems went deeper than the brain injury and might still be there after I recovered from it. He could tell that I was "off." He first mentioned this to Wanda, who suggested he talk to me about it.

The next day he asked me to join him for lunch, then get some appliances. That's right, Mr. October needed a gas range, a refrigerator, and an oven, just like the rest of us. In the process I got a taste of what it's like to *be* Reggie Jackson. At a popular deli in Westchester Reggie walked quickly through the door and to our table before the patrons could fuss over him, but the owner grabbed his arm to pose for a picture. Reg loves to tease folks, so he asked if the photo was good for a free lunch and pretended to back out when the owner said no, so Reggie joked that the owner couldn't display the photo until he was properly compensated with a free sandwich.

When we stopped to buy his appliances people seemed to come out of nowhere to ask for his autograph. When Reggie asked one lady where she had come from, she said the place next door.

"Wait—you came in here, and you don't work here?"

She said, "Yes!"

"That's it!" Reggie said. "Lock the store!"

I couldn't resist. "You should have only hit two homers that night against the Dodgers." That got a Hall of Fame laugh.

But before we left the parking lot he asked me, "Are you okay?"

I said, "I'm great!"

Instead of nodding or arguing, Reggie started asking specific questions about my treatment. What types of therapy was I getting? Had my doctors told me to slow down my schedule? How long before I thought I'd be 100 percent? How long before my *doctors* thought I'd be 100 percent?

Trust me when I tell you: there is no bullshitting Reggie Jackson.

After I gave him real answers, he told me he had a friend at Columbia University who could recommend someone who could help me, and gave me her number. As soon as we returned home I called her for an appointment. Reggie's friend got me in two days later, and after running some tests she asked me several questions that made it clear that she believed my head trauma was making my depression worse. She put me in touch with a psychiatrist, Dr. Carolyn Douglas.

At my first appointment with Dr. Douglas about a week later I met a tall, attractive, precise, and caring woman, whom I liked immediately. She started by asking about my medications. I ran down the list, which was pretty long. When I mentioned Klonopin, which Dr. Dangerous had increased every few weeks, she asked, "How much?"

"Four milligrams a day," I said.

She looked up. I could tell she was trying to hide her alarm.

"Why are you on such a high dosage of Klonopin?"

I didn't even know it *was* such a high dosage. "I don't know."

"You realize that's the maximum dosage? Do you get panic attacks?"

"No."

"Did you get them before you started taking Klonopin?"

"No."

She said, "We may want to talk about that at a later date."

A few weeks later I met with a neurologist named Dr. Martin Goldstein, who deals with the complications that often follow head injuries, from being physically off-balance to suffering depression. When Wanda and I told Dr. Goldstein about my medications, including 4 milligrams of Klonopin every day, he was clearly alarmed too.

"John, do you realize that's the equivalent of taking 20 to 40 milligrams of Valium a day?"

Of course, I had no idea what Dr. Dangerous was prescribing, or why. I would soon learn that Klonopin is five to ten times more powerful than Valium, which means I was taking roughly ten to twenty 2-milligram Valium tablets a day.

It was also potentially dangerous because Klonopin is a powerful sedative, which can make you fall asleep when you're just sitting on the couch. It can also affect cognition and balance, particularly in someone who's suffered traumatic brain injuries. And for those with severe depression—which is what I came to Dr. Dangerous to address—it can also adversely affect their mood, although I didn't know it then. Throw in Klonopin's reaction to even moderate drinking, which can lead to respiratory arrest and even death—which they tell you right on the label—and you'd have to conclude this was the perfect drug for me not to take.

"Oh my god," I said.

"Do you fall asleep a lot during the day?"

Wanda interjected. "All the time now. Watching games, trying to read."

"I never used to," I said.

"I'm amazed you can function at all, let alone do your job," Dr. Goldstein said. "We're going to have to adjust this to a more sensible regimen to enable you to function closer to your full potential."

The problem is that Klonopin is so potent that getting me down from 4 milligrams a day wasn't going to be simple or fast. It could take months, even years. And in case I didn't believe them, I recalled the day I ran out of Klonopin, which quickly became one of the worst days I've ever had. I was totally disoriented, with blurred vision and uncontrollable shakiness. They were right: it was going to be hard to bring me down, and we'd have to do it slowly and carefully.

The first baby step was simply to change the timing of the dosage. Instead of taking 2 milligrams in the morning and two at night, Dr. Goldstein had me take 1 milligram in the morning and 3 milligrams at night. We did that for three weeks, and I immediately noticed a difference in my ability to stay alert. We then shifted all 4 milligrams to night, with none in the morning—a big help.

Then we started bringing the dosage down, very slowly, to 3.95 milligrams—literally just chipping off pieces of each pill, which the doctors showed me how to do with a pill cutter—and then by another 0.10 mg every month or two. It would be a very slow climb down, indeed.

My doctors felt that the high dosage of Klonopin contributed significantly to my depression. I was always medicated, always tired. It was like going to bat every game with the metal donut still on the barrel.

And there's a lesson in this too: always know who's giving you the prescriptions and what the pills are supposed to do. Ask questions and get answers before you take any medication. I didn't, and I paid a price.

CHAPTER 32

Let the Bad Times Roll

NEW YEAR'S EVE 2011.

Wanda, the girls, and I went out with Uncle Reggie to Sylvia's, a famous restaurant in Harlem. But at 11:30 I wanted to dash home in time to see the ball drop.

"Why do you want to leave, Daddy?" my daughters asked me. "You don't care about that."

It was true. I usually spent New Year's Eve at a bowl game somewhere warm. It had never been a big deal to me. But this time, I explained, "I don't want to see 2012 *start*. I want to see 2011 *end*."

It felt good to see that ball drop and get 2011 officially behind me. I didn't know what the New Year would hold, but I was certain it couldn't be worse than 2011.

Four hours later I was getting up to do *The Sports Reporters*. The car came at 4:30, but the roads were icy. The driver was going slowly and carefully to Bristol when my phone rang. It was Joe Valerio, already worried about the show starting on time.

"How close are you?" he asked.

"Very," I said. "I'll be there in ten minutes."

But no sooner had these words left my lips than the car started spinning on the ice. Still on the phone, I told Joe, "I don't know if

I'm going to make it." I meant that in two ways: not to the show, and maybe not make it at all.

We smashed into the concrete divider. My head hit the window as a car smashed into us, sending us spinning again. Then a second car hit us, propelling us hard against the guardrail. The smashed front of our car was now pointing toward the traffic coming toward us, the corner sticking out into the right lane.

Then I blacked out. The next thing I knew I was lying in a hospital bed with another concussion.

I was supposed to host the Fiesta Bowl on January 2, and needless to say, I missed that. But I felt good enough—or desperate enough, take your pick—to travel to New Orleans on January 3rd to take part in our lead-up coverage for the national championship game that year, between Alabama and LSU. I stayed for the game too. I did all of this against the strong advice of my doctors, Wanda, and Uncle Reggie.

ESPN installed our temporary set in the French Quarter, with an office on the other side of Canal Street, about a five-minute walk. Between shows we headed to the office, where they'd created a makeshift green room so we could relax and get a soda.

Now this is usually one of my favorite weeks of the year. I spend a few days working and hanging out with my friends, then top it off by handing out that championship trophy to the winning coach—often a friend of mine, like Texas's Mack Brown. I never ask Wanda to watch me on TV, with that one exception: after the title game I always ask her, "Did you see me?!" as giddy as a cub reporter starting out in Espanola, Ontario.

But not this time. The day after I arrived in New Orleans I made six appearances on the set. After all six shows I walked across Canal Street toward the office—and I got lost, every time. I couldn't find it by myself, even though everyone else could. I required an escort, one more sign that I still wasn't right.

During the first of our lead-up shows I was on the air with Jesse Palmer and Lou Holtz. When we came back from a break

I couldn't remember their names—I just blanked. I had enough presence of mind to dance around for a bit until their names came back to me. I could tell Jesse noticed, but the viewers couldn't, and I got through the broadcast without any major gaffes.

That night, after we all went back to our hotel rooms to change, Jesse called to invite me to dinner with the whole crew: Kirk Herbstreit, Chris Fowler, Rece Davis, and Erin Andrews. I've always enjoyed these guys, so it was good to get together again.

From there we walked to an ESPN party for the entire staff, the unsung heroes who put the shows together, then on to Pat O'Brien's on Bourbon Street. The place was rocking: lights and loud music and a big crowd going crazy, mostly Michigan fans still celebrating their 23–20 upset over Virginia Tech the night before. I hadn't had a drink in almost a year, so I was happy to abstain, but when we went to another club with live music, my head felt like it was about to explode, just like it did at Madison Square Garden when Bob Knight told me to go home.

This time I didn't need the General to know I'd reached my limit. I shouted to Jesse, "I have to go!" and started walking back to our hotel—my first smart decision in some time.

On my walk back I started getting depressed. Block by block I was dropping from functioning to almost incapacitated, like someone had injected me with poison and it was starting to take effect. I wasn't getting depressed *about* anything in particular, but by the time I got back to my room I was crying.

I felt like hell, physically and emotionally. I didn't want to go outside because everything I saw just made me feel worse: people drinking, joking, having a good time. So I spent the weekend lying there on my hotel bed, missing my wife and kids, and wondering why so much shit had happened to me in my life.

During my self-imposed "house arrest" I started emailing back and forth with my brother. When I brought up my shoulder injuries and how I felt it impeded my hockey career, Bernie pointed out that I'd made some bad decisions too, but it didn't matter anymore, anyway. He kept telling me to leave the past behind and live in the present. Good advice, but I had a hard time following it.

But his bigger point was this: "Forget about hockey. Look at your broadcasting career and how successful you are, and your daughters, and your family. Be happy for what you have, not what you don't have."

To reinforce this Bernie tried to get me to do an exercise he'd read about in a self-help book recently, but I couldn't get into it.

Even when I'm depressed, I'm still grateful for my wife, my kids, my career, and my home. I can usually still appreciate life's little pleasures, whether it's enjoying dinner with Mack Brown every Friday night before our Saturday college football broadcast, flying to Toronto with Chris Berman to witness the closing of Maple Leaf Gardens, or just watching a movie with my family at home.

But sometimes my depression is so bad that I'm reduced to a point where happiness is nonexistent. Nothing can cheer me up. The good things in life can't reach me because I'm too far down. It's like the world used to be in color, and now it's black and white. Everything still *looks* the same, but nothing *feels* the same. There's no color, no joy. That's why even rich and famous people suffer from depression and sometimes attempt suicide. When that happens it always surprises people who aren't depressed, but not those who are. We get it.

And this is why "cheerleading" doesn't work. So when my brother wrote, "You just need to get up in the morning and tell yourself you're going to have a great day," despite his good intentions, it didn't help.

After Bernie and I finished emailing I called Wanda looking for sympathy, but she said, "Well, your brother's right. That's what you need to do. You just need to talk yourself out of it. You know you have a family who loves you, you've got great friends who care about you, and you've got a great career."

Unfortunately it's not simply a matter of bucking up. You're not just "bummed out." Again, it's like you've been poisoned, and you want someone to give you the antidote. Everything else that people tell you just feels like—pardon me—happy horseshit. And then I feel guilty on top of the depression because no one loves me more than my wife and brother.

◆ ◆ ◆

I stayed in bed the entire weekend. No more Bourbon Street for me. I got my act together enough to get out of my room that Monday for the BCS title game between top-ranked LSU and second-ranked Alabama. That's what's great about my particular line of work: you *have* to get up enough to do it, because who wants to see a grown man cry on national TV?

After the Tide swamped the Tigers, 21–0, I stepped up to our temporary stage on the field to hand out the national championship trophy to Alabama's Nick Saban, one of the plums of my work. I got a booster shot just from being up there, but that night it gave me only temporary energy, very temporary. Once the lights went off and I stepped down from the stage, I was right back to where I was before.

After having a Diet Coke at the hotel bar with Jesse, I went back to my room, packed, and got on the plane.

The next day I went to see Dr. Goldstein and related the conversations with my brother and my wife.

"They love me so much and mean so well that I felt bad about rejecting their advice," I told him. "They're telling me to get up and just say, 'I'm going to have a great day.'"

"If it were that easy," he said, "I wouldn't have a job. Everyone could just talk themselves out of it. There is scientific evidence that depressed people are actually wired differently, so telling a depressed person to talk themselves out if it is like trying to persuade yourself to be taller. This is why healthy people sometimes have a hard time understanding depressed people."

That was helpful to hear, something I've gone back to more than once. But it still didn't answer my bigger question: What *did* work? What *would* help?

CHAPTER 33

Stumbling Toward Unhappiness

AFTER MY TRYING WEEK IN NEW ORLEANS, IT WAS GOOD to get back to our nice, quiet, comfortable home and get some rest. But things took a downturn when I started doing college basketball games again.

Given the speed of the sport and its many substitutions, I prepare for these games like no other. I get DVDs from each team, record recent games at home to study, and get still more from ESPN's library or from the ESPN app. Then I take about three hours to prepare a board that I'll have in front of me on game day, with each player's name, stats, and anecdotes attached, color coded by team. By game day I feel as prepared as anyone possibly could be. As the coaches all love to say, confidence comes from preparation.

My homework complete, on January 19, 2012, I traveled to Blacksburg, Virginia, to cover an ACC clash the next night between the University of North Carolina and Virginia Tech. I'd be working with Jay Bilas, a close friend and one of the best in the business. As is our custom, we met that day with UNC's Hall of

Fame coach, Roy Williams, and Virginia Tech's Seth Greenberg, who's now an ESPN analyst.

I felt a bit off, and I've wondered since if the coaches could tell, but I ignored my nagging doubts. After tip-off I was feeling a step slow—not a good thing when you're covering a basketball game. But thank goodness I had Jay Bilas with me. He was sharp as always, picking up whenever I fell behind, as if he realized his point guard wasn't on his game, so he took over the offense. He covered the gaps so well that probably no one but us noticed.

With just 0.2 seconds left in the first half, Carolina got the ball out of bounds. The rule here is very clear: if you have 0.3 seconds left, you can catch it and shoot it, but with 0.2 you can only tip it in. I've seen the exact same circumstance play out dozens of times. I *know* this rule, and I *know* this play like I know my daughters' names.

While the Carolina players were getting set to inbound the ball Jay said, "The only thing they can do here is an alley-oop." Of course, he was exactly right. Before I could I formulate my thoughts, Carolina launched the ball toward the hoop, and John Henson jumped up and slammed it in. Two points for Carolina at the buzzer.

Easy call—but I froze. My mouth didn't move. At that instant— on national TV, no less—it was obvious I was still missing part of my mental library. I couldn't figure out whether the bucket had counted. To make matters worse, the ref was signaling that the bucket was good, rightly—but for some reason it looked to me like he was waving it off. Finally, I said the exact wrong thing: "They're waving that off!"

By this time Bilas must have figured out that he might have to cover for me at any moment, and he was ready.

"No, no," he said, calmly. "I think they're going to count it."

He handled it perfectly, cutting off my mistake before it got worse, without embarrassing me. I quickly realized he was right, but I was thinking about my gaffe throughout the second half.

Normally after the game we'd relax and talk about it back at the hotel. But Jay had to drive that night to cover another game, so I went back to the hotel by myself, where I whipped myself over my inexplicable mistake the rest of the night.

This is a disaster, I thought. *I'm totally incapable, and I'm not getting better.*

It's hard enough for any closed-head injury patient to recover their mental faculties, but it's a bit trickier to do it on national TV, with millions watching you screw up. It only magnifies the panic and despair. I just crawled into bed and pulled the covers over me.

◆　◆　◆

I went home the next morning totally discouraged and immediately made an appointment to see Dr. Choudhri—something I wouldn't have been wise enough to do just a year earlier. After I described what had happened at the game and how I felt about it, he said my improved physical health fooled me into thinking I had fully recovered and was ready to take on all these tasks. But my brain still hadn't caught up with my body. I was physically rested, but for my brain to start working at full capacity, it had to be re-trained too. I was trying to leap from my mental wheelchair to the Olympic steeplechase, and repeatedly falling down.

That made sense, but I was still in a panic. I all but pleaded with Dr. Choudhri. "You've *got* to tell me this is going to get better. I can't accept that this is going to be the rest of my life."

"You're going to get better," he reassured me. "But you can't keep piling on the assignments. You just have to take it slower."

At his suggestion I scaled back a few assignments but still kept a pretty busy schedule. I had to walk a fine line between overdoing it, which made things worse, and not doing enough for the "drug of work" to kick in.

A month later, on February 21, I flew to Columbia, Missouri, to cover a game with Doug Gottlieb between Kansas State and second-ranked Missouri. I put in my usual preparation for the game, plus a little more, just to be safe. The game was a hot one, going right down to the wire, when Kansas State pulled the upset over the Tigers. Unlike the UNC–Virginia Tech game, I was on top of this contest throughout and felt truly connected to the action. I returned to my hotel room feeling great, allowing myself to think that perhaps the Carolina mistake was just an aberration.

When I got online I saw that I had received some Twitter alerts and clicked on my feed. Although 99 percent of the things people tweet about me are really nice, the 1 percent are ruthless, faceless critics. It seems to me—perhaps because I'm Canadian!—that you shouldn't say anything on Twitter that you wouldn't have the guts to say to someone's face. But that's what Twitter is. You've got to have thick skin to be on it in the first place.

But when I read five or six K-State fans complain that I'd called Angel Rodriguez, their point guard, "Hernandez" a half-dozen times, I was shocked.

"Have you ever watched a KSU game?" one wrote. "Do your homework!"

I went back and looked at the game. I hadn't called Angel Rodriguez "Hernandez" a half-dozen times, but I had done it a few times—and that was enough to get them tweeting, and make me feel incompetent. Now, even when I *felt* like I was doing a good job, I wasn't! That scared me even more.

I sat up in bed the rest of the night, wondering if I should pull myself out of ESPN's college basketball rotation. I went through a dozen emotions, but the strongest was a sense of loss: feeling that I was being robbed of something I had taken for granted, something that I had prided myself on for so long. There didn't seem to be anything I could do about it.

My doctors, family, and friends kept telling me I was going to get better, but I could see little evidence of improvement. Six months after I had fallen, the promise that I was going to recover fully was starting to feel like a lie.

Around this time I was talking with Merril Hoge, the former Pittsburgh Steeler and Chicago Bear who is now one of our NFL analysts. He suffered several serious concussions himself, including one that ended his career. After I told him what had happened to me, he shared how hard and long his recovery was, with symptoms just like mine.

"It's like you're living in a fog," he told me. "But one day—I can't tell you when, I can't tell you why—that fog is going to lift, and you'll be amazed."

I really needed to hear that.

◆ ◆ ◆

A week later, after a few days of strenuous preparation, I flew down to Chapel Hill to cover Maryland against the Tar Heels. I'd be working with Bilas again and meeting with the coaches during the day, one of my favorite parts of the job.

In fact, if I can say this without tooting my own horn, one of the keys to my career has been simple sincerity. A couple of years ago at Dick Vitale's charity event Rick Pitino pulled Wanda aside and said, "Your husband, of all the people in this business, is the nicest guy. He's the one guy I really enjoy talking with."

That made me feel good. And with few exceptions, the coaches have been great to work with. Sitting down with Roy Williams that day felt like old times. He was funny, and we were having a good visit. I allowed myself to feel that, just maybe, things were getting back to normal.

The game that night wasn't a great one. Maryland wasn't that good, but Carolina struggled until late in the game. There wasn't much ESPN could do about that, of course, but I felt like I'd done a good job, a lot better than I had at Virginia Tech. But when I got back to my hotel room and turned on my Twitter feed, it was buzzing again.

"John Saunders obviously didn't do his homework tonight."

"He kept messing up the Maryland players' names!"

But this time I had a little defiance in me. "Wait a second," I thought. "I *know* I didn't screw up these guys' names!"

But Twitter kept going, with maybe eight or nine people making the same comments. I'm not used to that. I had to concede that I must have made some mistakes again, which was very, very disturbing to me.

I was totally distraught. Not only had it happened for the second game in a row, but it happened after I made *damn* sure it wasn't going to happen again. I just couldn't believe it. But the people on Twitter had no reason to make it up. At this point I'm thinking, *That's it. I'm done. I can't work anymore.*

I called Wanda and said, "I am an idiot. I've totally lost my mental capacity. And to make matters worse, I don't even have the ability to recognize it anymore."

She tried to console me. "Everybody makes mistakes," she said in her soothing voice. "The difference is that people talk about it now. When you made mistakes years ago, they weren't on Twitter. You can't determine where you are in your rehab based on a few strangers' comments."

Thinking rationally, she was totally correct, as usual. But when you're feeling as uncertain about yourself as I was, rational thinking didn't always work, and there was nothing anyone could say to make me feel better.

I feared the next game.

CHAPTER 34

A Day in the Doldrums

BETWEEN THESE GAMES I HAD STARTED THERAPY WITH Dr. Douglas and cognitive therapy with Dr. Emily D'Antonio, the psychoneurologist, to help get my memory back.

During my first few visits to Dr. Douglas we covered the major events of my life. While I'd confessed a few things to a few people over the years, especially Wanda, Dr, Douglas was the first person I told everything, including my early sexual encounters with my father's friend's daughters. I had no idea what Dr. Douglas's reaction might be, but I was surprised when used the word *molested*.

Growing up I'd never heard about women molesting boys, so I walled off the confusing memory as just another part of my strange childhood. Dr. Douglas helped me recognize the incidents for what they were—sexual molestation. It was the first time I'd ever thought of it in those terms. She asked me to imagine my own children going through what I had. What would I call that? That was an easy answer!

With Dr. Douglas's help, I started to understand that being molested played a major role in my sexuality, having taught me that sexual pleasure was something to hide and keep in dark rooms. Sex, I thought, was strictly for physical pleasure and wasn't connected to love. That meant I had chased casual sex but had difficulty connecting sex with a loving relationship. Looking back, it explained a lot.

In my cognitive therapy sessions with Dr. D'Antonio we started working on simple things, like detecting when a sound is going up and when it's going down by following a computer-generated slide whistle. The computer would play a sound going up or down, and I was supposed to hit the button if it was going up and not hit the button if it was going down. This was not a hearing test—I could hear the sound just fine—but a cognitive test: Could my brain send the correct signal to my hands to push the button or to *not* push the button?

I was appalled how often I got it wrong, which isn't exactly a great shortcoming to have for someone who needs to detect a speaker's inflection during interviews. This tested another element of impulse control, and if your impulse control is not strong, you can get in a lot of trouble.

But of equal importance was Dr. D'Antonio's simple question, which started every session: "How are you feeling?" Unlike Dr. Dangerous, Dr. D'Antonio was very concerned about my emotional state—which is saying something when you consider that my emotional state was supposed to be Dr. Dangerous's domain, not Dr. D'Antonio's.

We'd spend a lot of our sessions just talking. As a cognitive therapist, part of her mission is to get me to think more logically. Each week I'd tell her more and more about my feelings, and sometimes I'd burst into tears. "I'm just so damn depressed," I said.

"Okay," she'd say, "tell me what you're thinking."

"I don't think I'm getting any better. I don't think I am *going* to get any better. I don't think I'm capable of doing my job. And I think I'm going to lose my job."

She took notes, then asked, "When you break all of those things down, John, do you truly have any evidence that any of that is true? Do you have evidence that you're not getting better, that you'll never get better, that you won't be capable of doing your job, or you're going to get fired?"

"Quite the contrary," I had to admit. "All my doctors are telling me to take my time, that I'm going to be fine. The people at ESPN are telling me my job will be there whenever I'm ready, and that's from the top on down."

These simple little exchanges were enormously helpful for me, an important start to turning my thinking around. But the sad thing about depression is that the shelf life for that kind of logical reassurance is about an hour. This wasn't because I was pessimistic. It was because the concussion had limited my ability to think logically and retain those rational conclusions after I'd reached them. Every irrational fear I'd ever had in my life came back to the surface: my fear of abandonment, my fear of being worthless, my fear of losing my kids, my fear of being a bad father.

Just about anything could set off this chain of fears. If I heard Aleah rushing to get to work, I'd start worrying she was going to be late. Then I'd think, *I should I have gotten up and helped her.* Then I'd go to a bigger issue: *As her father, I could have taught her to always be on time, so she wouldn't be late. Therefore, I'm a bad father.*

I told Dr. D'Antonio that this spiral of doubts started the minute I woke up, so she asked me to describe a typical day.

"After indulging every fear I've ever had for an hour," I told her, "I often find myself in bed, sobbing uncontrollably. I can sleep better since we've started cutting back the Klonopin, but I wake up in worse shape than when I went to bed.

"The kids are off to school or work, and Wanda works three days a week, so I'm often by myself. I have a lot of self-destructive thoughts. I have a lot of suicidal thoughts. Not to the point of actually fearing that I'm going to do them, but just being obsessed with the idea that I don't want to live like this anymore."

Whenever I said this Dr. D'Antonio would follow up with detailed questions. "Do you have any plans to take action? Have you thought about how you would do it?"

As long as I assured her I wasn't going to do anything, she promised not to admit me into a psych ward.

I continued. "I feel like crap, I'm not working as much as I want to, and even when I do work, I suck at it.

"All these memories are coming up about my father and all these issues that can no longer be addressed with him because he's gone. Then every single fear and monster that I've ever had overtakes me, like a thick fog coming in. I just can't take this stuff anymore."

After I described a typical day Dr. D'Antonio said, "Okay, here's what I want you to do. When you have a moment of clarity, I want you to go back over your day and write down how you felt at each point during the day, giving each point a number on a scale of one to ten, with ten being your highest level of depression."

I did my homework three days in a row and then presented two copies to her at our next session. She asked me to read it out loud so she could track my emotional response while she read along.

"Woke up this morning. Depression Level 10. Stayed in bed for an hour crying. Sat on the edge of the bed. Depression Level 10. Stayed there for an hour. Got up, went downstairs, and got on my computer. Depression Level 8."

She stopped me right there.

"Okay, what do we know, right now? Those two things—lying in bed and sitting on the edge of the bed—those don't work. Getting out of bed will not solve all your problems, but it will help."

After this session I started getting out of bed as soon as I woke up. This simple act prevented me from starting my day with a depression spiral.

This change shows why several different methods can help address extreme cases of depression. Like a coach who draws up multiple defenses, I had Dr. Douglas handling my medication and the causes of my depression, Dr. Choudhri dealing with the concussion and its neurological effects, and Dr. D'Antonio providing tools to deal with what was happening in the present.

However, few solutions lasted for very long, and Dr. D'Antonio knew we had to work on that, too.

But the brain injury had created basic functioning problems, which, combined with an intensifying depression, would continue to pull me downward if something didn't give.

CHAPTER 35

Peering Over the Tappan Zee Bridge

IN LATE FEBRUARY OF 2012 I WOKE UP ONE MORNING AS deeply depressed as I'd ever been. That's when I decided to drive to the Tappan Zee Bridge, which is notorious for suicide attempts.

To prevent this they've installed traffic cameras, tall fencing, four emergency phones, and signs on both sides that say things like, "Life is worth living," and "When it seems like there is no hope, there is help." They've trained the bridge staff in suicide prevention, but even so, several times a year you hear about someone who jumped, or tried to. Since the bridge opened, more than two dozen people have jumped to their deaths. It's for this reason, not its appearance, that they call the Tappan Zee "The Golden Gate Bridge of the East."

Every time I've driven over the Tappan Zee I've looked over the side. If I have a passenger, I look past them, over the edge, through the bars and the metal netting, down to the icy waters below.

When I got up that morning I sat on the end of the bed for an hour—against Dr. D'Antonio's advice—sobbing. I felt hopeless, dumb, and depressed. I simply could not imagine any way out of this situation. I wasn't just losing hope that I'd get better any time soon. I had become convinced I would never be whole again.

I felt like I'd waged a war—and lost it, for good. I felt battered and bruised, like one of Mike Tyson's sparring partners. When you're deeply depressed, your emotional pain can create physical pain, which doctors call somatic symptoms. I constantly felt nauseated, my chest felt as if an elephant was sitting on it, and my whole body ached. I was done.

My thoughts had turned extremely dark. The desire to end my life was getting harder and harder to suppress.

◆　◆　◆

In order to allow myself to drive to the bridge, I had to promise myself I wasn't going to jump. I wanted to take a closer look over the side. That's all, I told myself. I was just going to take a look.

Whatever my intentions, I knew that if I stopped my car on the bridge, within minutes other drivers and the police would try to pull me away from the edge. That alone could make the national news.

So before I left home I had to come up with a plan. I decided to put an orange in the car. If I got stopped by the police, I'd just say, "Hey, I'm a diabetic. I needed to eat this orange, and I didn't want to try to peel it while I was driving."

I got in the car and headed out for the bridge.

As I approached it an impulse sparked in the pit of my stomach and started spreading throughout my body and soul. It gained a power I struggled to control, pushing me to do something I knew was wrong for me—the opposite of everything my friends, my family, and my doctors had told me was good and healthy.

I knew better, but whatever this impulse was, it was getting stronger, pulling and pushing me to do what I knew I shouldn't: go to the bridge and jump off. Right here. Right now.

But I kept driving toward the bridge anyway.

◆ ◆ ◆

When I got to the Tappan Zee I drove to the apex and stopped. I knew that if I got out of the car and looked over the edge, the voice inside me—telling me to do it, telling me to jump—could get even stronger. I felt like it could physically overtake me, like two strong hands on my back, and push me over the railing.

But my curiosity was too great. I just *had* to peer over the side of the bridge to see what it looked like, and what it felt like. It was a risk I was willing to take.

Okay, I reminded myself before I opened the car door, *if you're going to take a look over the side, you need to be stronger than the evil thing that's trying to kill you.* I told myself—again—that I just wanted to see what it would feel like to look over the edge. That was all.

Then I realized that if I tried to get out right away, I'd get hit by another car. So I sat in the driver's seat for a few seconds while traffic whizzed by. But I really, *really* wanted to look over the side.

Sitting there much longer wasn't an option either. Soon I'd hear the sirens of police cars headed my way. I waited for a gap in traffic, grabbed the orange, and got out of the car. I walked around to the passenger side, opened the door, and acted like I was searching for something. Then I turned to take a look over the edge of the bridge.

From inside the car the water seemed distant, like a scene from a postcard. But standing there, it looked dark and beautiful, almost calling to me.

It was only then that I saw parallel rows of guardrails—the same kind you see on a highway shoulder—between the roadway and the edge of the bridge. A chain link fence spanned them, like netting. Standing at the first guardrail, I couldn't look directly down to the water, but I could see past both rails to the Hudson beyond. It wasn't hard to imagine falling off the bridge like someone's discarded piece of trash, tossed from the window of a passing car.

It wasn't as simple as I'd thought it would be, but I saw that I could climb through the girders and around the fencing. If I was determined to end my life, those girders wouldn't stop me.

I got close enough to get a good look at the slate-blue waters, 140 feet down. I was relatively calm, considering how close I was to the spot where others had chosen to end their lives.

I could feel the air whip up from the other side of the bridge, gaining momentum as it swooshed over the edge. I closed my eyes briefly and imagined I was going over the edge of the bridge with the wind. This image was a little too real, and I began to worry that I was losing control and wasn't going to make it back.

The impulse was still urging me to jump. Perhaps if I'd listened a moment longer, I might have let it give me that final push.

But somehow I gathered enough strength to overcome it. My self-destructive impulse had made me drive to the bridge, get out, and look over the edge. But it couldn't make me jump. Not today.

I turned around, moving quickly now, and got back in my car.

As I headed home my first thought was this: anyone who thinks people who end their lives are cowards hasn't looked over the Tappan Zee Bridge. They haven't seen and felt what I'd just seen and felt. Suicide victims might not be able to face the rest of their lives, but I'd just learned that it took a certain kind of courage to jump.

I also felt, for the first time in months, a sense of accomplishment. I hadn't just *thought* about looking over the side of the bridge—I'd actually done it, satisfying my aching curiosity. And I'd been stronger than the compulsion to jump.

I was still alive, but all I had really done was eliminate one option. I still hadn't figured out how to get out of the trap I was in.

◆　◆　◆

I knew I had to admit what I'd done to my doctors. They all had the same reaction: "John, do you need to be hospitalized?"

To which my response was, "No."

Each of them had questions and comments, but none were more pointed than Dr. Douglas's. She is a kind soul, but weeks earlier, knowing how depressed I was, she looked me in the eye and spoke as seriously to me as she ever had: "If you ever feel that you're in crisis, you must promise me that you'll call."

This was hard for me. As strange as it seems, I've never called any of my doctors in a crisis, or even if I just need to talk. It goes back to my old worry about being a burden.

When I told her about my trip to the bridge she was even more stern.

"John, you promised me you'd call," she said. "Why didn't you call?"

I shrugged. "I'd feel bad spoiling your weekend."

She was having none of it. "John, which call do you think I'd rather get: the one where you're feeling bad and you want to talk, or the one from Wanda, saying you're gone?"

I thought about it. "That makes a lot of sense."

This marked another crucial time when I was able to admit I was in over my head, and needed to ask for help. It worked.

CHAPTER 36

Back to the Bridge

AFTER MY MEETING WITH DR. DOUGLAS I WENT THROUGH a couple of days when I was beating myself up and feeling terrible. But that following Saturday morning I was in a pretty good mood, so I said to Aleah, "Let's go to the Palisades Mall." She needed to get something from the Apple Store, and Wanda wanted to come. I thought we'd all have lunch together.

It started out being a very good day. When Aleah got her shopping done Wanda asked me, "Okay, where do you want to eat lunch?"

This is a running joke in our family. Everyone's so flexible that no one can make a decision, so we end up saying, "I don't know. Where do *you* want to go?" We go around like this at least three times before someone finally picks a place.

But this time, as we were going around and around, I mentioned that my blood sugar was starting to get low. Wanda was annoyed with me because I hadn't eaten enough for breakfast, and then Aleah snapped at me about something small, though I can't even remember what. For some reason these little things all seemed to crystallize, and all my insecurities and doubts— already heightened by the results from Dr. D'Antonio's tests and piqued by a bad week behind the mic—came crashing down on me at once, and I started to lose it. Just like that, in a flash, I was reduced to feeling like my dad's son—stupid and worthless. I turned and walked away.

"Where are you going?" Wanda asked.

"I've just got to get away," was all I said.

I started walking from one end of the huge mall to the other. I found a bench, sat down, put my head in my hands, and started crying. I kept thinking, *I am just so freakin' stupid. I'm never going to be smart again. I've been exposed to the nation as a fraud, and now I'm being exposed to my own family. I'm just . . . stupid.*

My phone rang. "Where are you?" Aleah asked, clearly upset.

"I just need to be myself," I said.

"Tell us where you are so we can find you."

"You guys go get lunch. I'll walk home."

Now, it's about fifteen miles from the mall to our house, and you'd have to go across the Tappan Zee Bridge—and they don't allow walkers. But I was convinced that if I could just "walk it off," I'd get better. I had no plan other than to keep walking. Heck, my cloudy brain concluded, I could walk coast to coast like Forrest Gump until this feeling went away.

So I got up, left the mall, and started walking on the highway toward the bridge. I had walked two miles or so when Wanda's car came up alongside me. She rolled her window down and said, "John, get in."

At first I attempted to keep going, but it was pointless. Not because my will wasn't strong enough to keep walking but because I had nowhere else to go. I was getting pretty close to the bridge, about a mile away, where I'd be stuck. I knew I had to get in the car.

When I did I felt even worse because Aleah was hysterical. Wanda was understandably angry too, but she kept calm because she didn't want to make Aleah any more upset. So now on top of the emotions of feeling stupid, I felt like a terrible person too.

When we got home Aleah went up to her room, so I went up after her, walked in, and sat on her bed.

"Aleah, what I did was wrong, and I apologize for that," I told her. "But I want you to understand that I'm dealing with something that feels out of control right now. My head injury has me feeling really stupid, and the way you guys reacted to me in the mall—and I'm not blaming you, because it's all in my head, *because* of my head—where normally I would have argued back or laughed it off, my insecurities took hold, and I just felt really dumb. And the only thing I felt like I could do was walk away, and that's what I did.

"I apologize to you again, and just want you to know I love you, and I'm working to get better."

She told me I didn't have to apologize and that she forgave me. We hugged.

But I took away something else from that day: I was not in this alone. Obviously I knew that before, but I never felt it so deeply as I did that day. My earlier rationale that those who loved me would understand if I took my life, and might even be relieved of the burden of being with me, was revealed for what it was: a self-serving lie.

Whatever I did would affect the people I loved most, and affect them profoundly.

CHAPTER 37

Crunch Time

NEXT GAME: VILLANOVA AT RUTGERS, MARCH 1, 2012.

This contest was close enough for me to drive about ninety minutes and drive back the same night—a nice break for a man who flies as much as I do.

Villanova won, 77–71, and everything went fine, or so I thought. I had already learned the hard way that the more convinced I was that I'd nailed it, the more likely I was going to get slammed by a few self-appointed critics when I got online.

So after the game I drove home, went into my office, and opened my Twitter feed with all the enthusiasm of a man on death row awaiting his sentence. I was expecting the worst, but at least this time I was ready for it.

I got online, looked at my account, and found . . . nothing! I was either clean, or no one was watching! But I chose to think I was clean—assuming the best, for once.

There was hope for me yet.

◆　◆　◆

Just when it seemed like I was getting my game back, the biggest test of the year was coming up: NCAA basketball's Championship

Week, when all the conferences host their tournaments, with dozens of games going each day, leading up to Sunday's conference finals and the NCAA selection show that night. For sportscasters Championship Week is actually harder than the NCAA tournament, because *everyone's* playing, almost every day. So you're constantly updating games, cutting to this finish or that overtime, and continually trying to predict how each result might impact the NCAA brackets. This is air traffic control on speed.

Given my recent progress ESPN had assigned me all five days, Wednesday through Sunday. I still wasn't operating at full capacity, and nowhere near full confidence, but if I could do this, I knew I could do just about anything ESPN asked of me. And if I couldn't, I'd have to dwell on it all summer and wonder whether I'd ever be able to do my job again.

When I told my neurologist, Dr. Goldstein, about the upcoming Championship Week, he said, "Is anyone on the set someone you trust a lot?"

"Sure."

"Good. Don't ask a bunch of people, but just ask one person you really trust to give you an evaluation after your first day."

I thought that was a great idea. Before I went on the air the first day I sought out Rob Lemley, my good friend who was the producer on the *ABC College Football* broadcast when I first fell. He knew more about my situation than most, and I trusted him completely. He agreed to give me an honest assessment of how I was doing.

I thought our first day went pretty well, with no obvious problems. When I asked Lem what he thought, he said, "You're still not quite yourself, but today was a good start."

Amazingly I took him at face value, but I was still a little disappointed. I was hoping to get his unqualified, "Two thumbs up!"

The next day I asked Barry Sacks, another trusted pro who's responsible for all of ESPN's daytime studio programming, to do the same thing. When we'd finished that day's work I thought it had gone pretty well, but I was concerned that my give-and-take with our analyst, Adrian Branch, might have felt a little forced.

When I asked Barry, "So how did it go?" he just kind of shrugged and gave me an, "Eh."

Now I was concerned, so I walked back to the makeup room to find Rob Lemley.

"Rob, I have to ask: how'd I do?"

"Let me call you later."

Crap. If it was going to be bad news, I knew I couldn't wait that long. "No," I said, "you have to tell me now."

"You were not yourself."

"What do you mean?"

He paused, because he knew he had to be careful with me, but he also knew anything less than the truth wouldn't do.

"You were very hesitant," he finally said. "And when you were doing highlights, you sounded like you were reading them. That's not the John Saunders who can make it sound like you're ad-libbing as the clip rolls out. You sounded stiff, not conversational."

Recently that would have been enough to send me spiraling downward for a week. But not this time. Strangely enough I actually felt a bit of relief because I had been more concerned about my interaction with analyst Adrian Branch. Lem hadn't mentioned that, so I asked him about it.

"Oh no," Lem told me, "you were dead-on with that."

Amazingly, thanks to Dr. D'Antonio beefing up my ability to think rationally, I could handle this. In my mind the things Lem was concerned about weren't big worries because I knew I could rediscover a flowing delivery with the clips pretty easily. Those problems weren't based on my mental capacities; they just required a little more practice to get the rust off. What I thought would be the toughest part for me to regain, the repartee, I had down, according to him.

After our conversation I focused on my delivery on the clips for the rest of the week. By the end of the week Lem said I was doing those as well as I ever had. One less thing to worry about.

But on Friday, the third of five straight days of coverage, we had to cover a double-header from the same site. That means we would have almost an hour gap between games—about three times longer than a normal halftime—so we would have to fill in, one of the best tests for a sportscaster.

To increase the "level of difficulty" another notch, that day we had a producer I'd never worked with before. But Lemley, God bless him, was good enough to coach the new guy about working with me. Before we went on the air the new producer came up to me and said, "John, Rob Lemley told me to ask you if there's anything I can do to make things easier on you."

It was a nice gesture, from both of them. Learning my lesson about asking for help, I was 100 percent honest with him: "Do not take for granted, for one second, that I will remember anything you have told me—even if you told me five seconds ago. Do not take for granted that I know where we're going next. If you want to stay in my ear the entire time to make sure I get it right, you go right ahead."

He looked at me for a moment. He'd probably never heard *that* before from any of the pros at ESPN! Then he nodded. "Okay, fine."

Bill Graff, the old pro, was up in the booth backing the new guy. He does not suffer fools gladly. If I screwed up, he'd probably let me know—straight into my earpiece.

The stage was set for a great success, or a big, public face-plant.

The first halftime went great, and the bulk of the fill between the two games went great, too. But near the end of that hour-long gap the new producer got in my ear to tell me, "Talk about Kendall Marshall." But he didn't remind me Marshall played point guard for North Carolina, probably because I'd covered the Tar Heels twice that year, so I'm sure he felt he could take that for granted.

But I couldn't remember Kendall Marshall. Once again I went blank. Nothing.

Seeing my uncertainty, the producer said, "Kendall Marshall" again, but that's not the part I'd forgotten! I didn't know what to do.

Now what? Try to guess and get Marshall's position and team wrong and then hear about it from my producers and Twitter? Or just sit there, staring at the screen like an idiot—which would be even worse? I knew that whatever I was going to do, I had to do it *that second*.

I thought quickly and pulled something out of my ass. Although it didn't have much to do with anything, I started discussing the Big Twelve tournament for a few seconds—though it seemed like an hour, which is always the case when something is going wrong on TV. Kendall Marshall's position and team still weren't coming to me, so I moved right on to the next match-up.

While I'm doing this the new producer is in my ear, trying again to get me to go to Kendall Marshall—but he's still not giving me Marshall's team or position—and I don't blame him, because he was doing his job. With anyone else at ESPN or even with me a year earlier, you wouldn't need any more information. He was not used to working with rookies, which is about what I was.

Still, nothing came to me. I could not place Kendall Marshall for my life.

The producer finally put up a graphic of Kendall Marshall on the screen—and boom, in a flash I knew he was the point guard from North Carolina, and I knew where my producer wanted me to go. I asked Adrian Branch to talk about "the fine point guard from North Carolina, Kendall Marshall!"

We got past that bump without much damage. No one watching at home probably had any idea I had been completely lost. Then we sailed right through the rest of the fill, then the second halftime too, and everything was great. We didn't have any other glitches the rest of the night.

Bill Graff, who usually gives his edicts from the booth right into your ear, made it a point to walk down to the studio to talk to me face to face.

"John, you're doing a great job," he told me. "I know you got lost there a little bit during that fill. But I've worked with you for twenty years. *I* knew you were lost, but I doubt anyone else would know."

He was telling me the truth—Bill always does—and that meant the world to me.

"Bill," I felt compelled to tell him, "I'm working at about 50 percent brain capacity."

What he said next I will probably never forget.

"John, I'd take you at 50 percent any day of the week."

❖ ❖ ❖

The rest of the weekend our broadcasts moved from ESPN to ABC, which increases the audience. That included the SEC semi-finals on Saturday, a doubleheader with a fill, and Sunday's finals, which I did with Hubert Davis, who used to play for the Toronto Raptors. I hadn't worked with him much before, but if you want to get a laugh, Hubert's one of the best audiences you can have, so it was fun to get him going. We finished in fine style.

When I got home and analyzed as objectively as I could my last big test of the season—really, my last chance for months to prove I could still do this—I concluded that I'd started out a bit rusty on Wednesday, and I'd handled the hiccup on Friday, when I could have very easily spiraled downward. But Bill Graff was right: the rest of the weekend went great.

During my long recovery, handling Championship Week was one of the best boosts I received. By the end of the weekend I knew two things: I could do my job again, and I could enjoy it too.

Progress.

CHAPTER 38

You've Got to Admit
It's Getting Better

MY WORK DURING CHAMPIONSHIP WEEK MIMICKED THE experience of the athletes we cover: lose to your rival at the end of the season, and you have to stew on it until you play them again next year. But if you beat them, you can savor it all summer. As you can imagine, it was a great relief to have that big victory in my pocket going into the long "off-season."

My bosses at ESPN were happy too, and they planned to give me a full schedule for the fall of 2012. Until then, they said, except for *The Sports Reporters*, they wanted me to take off the rest of April and all of May. On top of that Bill Graff insisted I take at least one *Sports Reporters* off in April and one in May, which would give me two straight weeks away from the studio to travel, rest, or do whatever I wanted.

I decided I would spend one of those breaks in early April to see Jenna in Toronto. I told Dr. Douglas and Dr. D'Antonio I was feeling pretty good and looked forward to the trip. They were pleased and told me that when I came back we'd work on rebuilding my memory. That sounded good to me.

Minutes after I drove across the Canadian border I got a call from Gerry Matalon, one of our former producers who became an executive in the talent office. He's also one of my closest friends at ESPN, one of the guys, along with Graff, Lemley, and Berman, who kept in close touch with me throughout those rough months. To me, the ESPN family was just that.

Matalon had lived through a lot of that horrible half-year with me. He'd been at my home one time when I dumped my whole life on him in one visit, and I broke down. Well, he was about to get his reward!

As I was crossing the border my seven-month-long headache— which had felt like a little man with a jackhammer inside my skull since I'd fallen in September—had finally stopped, *cold!*

Merril Hoge was right: "One day—I can't say when, I can't say why—the fog is just going to lift. And when it does, it will be amazing."

And that's when Matalon called me.

"So how are you feeling?" Gerry asked.

"Gerry, I don't have a headache!"

"What?"

"Gerry, I don't have a headache!"

He knew what that meant. I tell you, that guy was as happy as anyone could be—except me, of course!

"John, that's fantastic!"

"I don't know whether it's because the headache's gone," I said, "or whether I'm in Toronto. But I just feel *good*."

◆　◆　◆

I'd love to tell you that I've lived happily ever after. To be honest, that's what I thought would happen. But that's not how this illness works.

It was great to have the headaches gone once and for all—a victory I could keep—but unfortunately my amazing mood lasted only about two days. For the next three weeks, for some reason, something got ahold of me, and I went through a particularly bad depression.

What the hell was going on? How could I feel so good for a couple of days, then come crashing down so hard? It gripped me even when I was with Jenna. My baby girl was off to college, and I felt I had wasted too much of my life with depression. Yes, it was depression causing depression, a vicious cycle if ever there was one.

When I met with Dr. Goldstein I described the roller coaster I'd been on. He wasn't surprised. I think he even expected it, which was a relief in itself.

"You are going to experience some 'extreme normalcy,'" he explained, "which to you, having been depressed so long, will feel like you're feeling *fantastic*. That's where you were after the headache finally disappeared. You felt normal, so you felt like you had the world beat.

"But because of the very traumatic injury your brain suffered, from which it's still not fully recovered, you are going to go through some extreme low periods. As those parts of your brain recover, they're going to lead your mind into certain behaviors and thought patterns that are going to bring you down."

Further, he said, weaning me from such a high dose of Klonopin, step by step, was going to affect my mood each time we brought it down a notch. Well, that wasn't great news, but it was good to know that my roller coaster could be explained, and was even expected. When you've had a brain injury, you think your downturn is due to the brain injury, which makes you think your whole life is going to fall apart when you're just going through the normal ups and downs of life. Throw my past issues on top of that, and I was dealing with a double whammy.

This brought us to a conversation about concussions, a topic that was just starting to get a lot of national attention due to the tragic deaths of former NFL players like the Chicago Bears' Dave Duerson, who shot himself in the chest to preserve his brain for research, and Hall of Fame center Mike Webster, whose brain damage from playing the game was becoming public. And right about this time, on May 2, 2012, NFL Hall of Fame linebacker Junior Seau also put a gun to his chest and killed himself at age forty-three. The National Institutes of Health studied his brain and concluded that he suffered from chronic traumatic encephalopathy, or CTE.

When I asked Dr. Goldstein about this he said, "Concussions are a very hot-button topic right now. We neurologists talk about this all the time. In fact, rather than use the word *concussion*, we're more often saying, 'What you have is a brain injury.'"

As simple as it was, that resonated with me. It was one thing to talk about concussions, a term people threw around without really understanding what it meant. But when you start calling it a brain injury, you look at it a little differently.

He then explained that brain injuries don't create depression directly, but the side effects could make you depressed. Combine that depression with a lack of impulse control, which can lead smart people to make foolish investments that cost them millions, get behind the wheel of a car after drinking too many, or forget their wife and kids when an attractive young woman starts flattering them, and it can destroy lives. People who have suffered from brain injuries are more likely to attempt suicide, which doctors believe is often an impulsive decision.

In other words, what I was experiencing was similar to what the NFL players were experiencing. That was pretty troubling, but it was good to know it wasn't just me and that there were actions I could take. Unlike Webster and Seau, my doctor and I knew what we were dealing with.

I came out of that meeting with Dr. Goldstein thinking I still had a ways to go, but I had good reason to be hopeful. I also couldn't afford to become complacent, so I kept up my regular appointments, visiting every week with Dr. Emily D'Antonio and Dr. Carolyn Douglas and every two weeks with Dr. Goldstein. I also had to stick to my meds, which were finally working the way they should.

But through all this it was starting to become clear that on most days I was going in the right direction, something I wouldn't have believed throughout that long, cold winter.

CHAPTER 39

Jimmy V, Dickie V, and Cardio V

I LOVE BEING INVOLVED IN THE V FOUNDATION, WHICH we created for my good friend Jim Valvano. You already know how important the man was to me. But every time I do a function for the V Foundation it reminds me just how much he meant to me, and how much I miss him, so it can be a little tough.

Given my relationship with Jim, I can't just sit in the crowd and be happy we're raising millions for cancer research in his name. I have to get up there and talk, and I can't do that without telling a little story about him, which can become very personal. I need to bare a bit of my soul in front of everyone, and despite doing my work in a very public sphere, I always have a bit of apprehension about this.

The funny thing about me is that, for someone who's in the public eye, I'm not really that outgoing. I have lots of good friends, I can make new friends pretty easily, and I always try to be cordial to fans who come up to me. But I'm really more of a homebody. I wouldn't even say I'm a people person, which is pretty rare in a business full of extroverts. Heck, compared to a lot of our viewers, I'm not even sure I'm that big of a sports fan! Some of those guys follow the stats, their fantasy teams, and the recruiting business more closely than I do.

Throw all of that together, and you can see why the V Foundation events always take a little out of me. So I try to be well rested and emotionally up before I fly down, and I give myself a day off, if I can, when I get back.

In 2012 they held the event on Friday, May 18, so Wanda and I flew down to Sarasota that morning, went to the hotel, and took it easy. When it was time to get ready for the main event that night, I was feeling a little off, but I figured that was due to the mild anxiety I always feel before speaking at the V Foundation. Nothing new there.

When we went down to the private reception it was loud and noisy, and my head started to hurt. I said to Wanda, "I don't get it. Normally, once I get around the people who knew Jim, I get up, but I'm not feeling that right now."

Wanda said, "Let's go for a walk."

We did, and that helped a little. When we came back the main event was just starting, so we sat at our table with Lorraine and Dick Vitale, Pam Valvano, Rick Pitino, Jay Wright of Villanova, Lou Holtz, and Gary Williams—an interesting group. Everything seemed fine.

When I got up to the dais I said, "I couldn't be here last year because my oldest daughter, Aleah, was graduating from Fordham. During her entire time there I thought she was going to be a lawyer. Now she wants to be a sportscaster. Heck, if I had known that, I wouldn't have wasted all that money on a good education!"

It got a good laugh.

"Jenna has just finished her freshman year at Ryerson, my alma mater, in Toronto. It's a great school—I love it—but I admit I was kind of interested in seeing her go to a school with a big sports tradition. I wanted her to look at North Carolina, Duke, Notre Dame," I said, working in the schools of the big-name coaches in the room. And then, looking right at Kentucky's head coach, John Calipari, whose best players tend to sign up for the "one and done" deal, I added, "I even tried to get her to go to Kentucky—because I knew I'd only have to pay for one year!"

Well, that brought the house down. My good friend Harry Rhoads, the president of the Washington Speakers Bureau, of which I'm a member, said it was one of my best speeches.

When I stepped down from the podium I was feeling pretty good again, and the rest of the night we spent socializing. The Foundation had invited the Spinners to perform their hits, including "Rubber Band Man"—the song I used to sing to the girls when they were little.

I had just gotten through the hardest parts of the weekend in fine style, so I was looking forward to enjoying the rest. But when I got up the next morning I wasn't feeling bad, as such, but I still wasn't feeling as up as I thought I should—almost the same sensation I'd felt the night before. Wanda suggested we walk around outside again, but this time I didn't feel any better. *Well, whatever,* I thought. *You gotta play hurt in this business, and it isn't that bad. You've worked through worse, plenty of times.*

That afternoon we went to a private reception at Vitale's house. Of course, when you live in a gorgeous mansion and you've invited over two hundred people there, it can only be so "private," but it's always fun.

We weren't there more than fifteen minutes when Dick gathered everyone into his family room and started talking about all the kids the Jimmy V Foundation was helping to get through cancer. He spoke with the kind of energy only Vitale can generate.

The night before I had met a sweet little child who had successfully battled cancer. At Vitale's house I met a teenage boy who was a really good pitcher and tennis player until he lost his right arm to cancer—so he taught himself to play tennis left-handed. Man, how could I possibly think I had it bad when I looked at these kids?

I was in the kitchen, listening to Vitale give his speech, when I heard him say, "Where's my partner? Get up here, Saunders!"

When I went up to the front of the room Vitale put me in a headlock.

"Let me tell you how special this guy is!" Vitale was shouting—because he's always shouting. "When I thought I had throat cancer, I went to Boston to see the best doctor in the field, the same guy who saved Adele's voice. My surgery was scheduled for nine in the morning, so I had to get there by seven. I was scared to death!

"As I was on my way to be prepped for surgery the elevator door opens, and who's standing there but John Saunders! He came up unannounced just to support me. That's the type of guy John Saunders is.

"I was so happy to see him, I had tears in my eyes. I knew after surgery I wouldn't be able to talk, so I told Big John, 'Just give me thumbs up or thumbs down to let me know if the surgery went well or not.'

"Well, after the surgery, when I start to wake up, Big John's right there. I look up at him, waiting for him to give me the signal. Well, the big guy's just standing there, with two big thumbs up! I coulda kissed the man!"

I spoke for a few minutes about how passionate Dick obviously was—not just for his job but for his family, his friends, and all these young children fighting cancer.

It all felt really good—Friday's event, all those nice things Dick said about me, getting the chance to reciprocate, and then spending some time with these amazingly courageous kids. I took some pictures with them—one of the kids called me the "Host with the Most" on her Twitter page, which was very cute—and I was feeling pretty happy.

When I realized I hadn't eaten all day, I went back to the kitchen to get a bite and ran into Bill Raftery, one of the funniest guys in our business.

But then, suddenly, I felt faint. Now, I've felt faint a hundred times before, but this was different. I started sweating profusely. I felt dizzy and unable to fake my way through it by just holding onto the table and nodding. But I had no chest pain, so I figured it couldn't be a heart attack.

"Bill, I apologize," I said. "I've got to go sit down."

When I sat down next to Wanda she said, "You look terrible." When I admitted I felt dizzy she said, "Let's go out by the pool and get some fresh air."

When I got outside, I felt like I was going to pass out, but I managed to get settled into a chair. Then I saw Vitale charging over with a friend of his. I stood up to shake his hand, but no sooner did I do that than I had to say, "I've got to sit down."

Vitale didn't like the sound of that. He went to get his son-in-law, a doctor, who came out, took one look at me, and said, "I think we should call 911."

"No!" I said, the hockey player in me coming out again—the same guy who thought he was going to finish his shift on *College Football* with blood shooting out the back of his head. "I'm fine! Just a little dizzy is all. I'm going to be fine in a second."

But before I knew it two other doctors materialized from the crowd, one of them Lou Holtz's cardiologist. If you're going to fall suddenly ill, it's a good idea to do so at a Dick Vitale party.

"You have to lay down," the first one said.

"No!" I said. "I'm not doing that at Dick's party!"

But they insisted, so they laid me down on the pool deck. After a little while I said, "I think I feel a little better," and they helped me to get back in my chair. One grabbed my right wrist, the other grabbed my left.

The first said, "He's barely got a pulse."

The other said, "And his blood pressure is barely there." I still don't know how he figured that out.

Holtz's doctor said, "John, my name's Kevin." It seemed like a strange time to make introductions, but thirty seconds later he asked, "John, what's my name?"

I didn't have a clue—another bad sign. He turned to the crowd gathering around me. "Could someone please call 911?"

"I don't need that," I said. "I'm feeling better."

I sat back up in the chair, then I remember lying back on the stone deck surrounding the pool. Next thing I knew I had an oxygen mask on, my shirt was open, someone had put EKG monitors on my chest, and paramedics were all around, getting ready to lift me to the gurney, get me into the ambulance, and rush me to the hospital.

I do remember turning to Vitale, who was white as a ghost at this point, and saying, "Dick, I'm so sorry for ruining your party." I must have said that three times.

"John—please, please." That was about all he could say.

◆ ◆ ◆

More luck: one of Vitale's doctor friends attending to me happened to work at the local hospital, just five minutes from Vitale's house. He called ahead to the hospital to get them ready for me, then called their top cardiac surgeon—a friend of his—to tell him to get to the hospital. By the time the ambulance dropped me off, everyone knew what to do, and the cardiac surgeon was already scrubbed up and ready to go.

After they got me to the operating room the doctor pointed to the EKG machine. "See that little blip there? That could be a heart attack."

That was the first time I'd heard anyone say those words. That got my attention. Then he turned to the nurse and said, "Catheter." That *really* got my attention!

Now, I realize, ladies, that you will not understand what I'm going to say next. But all the men will. The doctor just told me I might have had a heart attack, and that alarmed me a bit. But I didn't panic until he said, "Catheter." Short of becoming a popular prison inmate, this is just about every man's worst fear. And I'm thinking, "She's going to put that damn thing where I would least like to have her put it!"

And, just that fast, that fear eclipsed everything else. That's all I could think of! Heart attack, schmart attack—but a catheter, right where I don't want it? Now the *real* fear sets in. And I'm thinking, *How the hell can they get that device from my penis all the way to my heart? That's going to be terrible! And even worse, how can they get something like that* back *out?!?*

They told me I'd be awake through the entire procedure. Now, I just had the doctors at Mt. Sinai a few months earlier burn a pocket in my chest on local anesthesia, and I had my knee 'scoped on local anesthesia, and I was awake through both of those operations. No problem. I even watched the knee surgery on the screen. I had no reservations about staying awake through my surgery either—but damn it, if that doctor had any plans of sticking anything up my penis, he'd better have the best damn anesthesiologist in all of Florida prepared to knock me out for a day. It might even be a good idea for them to keep a room prepped for whomever I wounded when I reacted to my own procedure!

Then I got the best news of the day: they were not going to send the catheter up my penis but through my thigh. That was a great relief—one I will never forget. Gentlemen, you understand!

Even with a local anesthetic, I could kind of feel the catheter going up my leg, but I didn't care. The doctor told me I'd probably feel it when it got to my heart, and I did.

But amazingly, I could watch on the monitor and listen to the cardiologist talk to the other doctor, who had examined me at Vitale's house. I heard the first doctor say, "Oh, that artery looks about 50 percent blocked."

Then the other doctor said, "I'd say that looks like about 75 to 80 percent."

It turned out it was 90 percent blocked.

Holy smokes.

"Mr. Saunders," the first doctor said, "you have a blockage in your coronary artery. We're going to clear it out right now. And I'm going to put a stent in there, then we're going to run some tests today and tomorrow, but I have to say, it looks like you're pretty lucky."

I resisted the urge to say, "But you're not going to stick anything up my penis, right?"

◆　◆　◆

They had me in and out of the operating room in under an hour.

Back in my room I was still kind of out of it when both doctors came in to talk to me. I thanked them profusely, then asked, "What do I say when people ask me what happened? What do I tell them?"

The second doctor looked at me, then said, "You tell them you had a heart attack. And you tell them this guy saved your life," pointing to the first doctor, Vitale's friend from the pool party. "John, another forty-five minutes, and you could have been in serious cardiac arrest. Thank God you weren't somewhere by yourself or driving or on a plane, or we might not be talking right now."

If I wasn't surrounded by skilled doctors at Vitale's house, professionals who knew better than to listen to the silly, macho protests of a former hockey player, I'm pretty sure I wouldn't have done anything about what was happening to me. I would have laid down—and I would have died. It just didn't seem that serious. That's the kind of dumb guy I am!

And very, very lucky.

The next day they ran all the usual tests and came back with very good news: I had miraculously suffered *zero* damage to the heart muscle. Even the victims of small heart attacks almost always suffer some damage to the muscle. All of the arteries in my heart were pristine—they discovered no further collection of plaque—and even my cholesterol was good. They told me my heart attack was probably due to my diabetes, which makes all bodily functions slower, including your heart's ability to clear plaque out of your arteries.

Dick and Lorraine Vitale visited me in the hospital a few hours each day. When I got out of the hospital on Tuesday they picked us up. All the doctors who had saved my life came by to see me out, which was nice.

Before we went to the airport the Vitales took us to breakfast. I ate one whole-wheat pancake with sugar-free syrup. After everything I'd just been through, it tasted pretty damn good.

CHAPTER 40

Learning the Best Lesson

WHEN IT WAS TIME TO FLY HOME I WAS ACTUALLY FEEL-
ing pretty good, although I dreaded having to tell my daughters
I'd just had a heart attack. They'd had plenty to worry about.

I was smart enough to call Dr. D'Antonio and Dr. Douglas from
Florida to let them know what had happened so I didn't have to
drop that news on them when I saw them later that week.

After I sat down in Dr. Douglas's office, she said, "I was afraid
you were going to tell me you're sorry you didn't die."

"Nobody knows better than you do," I said, "that just a few
months ago that would have been the case. But sitting in that
hospital bed in Florida, I realized I've got too many people who
care about me, and I've got too many years left.

"I'm going to enjoy the rest of my life."

◆ ◆ ◆

After my heart attack I continued to recover from the lingering
effects of my brain injury, but my progress was very good, and I've
made a full recovery. By 2013 my doctors finished the two-year
process of weaning me off of Klonopin, which has improved my
energy, my clarity, and my moods.

About the same time I finished with Klonopin a White House staffer asked me to write and record a two-minute video for the White House's new website, mentalhealth.gov, part of a campaign to raise awareness of mental health issues. We have every reason to take this seriously: some 65 million people in the United States and Canada have a diagnosable mental illness, half of them suffering from a serious form of depression.

The staffer who called me had no idea that I've battled depression my entire life, but I jumped at the chance. This is what I came up with, in part, which we shot from the set of ESPN's *Sports Reporters*.

"Hi, I'm John Saunders.

"Take a quick look around: whether you're with family, co-workers, or in a room full of strangers, someone around you is dealing with a mental illness. They are living silently, but dealing with an issue that affects their lives and others.

"Asking a person suffering to move on is like asking a person with a broken leg to run a marathon. You wouldn't tell someone who can't walk to get out of bed.

"What *is* needed is understanding and help. And there is help. Tell your family, tell a friend, and, just as important, tell your doctor. He or she will be determined to get you the right person to change your life.

"Not only *should* you talk about it, you *need* to talk about it.

"We must learn to recognize the signs and reach out to those we know are in trouble.

"Be the one who reaches out to save someone.

"Or maybe it's you: be the one to save yourself."

The White House followed up with an invitation to the first National Conference on Mental Health on Monday, June 3, 2013. I had met President Obama during a shoot for ESPN when he made his NCAA basketball tournament picks, but this was something else.

I waited in the Green Room with Bradley Cooper, whose character in the groundbreaking movie *The Silver Linings Playbook* suffers from bipolar disorder, and Glenn Close, a longtime activist for mental health whose sister, Jennie, suffers from bipolar disorder. Glenn founded BringChange2Mind, a US campaign to eradicate the discrimination surrounding mental illness.

She told us when she tried to research her character for *Fatal Attraction*—before the Internet age, obviously—she was amazed how little she could find about the disease. She said the movie originally ended with her character taking her own life, but when they screened that ending with test audiences, they hated it. So they changed it, with Michael Douglas's character's wife killing her. The audience loved it, of course—but Close didn't. She was very upset and fought to get them to go back to the original ending, because it was clear to her that's what someone in that role would have done. No luck, of course—but that's Hollywood.

I talked with Glenn about my sister, Gail, and about Glenn's sister and her nephew, who also suffer from depression. Mental illness doesn't seem to have much regard for race or religion, wealth or education. It affects just about all Americans, one way or the other.

When I met the president, he said, "Hi, John! How have you been?"

"Mr. President, it's been a while."

"John, it hasn't been that long. You were just here six months ago!"

When he asked what had brought me there, I explained how mental health issues have affected my family through my sister. He thanked me for attending, then promised me we'd win this battle.

When the president took the stage before 150 people, he said we should treat mental illness the same way we treat cancer or diabetes—as a disease, and with the same organized efforts to reduce the threat.

"We wouldn't accept it if only 40 percent of Americans with cancer got treated," he said. "We wouldn't accept it if only half of young people with diabetes got help. Why should we accept it when it comes to mental health? It doesn't make any sense."

He added that people who suffer from mental illnesses still face a huge stigma, with 60 percent of Americans saying they wouldn't want to live next door to someone with a mental health problem—even though many of them already do.

When I took my seat on the train back to New York, Vice President Joe Biden happened to be standing right next to my seat, so I seized the opportunity.

"Mr. Vice President," I said, "I was just at the White House conference and heard you speak."

Before I could say any more he looked at me and said, "You work for ESPN! You're John Saunders, right?"

Then he took the seat next to me. When we discussed the conference he stressed how we must get athletes who suffer from depression to come out and admit their struggles. They're too often hidden, he said, because they fear how they'll be perceived in "the macho world of the invincible!" He puffed up his chest as he said it.

"Heck, John, right now it's easier for a pro athlete to come out and admit they're gay than it is for someone suffering from depression to admit *that!* We've got to do something about that!"

He was right, of course. I didn't tell him that I suffered from depression or that I'd already started working on this book, but I hope he sees it now—and I hope it helps.

◆　◆　◆

For someone like me who suffers from depression, life is never as simple as "happily ever after." Like cancer survivors and recovering alcoholics, our disease is rarely far away, and it can always resurface. I have gone through more ups and downs since then, but the ups have been higher, and the downs not as deep or as long. The overall trajectory of my health has continued upward.

These days there's nothing I love more than seeing old friends, playing golf with Bernie, and hanging out with Wanda and our girls, whether we're watching a movie, listening to music together, or just doing nothing. It helps that I listen to the same music my daughters do, and we've even gone to concerts together.

I don't go a day without telling my wife and daughters how much I love them, even during frequent trips. I do not leave the house without kissing them goodbye, whether it's six in the morning or six at night.

Aleah and Jenna are my life. They've given me far more than I could have imagined. They started calling me "Daddy" from the start. They still do, and it melts me every time.

My wife and daughters are doing great, and my work is going well. I still have bad days and even bad weeks. But bit by bit, day by day, I'm getting better and better.

Imagine that.

AFTERWORD

John U. Bacon

When John told Dr. Douglas after his heart attack that he intended to enjoy the rest of his life, he meant it.

Aleah and Jenna both moved home after graduating from college, which thrilled John. He knew he couldn't keep them forever, but he seemed determined to make the most of their time together under one roof. The family made it a point to travel more, taking trips to France and then Italy, followed by a theme wedding in Greece.

"The best part," Wanda recalls, "is that we made all these trips as a family, with our girls in their twenties, when most kids don't want to be with their parents. We were having so much fun that we were planning another trip to Italy."

John also promised to spend more time with Bernie, and he did. At John's urging, Bernie joined John's country club in Westchester, where they had adjoining lockers. Even during their happy rounds of golf, however, Bernie could see the damage diabetes had done to John's body. "His hands were so shaky," Bernie recalled, "that I would often have to help him tee up his golf ball."

On Monday, February 2, 2015—Groundhog Day—John turned sixty years old, which in itself could be considered a minor miracle. Bernie gave him a scrapbook filled with some of their favorite moments, which John figured was enough for any grown man's birthday. He didn't realize it was just a smokescreen for what was to come.

The following Saturday, February 7, Bernie and his old Western Michigan friend Neil Smith took John out for dinner. When John walked into the restaurant, he started recognizing people he'd known forever, from grade school to ESPN, but he was slow to process why they were all in New York, in this restaurant. Then it hit him—and yes, he was surprised.

Friend after friend got up to the front of the room and told him how much they loved him. They were funny, sincere, and real—and John often got choked up. The showstopper was Jenna, who pulled a few laughs and a few tears from the crowd. But the last speaker, naturally, was John himself.

"As I look around the room," he said, "I know you all have reasons for being here, and you know how difficult life can be for me at times. I tend to carry a little black cloud around with me. Thanks to all of you, it's getting easier for me to get rid of that cloud and allow me to enjoy life. I can't begin to tell you all how much you mean to me. I love you all."

◆　◆　◆

Before Bernie turned sixty the next year, on June 21, John had an idea. In May of 2016, without much warning, he took Bernie to Georgia to play thirty-six holes at Augusta National with Lou Holtz.

"I thought that was one of the best gifts I could get," Bernie said. But like the scrapbook Bernie had given John the year before, the golf trip was a setup for bigger things to come.

Another last-minute trip started a week later when John and Wanda flew with Bernie and his longtime girlfriend, Pam, to the Bahamas. They planned to stay at the place of former Texas head coach Mack Brown while John secretly rented another place a block away. Once the couples settled in, John suggested they go for a walk over to see Mack. When they stopped at the rental home, Bernie saw his three children, both of John's, and a few of Gail's.

"It was a huge surprise," Bernie told me, still smiling about it months later. "Couldn't have had a better birthday."

◆　◆　◆

Two days after they returned, Pam suffered a ruptured aneurysm, which required emergency surgery. Nine days into her recovery, while still at the hospital, she had a stroke, which kept her there nearly two months, with Bernie by her side. John often visited, and when he couldn't, he called. On July 10, during a trip to South Bend, Indiana, John arrived at his hotel too late to call, so he sent Bernie an email instead.

He wrote, "Although I want you to sleep well, I hope you roll over tonight and see this, because I feel like an idiot for missing you today. Anyway, hope you get this to know I didn't forget you and Pam. I hope she had a better day and thus you as well.

"During the drive I thought about how, if it's ok with you, I'd like us to examine getting a place either together or near each other somewhere as I can't imagine having a lot of fun without you around. And even though I know I get on your nerves sometimes, I'll try to be better so as not to make it too bad. Love you little bro and through this tough time I want you to know that and how much happiness it gives me to see you happy with Pam."

John was following through on his promises to his family and to himself to enjoy the rest of his life. That still wasn't always easy, but it was getting better and better every year. The future looked bright.

◆　◆　◆

At about this time John and I met again at my home in Ann Arbor to finish what we believed to be the penultimate draft of this book, and we liked how it was shaping up. After four years working together on this, John's dream of sharing his story with the world was almost a reality. We even talked about writing another book, this one exploring his relationship with Jim Valvano, tentatively titled, *Jimmy V and Me*.

Whenever one of the panelists on *The Sports Reporters* published a book, it was their custom to bring signed copies for the others at the next taping. John looked forward to handing all of them signed copies of his first book that fall and adding his book to the shelf alongside theirs.

In early August John started feeling under the weather, but that wasn't unusual. While Pam was still in the hospital, Bernie and John would often meet for dinner. On the night of August 7 they went to a rib place that John liked so much that he told Bernie they should revisit it soon.

"John sounded upbeat and supportive," Bernie recalls. "He was excited about what he was doing. When he drove me back to the hospital we hugged and said we loved each other, like always."

Those would be the last words they would share.

◆   ◆   ◆

A few hours after midnight on Wednesday, August 10, John walked into the bathroom of their home and collapsed on the floor. When Wanda found him, he was not moving. She called 911 and then Bernie, who immediately drove over to their home. When the paramedics arrived they told Wanda they needed a doctor to declare John dead, so Bernie called a doctor who lived nearby to come to their home and fill out the paperwork.

John's death quickly became national news, complete with the erroneous information and unfounded claims that seem to follow every national story these days. Partly for that reason the family wisely decided to have a thorough autopsy performed. The coroners concluded that John had died of a combination of an enlarged heart, complications from his diabetes, and dysautonomia, which affects the automatic nervous system that regulates breathing, blood pressure, and heart rate. John had asked that his brain be donated to Mt. Sinai for research, and his family honored his wishes.

Condolences came from around the country, including a personal note from President Obama. A week later the family held a visitation, which drew hundreds of John's family members, friends, and colleagues, representing the usual cross-section of society that John always seemed to attract.

Bernie initially decided to avoid seeing John's casket, but he eventually walked up to the front of the room to see his brother for the last time.

"He looked at peace," Bernie told me. "I'm glad I have that final memory of him."

◆　◆　◆

On November 1, 2016, ESPN hosted a ceremony to celebrate John's life. Hundreds of John's friends packed ESPN's KidsCenter Gymnasium, which can double as an auditorium. The audience heard from ESPN stalwarts, and John's close friends, Bob Ley, Chris Berman, and Barry Melrose, among others, and John's high school friend, Barry Stephens. Ryerson teammate Frank Sheffield talked about partnering with John on defense, and John's best friend, Neil Smith, told stories that spanned from Western Michigan to the past summer.

A few themes emerged. Everyone admired John's work because he focused his attention on his subjects, not himself. They also respected him for standing up for what he believed, having the ability to disagree without being disagreeable, and going out of his way to help his colleagues, especially those just getting started. Despite working in a shark tank of an industry where egos can run wild, John made hundreds of lasting friendships, but not a single enemy—almost unheard of in this business.

But the highlight of the day was Aleah Saunders, who usually avoids the spotlight. When she took the podium she was clear, strong, and sincere—a vision of what John had hoped she would become. She talked in detail about what a wonderful father he had been, thereby officially dispelling John's greatest fear, once and for all: he had not repeated the Saunders's family history.

◆ ◆ ◆

Now we are left with our private memories and John's public legacy. After John died, another spouse might have thought that revising the book for publication wasn't worth the trouble, especially given John's unsparing candor, but not Wanda. Another brother might have flinched at seeing so many family secrets divulged, but Bernie saw the greater good. They both decided it was more important than ever to let John tell his story. Everyone involved wanted to honor John's wishes, protect his legacy, and help those who could benefit from John's story—just as he'd wanted.

"Depression is a beast," Bernie told me in 2017. "Watching Gail and John, I could see how it could suck every ounce of energy from you. Through them I feel like I know depression, but on the other hand, I don't think anyone who doesn't have it can fully understand the anguish people with depression often feel.

"Some events in this book I saw in a different light than John did, but when you're depressed, it's difficult to let the light in. But in typical John Saunders fashion, he wanted to draw some good out of his experience with depression. John spent the last year of his life working hard on his story so he could help others in their battle.

"Although John was probably never going to be a 'glass half-full' person, I believe John found peace before he passed away. In the end he understood how lucky he was to have a loving wife and two amazing daughters, and he was grateful. He learned to appreciate his success and what his life had to offer. Our plan was to play golf and enjoy the rest of our lives together, and we were doing it: two brothers finding happiness, against all odds. He was the best brother a brother could have.

"What this book says to me is the same message that his good friend Jimmy Valvano said: 'Don't give up. Don't ever give up.'

"John never gave up."

John's doctors saw what Bernie saw. "I was always impressed by how hard John was working to get better." Dr. Goldstein told me. "He didn't come in with any of the entitled attitude you might expect from a celebrity. He was very down to earth, very likable, a good-hearted guy. When you asked him a question, he gave you an honest answer, and he made an honest effort. He didn't always succeed, but he was earnest. I think that inspired his doctors and his therapists to work harder for him."

◆　◆　◆

None of us has the ability to see ourselves in full, and John was no exception. Although many of us might be tempted to hold an inflated view of ourselves, John was inclined to do the opposite—one of the hallmarks of depression. As Dr. Carolyn Douglas, John's last psychiatrist, wrote me, "John had a tendency to emphasize his faults and overlook his many strengths. You hear stories about people who overcome serious childhood trauma and neglect and go on to lead remarkably successful lives, personally and professionally—but they are the exceptions, not the general rule.

"Certainly John did not come through his childhood unscathed. His chronic depression, earlier drug abuse, history of self-injury, intense self-recriminations, and difficulties with intimacy are all well-recognized consequences of the kind of abuse he endured.

"But what always struck me as admirable and remarkable was how John kept getting up again and again, pushing to overcome whatever adversities he faced over the course of his life, always striving to get better and be happier—even as he doubted this would ever be in the cards for him. He endured chronic physical pain throughout our treatment and almost never complained about it. In fact, he showed remarkably little anger and self-pity about his trials and tribulations in the time I knew him.

"He was also always intent on providing and preserving for his daughters—and nieces and nephews—the kind of family love and stability he never had. It is so hard to give what you never got, and John was able to do that to a remarkable degree."

To me, John was an alchemist, blessed with the uncommon ability to take the pain the world too often gave him, and transform that into love for his family and friends.

This book is John's ultimate act of generosity. Here he has bared his soul to give hope to thousands who face the same hardships he did. John wanted to save lives, and I am convinced he will.

That is no small consolation.

ACKNOWLEDGMENTS

John U. Bacon

John Saunders and I met almost two decades ago during Dave Coulier's charity hockey game at Joe Louis Arena. We dressed in adjoining stalls, started chatting, and kept it up for nineteen years.

About a decade ago John told me he wanted to write a book. We started working on a couple of sports-related ideas, but our focus changed after he fell on the set in 2011 and embarked on the long, hard recovery that followed. In the spring of 2012, not long after John's heart attack, we started working on John's story.

We worked for three years without a contract or even the promise of one, writing countless proposals and drafts. Because we were writing on faith, we needed the considerable support of our spouses, Wanda and Christie, and they supplied it in generous doses. Along the way we received first-rate guidance from a few great agents: David Black, Dave Larabell, Jay Mandel, and Eric Lupfer, who spearheaded the final effort. They went above and beyond the call many times.

In February of 2015, shortly after the proposal finally went out to the publishers, David Steinberger, the CEO of parent company Perseus Books, and Dan Ambrosio, an editor at Da Capo, expressed immediate and serious interest. Given this book's long, winding journey, we relied on their patience and loyalty throughout, and we appreciated both greatly.

A year and a half later we were close to finishing the manuscript when John died. The people at Da Capo couldn't reduce our sadness, but they were steadfast in their commitment to *Playing Hurt*. The list of talented people who made significant contributions to this book includes Susan Weinberg, Perseus Books publisher; and at Da Capo publisher John Radziewicz, publicity director Lissa Warren, marketing director Kevin Hanover, managing editor Fred Francis, Lifelong editorial director Renee Sedliar, editorial assistant Miriam Riad (who did great work with the photos), and Christine Marra of Marrathon Editorial Production Services, who coordinated the book's final production.

We naturally depended on many people at ESPN for help, including Gerry Matalon, Scott Turken, and particularly Josh Krulewitz. Chris Berman and Bob Ley, longtime colleagues and close friends of John, both read the manuscript and offered their endorsements, while Mitch Albom generously agreed to write the foreword for his old friend.

After John died I relied on several friends, physicians, and experts to improve the manuscript. Hockey friends Dan Farrell, Rob Palmer, Dave Shand, and Neil Smith all helped. Dr. Carolyn Douglas was everything John always told me she was: smart, professional, caring, and extremely helpful. She brought all those traits to this effort too. Drs. Choudhri, Gerdis, and Goldstein helped clarify many medical aspects of John's story while demonstrating their obvious affection for John.

Dr. Richard Dopp at the University of Michigan Depression Center gave me a careful reading, providing a professional sounding board and lots of good insights. I also asked my wife, Christie, and a few trusted friends to weigh in on the penultimate draft, including L. Todd Johnson, Thomas Lebien, John Lofy, Ivan Maisel, James Tobin, and Pete Uher, and they came through in spades.

There wasn't much about this book that was easy, which might explain why it took five years to finish. But it was particularly hard for John's wife, Wanda, and John's brother, Bernie, to read the manuscript, share their reactions, and give the book their blessings. They did so out of their love for John because they knew how much this book meant to him.

Throughout this often arduous process two things kept me going: my belief in the good it would do John to tell his story, and the good it could do others to hear it. That group includes the millions of Americans who suffer from depression, and those who love them.

John had many admirable qualities, including a sharp intelligence, a quick wit, and a great warmth with those lucky enough to get to know him well. But I believe he will be remembered mainly for his resilience, his courage, and his generosity, which will live on long after his passing.

John, we have finally fulfilled your dream of telling your story. Thank you for giving us that chance.